T0329471

ORION'S GUIDING STARS

ORION'S GUIDING STARS

THE MYTH OF THE HERO AND THE HUMAN INSTINCT FOR STORY

MARC LADEWIG

Algora Publishing
New York

Library of Congress Cataloging-in-Publication Data —

Names: Ladewig, Marc.
Title: Orion's guiding stars: the myth of the hero and the human instinct
    for story / Marc Ladewig.
Description: New York: Algora Publishing, [2017] | Includes bibliographical
    references and index.
Identifiers: LCCN 2017001399 (print) | LCCN 2017006952 (ebook) | ISBN
    9781628942767 (soft cover: alk. paper) | ISBN 9781628942774 (hard cover:
    alk. paper) | ISBN 9781628942781 (pdf)
Subjects: LCSH: Heroes—Mythology. | Mythology. | Myth. | Folklore. |
    Storytelling. | Orion (Constellation)—Miscellanea.
Classification: LCC BL325.H46 L33 2017 (print) | LCC BL325.H46 (ebook) | DDC
    201/.3—dc23
LC record available at https://lccn.loc.gov/2017001399

All photos and graphics are in the public domain. All illustrations by the author.

To Fred Cahill, who took me out hunting as a kid,
and to my children
Mara and Lars
and the dear memory of enjoying folk tales
with them at bedtime.

TABLE OF CONTENTS

Table of Contents

Introduction: A Footnote in History

A book about mythology should begin with a hero. Maybe with a story about someone who risked it all and went somewhere or did something that nobody else ever did. Perhaps someone to emulate. But Filippo Sassetti never made it back to Italy from his travels in India. So did dying far from home make this hero an explorer or a mere adventurer?

Out of the plague years when perhaps thirty percent of the people in Western Europe died, the Renaissance flowered. The vigorous Irish clergy had preserved and spread lost Latin works throughout the continent wherever they built a new monastery. The conquering Moors in Spain had translated many works of Aristotle from Arabic into Latin and other European languages. Refugee Greeks fleeing the Turkish conquest of Byzantium had brought copies of Homer's *Iliad* and *Odyssey* with them to Italy. Everyone was obsessed with the reemerging literature of the ancients.

The imaginations of young Europeans were fired by Vasco da Gama's discovery of a sea route around Africa that led to India. With the drawing of a single map, the long, expensive and dangerous overland route on the Silk Road from the Far East was no longer the only way to caravan goods through hostile Arab lands to European markets. With the drawing of a single map, Italy surrendered her privileged position as the middle man for all Far Eastern trade with Europe to the new kingdom of Portugal, which lay beyond the old Mediterranean world on the Atlantic Ocean, the new global highway of its day. Da Gama's voyage proved that sailing around Africa was a faster and easier route to India than plying the pirate haunted Mediterranean and caravanning pestilential deserts. An appetite for silks and spices, perfumes and precious gems had sprung up in Europe. With this also came a burning curiosity, a hunger for the world based upon scientific thinking

1

and a reawakened acquaintance with ancient Greek and Roman literature. It was a world that was proving not to be flat like common sense, experience and tradition dictated. Magellan's fleet departed Portugal and sailed west out into the Atlantic, around the southern tip of South America and across the wide Pacific. If Magellan had survived the Philippines, he would have ultimately ended up a couple of years later right back where he had started from in Lisbon. Circumnavigation proved Copernicus's theory that the world was a globe spinning in empty space in orbit around a central sun. The world was also vaster and stranger than that depicted in old travelers' tales like Marco Polo's. Earth was full of people, languages and cultures that nobody in the West had ever seen or heard of. There were whole races of people that the Bible made no mention of in any of its genealogies. Many Europeans of the day seriously wondered aloud if such newfound people even had souls. The insular, Mediterranean centered world of the past no longer dominated European thinking and imagination.

Florence, Italy was the birthplace of the Renaissance and the modern Italian language. It was the city where Dante wrote *The Divine Comedy* and shaped the West's notions of heaven and hell. Machiavelli wrote *The Prince* and shaped the West's ideals of political leadership. Florence was the home of the Medici's, the family which dominated the ecclesiastical politics of the day. It was the city of Michelangelo and Leonardo da Vinci. Into this roiling intellectual environment, about one generation removed from the discoveries of Christopher Columbus, Filippo Sassetti was born in 1540. He was the son of a prominent, well-to-do Florentine family of merchants. Filippo graduated from the University of Pisa in 1568 after having pursued studies in Greek and Latin. The elders of his family obviously read the handwriting on the wall. Italy was no longer the only middleman brokering European trade with the Far East. The Sassettis sent young Filippo to Lisbon, Portugal where the new action was. In that teeming seaport, he went to work for a merchant house. While he learned the office side of the import export business, he continued his studies and dreamed of traveling to India.

Filippo tells the story of witnessing a man of good family who wandered down by the docks where ships were preparing to sail for India. The man counted his money and sent word to his family that they should not expect him home for dinner. He went on board one of the vessels and did not set foot on land again until he disembarked on Indian soil. This incident reveals that there was a deep seated hunger for the strange and the exotic in Filippo's mind. Concerning the books that he read, he wrote, "...while I read I build castles in the air from which better to see, touch and write." There were dreamers before Don Quixote tilted at windmills.

His first attempt to reach India almost ended in disaster. The ship rode the prevailing winds south along the African slave coast past Madeira, past the Canary Islands, past the Cape Verde Islands until it crossed the equator, lost all sight of land and pushed further out into open ocean. The prevailing winds veered to the west and swept the ship all the way across the Atlantic. Filippo's ship beached on the far shores of Brazil in the New World. Forced to return to Lisbon, he had to wait a full year until he could book passage on another ship bound for India. What could this period of hunger and yearning have been like for him?

The second voyage took seven months. This time, the ship successfully reached across the prevailing west winds and made landfall in southern Africa on its fierce Skeleton Coast, the future graveyard of many a merchant ship. Then around the Cape of Good Hope and a turn northeast up the coast to Mombasa on the Indian Ocean. From there, the ship caught a trailing monsoon wind across open ocean. It took da Gama's fleet twenty-three days to make this last stretch between landfalls. The route had been in use for centuries by Africans, Arabs, Persians, Indians and Chinese. It was a tried and true passage long before its Western "discovery."

In 1583, at the age of forty-three, Filippo landed at Cochin on the Malabar Coast. Coconut palms and sandy beaches divided dense jungles from the sea. Stationary butterfly nets lined the shore like giant winnowing hands and scooped the tides for fish. This innovation had been introduced by the Chinese. There was a thriving Jewish community with a synagogue that had been in India since Roman times. There was a church of Thomasine Christians and legends that the doubting apostle had made it all the way to India on his mission before he was killed by a spear in battle. How could the fabled Christian kingdom of Prestor John not be very far off? Filippo was in India to negotiate for pepper and cinnamon and ship these novel spices back to Europe at a handsome profit. He was also there to see the sights and learn the languages and the customs of the people with whom he was doing business. He was a merchant anthropologist, an expatriate extraordinaire, a true Renaissance man.

Filippo Sassetti is a famous footnote in history because of the letters that he wrote while he stayed on the Malabar Coast between Goa and Cochin for the last five years of his life. Every year in November, the Portuguese India Armada departed with cargos of spices and letters for home. Filippo wrote "animated and judicious" letters to his employers and friends from his university days about his observations concerning all things Indian. If he had a wife and children, he addressed no letters to them. He did write to his sister Maria four times over the course of his stay.[1]

---

1 Sassetti, Filippo. *Lettere di Filippo Sassetti*. Reggio, Dalla Stamperia Torregiani E.C., 1844. p. 221.

Filippo wrote about customs, astronomy, religion, commerce, business opportunities, the plants and animals of the region. He also wrote down a remarkable observation that made his informal ethnography a milestone in Indo-European studies. He only wished that he had gotten to India while he was younger so that he could have become more proficient in the local languages. He was a scholar of Greek and Latin and knew the classical authors Herodotus and Pliny. Both had written of far off, fabled India and its Brahman priests. Filippo could only wonder at comparisons. He developed an interest in Sanskrit, the ancient language of the *Vedas* and the *Upanishads*, the holy books of the Hindus. Writing to his old school chum Bernardo Davanzati, Filippo observed that the numbers six, seven, eight and nine and the words for god and serpent were very similar in all three languages.

These letters were promptly filed upon receipt back in Italy. They were shelved in a library until they were found and published in 1844, almost three centuries later and then only in Italian. His complete works were not published until 1970. To date, there is still no full English translation. But Filippo Sassetti's observation marks the first instance in recorded history to date that Greek, Latin and Sanskrit all appear to share similar word origins. It was common knowledge that the ancient Greeks and Romans knew about India and traded with Indian merchants. However, no European before Filippo had put his or her observations to pen and paper. His remarks form the historical starting point of Indo-European studies. He never knew the part his intuitions would play in the understanding of historical linguistics. His observations remained unnoticed on dusty shelves for three centuries. They only give us pause for wonder in our day. Sadly, Filippo's flash of insight did not even give rise to a new field of Indo-European studies. Englishman Sir William Jones, also a scholar of Greek and Latin, performed that service in 1786. He published similar observations about linguistic connections East and West in the *Third Anniversary Discourse to the Asiatic Society* while he was a magistrate in Calcutta. He too had taken up the study of Sanskrit in his spare time. "The Sanskrit language, whatever be its antiquity, is of a wonderful structure; more perfect than the Greek, more copious than the Latin, and more exquisitely refined than either, yet bearing to both of them *a stronger affinity, both in the roots of verbs and the forms of grammar, than could possibly have been produced by accident; so strong indeed, that no philologer could examine them all three, without believing them to have sprung from some common source, which, perhaps, no longer exists;* (italics mine)."[1] Almost sixty years later in 1844, once Indo-European studies were well under way in many European countries, this apparent connection between far flung languages was discovered to have been already

---

1 Jones, Sir William (1824). Discourses delivered before the Asiatic Society: and miscellaneous papers, on the religion, poetry, literature, etc., of the nations of India.

noticed centuries earlier. Darwin was to have his Wallace, someone who would independently arrive at similar conclusions about natural selection. Jones had his Sassetti, but totally unbeknownst to him.

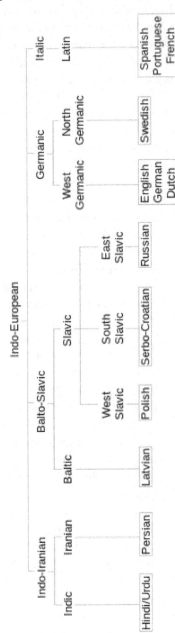

Filippo anticipated Indo-European studies. He had an inkling that the languages heard from India to Italy were related somehow. Centuries later, scholars like the Brothers Grimm and Max Müller would validate Filippo's intuition with scientific proof. They would go on to speculate that in misty antiquity, there must have been a population of people in eastern Europe or southern Russia who spoke a language which was the mother tongue of virtually all modern Indian and European languages. This hypothesis forms the foundation for the theory of the Indo-European language family. However, it was beyond Filippo's ken to solve the puzzle of his canny observation.

Death came suddenly to Filippo Sassetti in 1548. He was just 48 years old. Was it fever, food poisoning, diarrhea or tropical infection? Forty-eight is not old by modern standards. Did Filippo think that he was an old man upon his deathbed? Did he worry that he would be lost and forgotten because he never got back home?

A "Sassetti," is an observation, based upon experience and intuition. It is hard, even impossible to prove by empirical evidence or experiment. Though the parallels are close and the linkages natural, it is only suggestive by analogy. A "Sassetti" is a subspecies of the human capacity to make a hunch. A hunch is a feeling about something that is going to happen. A "Sassetti" is a hunch about connections between apparently dissimilar things. Take, for example, the fact that the words *sarpe, serpe* and serpent all refer to snake in Greek, Latin, Sanskrit and English. Logically, these languages must ultimately share similar historical borrowing or historical origins. This was a mighty leap of faith based upon homophony. It is the simplest explanation. Similarity has better odds than coincidence. But the assumption that became the foundation of Indo-European studies could not be proven true or false beyond this intuition based upon apparent similarity of sound. As interest in this obscure linguistic fact evolved into an academic discipline, it became evident that there was no way to check many of the facts directly beyond laying all the evidence out side by side and noting what patterns emerged. Mitigating evidence was easier to imagine than to obtain. How to make common sense of sound and fantasy?

Filippo had insight but the linguistics of his day was incapable of validating his intuitions. However, he was more than a mere adventurer. He was ahead of his time and a full-blown explorer. A scout. He got news back of his observations though they moldered on the shelf for a long, long time before they were recognized and appreciated. Filippo was a man whose curiosity led him halfway around the world. He died far from home. He saw much further than he could reach. But he was an explorer in every sense of the word because he left us his brilliant letters, and the people to whom he sent them had the wisdom to preserve them so that they could be rediscovered.

Filippo Sassetti is a prime example of the scholar hero. He worked diligently in obscurity for little more than to satisfy his own intellectual drives. He remained faithful to his interests. He shared all that he observed generously. He made canny connections the truth of which time and improved methodologies have confirmed. His work never achieved recognition until long after his death. Filippo is a lonely curiosity, a recurring hunger pursued vigorously. His life exemplified the adventure of seeking knowledge for knowledge's sake in faraway places. The discoveries of Columbus are of world historical significance, not because he was the first European to reach the shores of the New World. We have archeological evidence of Norsemen in Greenland and at L'Anse au Meadows in Newfoundland that pre-date his voyages by 500 years. As of the publication of this work, a Roman *gladius* or short sword has been produced that is purported to be the heirloom of an old Oak Island family who found it on their land generations back. In the waters off of the eastern Canadian seaboard, investigators have discovered a shipwreck that expert speculation allows could be Roman.

The discoveries of Columbus are of world historical significance because he spread the news of them. He made his discoveries common knowledge to everybody and thereby changed the course of the everyday world from then on.

Filippo made equally exciting discoveries but they did not get broadcast. His achievement was not recognized until centuries after his death. Nevertheless, Filippo Sassetti, on a personal level, is an explorer and discoverer of equal stature with da Gama, Magellan and Columbus. His experience reminds us that it is not always the first to discover who is remembered and celebrated for the discovery. Columbus might have "discovered" the New World but it was named America after an obscure Italian navigator called Amerigo Vespucci, yet another son of Florence. A German mapmaker named the empty landmasses on his map of the New World Amerigo's Land. At least a few centuries later, Columbus got Colombia. Nobody bothered to ask the conquered people what they had called their lost homelands. The largest land grab in history started with a name grab too. Perhaps all of us are, in fact, discoverers, but only a few of us get famous for it.

As a writer, I may hope but cannot expect to surpass the destiny of Filippo Sassetti. Books are validated by their readers, not their writers. Happily, it is out of my hands now that my work is done. Scientists often reveal that at the moment of their greatest discovery, he or she reveled in the knowledge that, for the briefest of moments, they were the sole possessors of this knowledge among all of humanity. However, it is not the having of knowledge that matters. It is sharing that knowledge. Filippo tried to share what he discovered. His lost letters became a buried treasure. That would define his destiny and his legacy.

Orion's Guiding Stars is a book about mythology. To be more specific, it is about the myth of the hero. Why is this particular story pattern the same, everywhere, always, pole to pole across the globe? What are the essential features of this sameness? Who made up these stories and what are they really about? Why does the myth of the hero continue to resonate in the digital age, not only for children but for adults as well? Finally, is the myth of the hero a bestowal of the spirit or an expression of our animal instincts? Many ancient assumptions will be revisited here under new, comparative lights from a multitude of viewing angles.

An author who embarks upon such a topic can reasonably be expected to be a classicist, folklorist, anthropologist or historian. Perhaps even a philosopher or a journalist. I am none of these by profession. Neither am I a biologist or a geneticist, though the latter half of the book will draw heavily from these fields. I am a classroom teacher of English and Spanish in a small school district near the sea in central California. My perspective is that of a layman who loves books and myths. My explorations of the myth of the hero began while I pursued a B.A. in Anthropology from the University of California in the early eighties. My courses took a folkloric bend in the trail. The myth of the hero had always intrigued me as a young reader. I was born with a hunger for story in my mind. At U.C.S.D., I was introduced to the eminent writers in the field: Carlyle, Tylor, Boas, Frazer, Rank, Raglan, Campbell, Eliade, Freud, and Jung among others. However, I thought that they all missed something essential in their attempts to explain the myth of the hero. All of these writers operated as if the most important features of the phenomena could be explained completely within the confines of their own particular discipline. All scholarship claimed, to one degree or another, that the myth of the hero was universal among human cultures. However, they never explained how or why this was true. Most despaired of even attempting to answer such questions. They focused on their particular interests, most often, how a cultural trait functioned within a society expressed in myth and folktale. Search for origins was abandoned as largely impossible to demonstrate empirically.

I always felt that human beings' essential hunting nature was never given its full due in the writings of any of the scholars mentioned above, nor in any other writers on mythology. At first, I wondered if the hunt was so apparent in myth that it was, at best, of too broad a scope to help much in working new and unexpected facts into a broad, coherent understanding. At worst, I worried that it just might be uninteresting because the notion did not really tell us anything that we did not already know about ourselves factually. After all, all humans know that they are hunters at heart. Some like it, some do not. Some are good at it, some are not. No one can seriously deny it for long. Inescapable hunger will make each survivor hunt, or depend upon others hunting, if ever one were to find oneself lost out in the wild. On the other hand, it is a very easy notion to parody and to dismiss in our state of civilization. The Old Sitting 'Round the Campfire Theory, for instance. I also had no interest in going down the path of Dart and Ardrey and represent the hunter-forager life as one of an intelligent killer ape, the alpha predator of the savannah. What could I discover new and of value to add to this fundamental perspective concerning the human hunter-forager as storyteller and mythmaker? The question grew with the journey. Where would I not find the hunter-forager in any aspect of human life? But did not being a modern human being in the super-civilization of science and technology render our past hunter-forager heritage as something of slight relevance to our present, urbanized, mechanized daily circumstances? The more that I pursued it, the more I came to wonder if civilization was little more than a thin veneer upon humanity's essential being. I wondered if the myth of the hero was the echo of our hunter-forager heritage and our daily lives. I came to understand it as representing the best and worst and most unique about us as creatures on this Earth. The best is that we can serve others, the worst is that we kill in order to live and the most unique is that we can sing it all in a story for others of our kind, so they can experience at one remove, our lives and our dreams, in their own hearts and minds.

Upon graduating, with subsequent marriage, travel, family, and teaching, I continued reading on the subject on my own. I watched *The Power of Myth*, Bill Moyers' interviews with the pre-eminent mythologist of my day, Joseph Campbell. I came away thinking that nothing more could be said about the myth of the hero. Almost. "Symbolically or unconsciously, the hero is either the creator of the myth or anyone stirred by it. In identifying himself with the literal hero, which he (or she) can do consciously, the creator or reader becomes the true subject of the myth." [1] If what Campbell says is true, then any layman with a hunger for the subject is qualified to think about and write about it. The myth of the hero is about every single individual of us. Further, the myth of the hero is in us before we ever listen to the first story in our lives. But how?

With every myth that I read or read about, I could never shake the feeling that the origins of the myth of the hero must be rooted evolutionarily in our hunting experience. As my thinking upon this subject matured, I became interested in writing the natural history of the myth of the hero from the perspective of human biology. This took my reading into many fields of expertise where a layman such as myself is not necessarily qualified to critique or challenge the data. However, the further afield I pushed my inquiries, the more convinced I became that only a layman, non-specialist perspective upon the myth of the hero could tie it all together and reveal its true structure and origin and meaning. Why so?

Laymen are outside of established institutions, church, state and collegial. They are interested in the gist of things, in the big picture, the forest for the trees. They want a "take-away" that reduces complexity to a pithy phrase that is easily remembered, applicable to daily life and has a way of popping up in everyday conversation. They are lumpers, not splitters. Laymen are attracted to the most general plausibilities of a field rather than to their hairsplitting controversies. Expert opinion is almost always divided down the middle and laymen must rely upon their instincts rather than their expertise in order to see their way clear to an understanding. It is more pleasing to compare similarities than to contrast differences. Particularists insist that all that exists in nature are individuals. They are correct. Comparativists insist that the taste of the sea can be captured in one drop. It can. Laymen want the sum total, the whole, the Gestalt. For some searches, this approach results in a blur. For others, it is the only way to uncover the cogent outlines of seemingly dissimilar phenomenon. It must

---

1 Segal, Robert A. *Joseph Campbell: An Introduction.* Penguin Books USA Inc., 375 Hudson Street, New York, NY, 10014, USA. p. 45.

necessarily be grand and overarching. Broad rather than deep. Hopefully, a multiplex of reasonable compromises. Perhaps a layman can only attain to a string of plausibilities. Considering the myth of the hero from a number disparate disciplines resulted in a string of plausibilities that came together with a surprising twist at the end. This twist will reflect the true value of my thoughts upon this subject as they relate to the day to day existence of each and every one of us as family members, workers, citizens of a democracy and as spiritual seekers.

My readings and ponderings also made me realize that in order to answer my original questions, that is, what is the origin of the myth of the hero and why is it universal and exactly how the hunt tied into it all, I would have to drastically expand the field of inquiry. I would need to examine storytelling, or narrative thinking, under the light of evolutionary theory, as a feature of human biology. The most insightful discipline of human biology's toolkit was ethology, the science of "interviewing an animal in its own language." Ironically, it was the ethological perspective upon the myth of the hero that revealed its origins most clearly and definitively. Comparing why animals communicate with why people tell stories was the most revealing exercise of all. This is a controversial take on the subject. A sizeable number of human beings do not accept the fact that man is an animal like all other animals on Earth. They resent, or hold as ludicrous, what has been mocked as the Martian biologist perspective. Initially at least, *Orion's Guiding Stars* does nothing more than consider *Homo sapiens* as a member of the kingdom *Animalia* and as such, represents the sum total of cognitive evolution of all life. "...the difference in mind between man and the higher animals, great as it is, certainly is one of degree and not of kind."[1] There is no behavior unique to humans that an analog in animal behavior cannot be discovered and used for comparison and insight. This includes manipulating symbols. Perhaps the only behaviors unique to humans are playing with fire, cooking and storytelling. There is no understanding the myth of the hero without considering language, but at the highest levels of cognition, as story, and story too has animal origins.

These are my "Sassettis" concerning the Orion Complex and its verbal manifestation as the myth of the hero.

The Orion Complex is a universal in human behavior and is therefore found in all human cultures in all Earthly climes from the misty depths of time until the day of our super-civilization of science and technology.

---

1 Darwin, Charles. *Descent of Man*, 1871. p. 105. See also Frans B.M. de Waal, *The Need for a Bottom-Up Approach to Chimpanzee Cognition* in The Mind of the Chimpanzee, University of Chicago Press, 2010. pps. 296-306.

People tell the kind of stories that they tell because they are part of the kingdom *Animalia*, and more specifically, of the order of Primates.[1]

The Orion Complex originates in Africa.

The Orion Complex is as old as the group of modern human ancestors that originally left Africa. Perhaps it is as old as *Homo Erectus, Homo heidelbergensis,* the Neanderthals and the Denisovans. It could be a feature of the genus *Homo* and not confined to the modern human species. However, we can never know. If any unique qualities of these more ancient peoples' stories survive, they are buried so deep in modern human mythology that they are beyond sorting out in our present state of knowledge. All hominids shared the same hunter-forager lifeway. More than one human species may have sung the myth of the hero. The simplest conclusion to draw is that myth of the hero is as old as human speech.

The Orion Complex is rooted in daily human behavior surrounding the hunt.

The Orion Complex is a three part pattern of Leavetaking–Adventure–Homecoming that can be detected not only in the myth of the hero but also in many other human behaviors. Analogs of this pattern are to be found in many animal species.

It is in the Orion Complex that the true meaning of all myth lies.

The Orion Complex has an evolutionary, developmental history.

The Orion Complex has a genetic basis as much as a divinely inspired one. It is the human instinct for story. It is a pattern deeply rooted, hardwired in the circuitry of our motor functions and basic instinctual drives. It is the Gestalt the sum total of human instincts.

The Orion Complex and the myth of the hero represent the physical, psychological, cognitive and emotional imprint of the Earth upon each living human being.

The Orion Complex is a broader term and encompasses many aspects of human behavior. The myth of the hero is the Orion Complex as manifested in speech and story and myth.

The myth of the hero was originally an artifact of oral tradition and was composed during public performance in a blend of spontaneity and recall, tradition and individual artistry.

---

1 Xenophanes. Fragment 15: "But if oxen (and horses) and lions had hands or could draw with hands and create works of art like those made by men, horses would draw pictures of gods like horses and oven of gods like oxen ande they would make the bodies of their gods in accordance with the form that each species possesses." Also, Fragment 16: "Aethiopians have gods with snub noses and black hair, Thracians with grey eyes and red hair." *Ancilla to Pre-Socratic Philosophers*, translator: Kathleen Freeman, Harvard University Press, 1956. pp. 22.

What the song is to the songbird, the cry is to the wolf and the waggle dance is to the bee, the Orion Complex and the myth of the hero is to humans.

The writing that follows is divided into three sections. *Bones* will critically examine the myth of the hero through scholarship traditional to its study. This will define the essential mystery and provide a solid counterpoint to what will follow. *Flesh* will attempt to explain the myth of the hero in light of modern developments in the more empirical sciences such as genetics, epigenetics, ethology and evolutionary theory. The Orion Complex will be examined as a feature of human biology. *Spirit* offers up the logical and ironic implications of the structural, functional, empirical, materialist point of view as applied to the myth of the hero. This study suggests that an agnostic frame of mind resonates most sympathetically with our evolutionary design as a hunter-forager and as a spiritual creature upon Mother Earth. The journey that we have in mind will define our terms, review traditions and meet some of the great minds of the past who shared an interest in the myth of the hero. As the first step we can only wonder, what are children's first experiences of story and myth like?

BONES

GROWING PAINS: STORY AND MYTH

Healthy human babies attentively watch the people mothering them as they go about their tasks. They listen to the sounds that pour out of family members' mouths as their caregivers wipe up spills, close windows and let the dog out. Once they can smile, they start babbling in earnest, imitating the vocalizations around them. Babies raised in English speaking homes do not babble like babies in Japanese speaking homes. For language to emerge as speech in a healthy human baby, all the parents need to do is to speak to, and just as importantly, speak around the baby while doing this or that. After around two years of ardent listening and trial and error, toddlers have started to associate the vocalizations with objects and social contexts. They begin to join in with, respond to, and experiment with the ongoing conversation of life in their own words, haltingly at first, then with greater fluidity with experience. Speech emerges like an instinct triggered by social interactions.

When the budding speaker gets questioned as to what happened on the playground, the simplest report becomes a story. The first stories children tell are more melody than meaning. Then come beginning, middle and end. Conflicts become artful, resolutions often never quite resolve. Escapes, rescues, failures grow in elaboration. Sometimes the story brings delight. Sometimes the story is called a fib. People learn with every story that they tell. By the time children are taught to read, they already have definite ideas about what is a good story and a well told story and what is a bad story and one which is poorly told.[1]

---

1 Sarbin, Theodore R. *The Narrative as a Root Metaphor for Psychology.* Narrative Psychology: The Storied Nature of Human Conduct, Praeger, Westport, Connecticut, 1986.

Language is considered to be rooted the nervous system as an instinct. Speech is a behavior and all behavior can be tied to DNA triggered by the environment. How about story and the myth of the hero? Is narrative thinking, storytelling, the myth of the hero acquired solely by learning? Or is the myth of the hero as deep a part of each human being as is the color of his or her eye? Was the scaffolding for the myth of the hero already present in the nucleus of each cell at birth waiting to be evoked by the needs of survival in nature and social life among family members?

For most of us, our first experience of myth typically comes as a story read at bedtime by our parents or in a classroom by a teacher. And so we meet Odysseus, Achilles, Hercules and Thor. We sympathize with the unsettling circumstances of the hero's birth and the trials of his youth lost among strangers. We thrill to the undeniable call that compels him to adventure and his magnificent exploits slaying villains and monsters. We bask in his triumphal return home, his winning of love and his rise to kingship. Finally, we rue his tragic fall from grace and power at the end of his life.

These myths of heroes with strange names were soul stirring. They also seemed wondrously familiar and somehow larger than their brave deeds and their purported divine parentage. And though they come down to us on the wings of an esteemed elder's voice, these heroes emerge from between the covers of books. The stories about these heroes were written down so long ago that the original authors, with the notable exception of Homer, are largely forgotten. Yet the same hero tales have been written and rewritten across continents, languages and historical epochs. Our first books were myths full of heroes; *Gilgamesh, Genesis, Exodus, Iliad* and *Odyssey.* All are still widely read today.

The oldest literary works grew out of thriving oral traditions of storytelling and myth found worldwide. The first stories committed to writing have been told and retold in different guises since humans first started to speak. They go back to the time on the African savannah of our origins, when sharp eyed foragers knew the use of every plant in their territory root to fruit. Back when long distance runners still chased the eland to exhaustion and throttled them by hand in the shade of the last tree. Back when strong arms still threw spears at big, dangerous animals in order to provide meat for their loved ones.

How different it was to hear the myth of the hero around a hearth fire, in places where myth was openly part of the daily fabric of life and not kept safe on a shelf in books. Myth was an oral tradition. The events of myth did not seem so far removed from waking life. Myths were direct reflections of reality. A story was a patterned public speech act. It was entertainment for adults as well as children. The listener assumed the active role of an audience member of a performance. He or she could laugh or cry, sing along, whisper to neighbors, get up and leave, or even fall asleep. The storyteller was generally an older family member eager to please his or her audience. His or her facial expressions were not hidden behind a book. There was eye contact and gestures in flickering firelight. All the crucial dynamics of the art of storytelling were worked out in the humblest of circumstances long before evolving into rituals, ceremonies, epic poems, plays, novels and films.

In these pages we will meet with one of the grandest mysteries of human thinking and of natural history. The myth of the hero is the foundational motif of folklore and it is fundamentally the same in all cultures and times. It is the stamp of the Earth upon human evolution. It is our accumulated experience as a creature in the natural world as it pours out of our mouths in stories conveyed by speech. Humanity did not invent the myth of the hero lonely individual by lonely individual in the grips of sudden inspiration. It was not made up as an artistic act of sheer imagination to be memorized word for word down the generations. Rather, we evolved as a species and in the process, came to realize the myth of the hero consciously in ourselves and celebrate it verbally in our lives. The myth of the hero was the driving force of our daily work lives as hunter-foragers. It is instinctively what each person knows he or she must do out in nature in order to survive. It still resonates with us as farmers, craftsmen, mechanics and clerks.

Humans, compared to our sibling species, only begin to reflect our unique qualities when we are telling stories. This is how high up out of our animal origins that we must reach in order to fully distinguish ourselves cognitively from our closest relative the chimpanzee. Many animals have communicative cries that produce predictable reactions in others and chimpanzees tantalizingly demonstrate the beginnings of language in their cognition. The art of storytelling reveals the human cognitive achievement of open-endedness, the ability to juggle and juxtapose a limited number of elements into infinitive structures. We are the only known creature on Earth capable of narrating a sequence of events with a beginning, a middle and an end. The capacity for narrative provided recreation for our leisure time. More importantly, the ability to tell stories also helped us to teach our young and to work in teams. With stories, humans remember the past and predict the future. Excellence in narrative reflects a high degree of social intelligence in individuals and singles out leaders. Lovers are more attracted to storytellers. Storytelling and the myth of the hero helped humans survive and thrive wherever they ventured as hunter-foragers upon the Earth.

Every human is born with the myth of the hero flowing materially in his or her veins. It comes with us into the world at birth as ready to find expression as does language and speech. The immediate environment will inexorably trigger it in our cognition and in our behavior. The myth of the hero might be called the life that the Earth inflicts upon each individual whose fate it is to be born a human being. The myth of the hero is so deep in the individual psyche that it almost represents the biography of Everyman.

Ultimately, though most heroes in myth are portrayed as male, the hero as a concept is beyond masculinity and femininity. It speaks to the species, not only to the gender, nor to social roles assigned to gender. The myth of the hero is no sanction for the repression of women because the stories are mostly scripted for and cast by male actors. In modern urban society, when mister becomes mom, then missus often becomes hero. Now, as back then, the hearth fire adventure is a complex story. With all due respect, gender issues associated with the myth of the hero are outside the focus of this work, except to acknowledge that lamentably, in this aspect of life as well, female heroes are unequally represented in the cavalcade of myth.

From the beginning, all of us knew that myths were special stories. Perhaps it was the awe in the voices of the adults who read them to us. When pressed to account for this special quality, we can only faithfully maintain that somehow, myths pertain to the spirit. They somehow explain you to yourself against the backdrop of the great beyond. This same feeling is what prompts mid-life crisis adults to go back to myth in their search for meaning during their post-child rearing years. All bookstores regularly restock their shelves devoted to serious collections of mythology aimed at the adult reader. The myth of the hero continues to pertain to our lives beyond our childhood and to be a source of revivifying energy. It feels right even though we might not know why. And just as strongly as anything else that we felt in our childhood experience of myth is the fact that these stories pointed to something mysterious and greater than ourselves. The Orion Complex works these nagging inklings into a coherent overview.

Is the myth of the hero only a literary experience? Or can it be lifted off of the pages and traced to our bodily structure and our evolutionary past? The journey will follow the material science as it leads away from speculative metaphysics. We will keep trailing the science until it naturally, inevitably circles back to metaphysics, like a melody begins and ends on the same note. It is in the myth of the hero that science and spirit can gaze upon each other with proper esteem and embrace as siblings of one mother. The trail ahead opens out into a radical vision of unity.

In the Beginning

A forensically sound discovery process requires searching out the oldest stories that we can find from literary sources. These stories come from the creation myths that have been written down in the holy books of religious traditions from around the world. These are the oldest stories to which we can gain access in books. What follows is a sampling of creation mythology with no pretense of being comprehensive. It is broadly representative and forms a general mythological account of two issues, man's material origin and the origin of speech. Upon the material origins of humans, science and religion are in general agreement. This is evident in the myths of the hero which follow.

In the ancient Babylonian account of creation, one of the oldest pieces of writing, first came the cosmos, then the gods. Tiamat, the originator, separated the primordial sea and the land. It was she who created the gods. Marduk, counselor of the gods and one of Tiamat's grandchildren, rose up in rebellion. He slew her and became the supreme god. Marduk's very word had the power of creation. From Tiamat's severed body parts, the earth and sky were created. Her spouse Kingu was sacrificed and from his blood, human beings were created.[1]

The Epic of Gilgamesh of ancient Sumer in Mesopotamia is one of the first stories in world literature. It predates the Hebrew Bible by over a millennium. It was preserved on clay tablets and written in cuneiform. There is an allusion to the power of thought and language in creation. The gods cry out to the creator goddess Aruru. "So the goddess conceived an image in her mind, and it was of the stuff of Anu of the firmament. She dipped her hands in water and pinched off clay, she let it fall in the wilderness, and noble Enkidu was created." Man is

1 Pritchard, James B., ed. The Ancient Near East, Volume I: An Analogy of Texts and Pictures. Princeton University Press, 1958.

created from clay to serve and provide food for the gods. There is one of the first recorded instances of a world flood in Gilgamesh.[1]

Ancient Egyptian mythology is rich and variegated. It is magnificently inconsistent viewed as a whole. One tradition had Khnum, the god of the source of the Nile as the creator of man whom he shaped out of mud. Another tradition had man spring from the tears of Atum, the god of the sun. The earth itself was personified as the god Geb. The god of writing was the ibis headed god Thoth. His wife was the goddess of scribes, Seshat. Their child Hornub was a god of language. The implication is that speech came from divine writing rather than the reverse.[2]

The Bible is one of the foundational documents of Western civilization. It does not deal with the origin of language itself much less the origin of storytelling. However, language was important. It was the word of God which brought about the whole of creation. "And God *said*, 'Let there be light.'"[3] Later in the New Testament, this notion of the power of language and speech was repeated. "In the beginning was the *Word*, and the *Word* was with God, and the *Word* was God."[4]

The first man Adam was created from dust as a fully developed speaker. "And the LORD God commanded the man, saying, of every tree of the garden thou mayest freely eat: But of the tree of the knowledge of good and evil, thou shalt not eat of it: for in the day that thou eatest thereof thou shalt surely die."[5] God spoke to Adam when he wanted to communicate with him. Biblically, language originated with man himself simultaneously at the moment of his creation like his eyes and his hands. He was a speaker from birth and understood God's original spoken commandments. This presupposes that man was fully cognitively human at the moment of creation. Later, "And out of the ground the LORD God formed every beast of the field, and every fowl of the air; and brought them unto Adam to see what he would *call* them: and whatsoever Adam *called* every living creature, that was the *name* thereof. And Adam *gave names* to all cattle, and to the fowl of the air, and to every beast of the field."[6] Language was part of the miraculous original creation of man, not an afterthought or a development of a budding skill inherited from ancestral forms or an attainment of innate learning abilities. Animals were created from the same stuff as were human beings, earth, but they were nothing special otherwise. Souls were not attributed to animals.

---

1 *The Epic of Gilgamesh.* Assyrian International News Agency Books Online www.aina.org. Tablet I.
2 Wilkinson, Richard H. *The Complete Gods and Goddesses of Ancient Egypt.* Thames & Hudson. 2003 (Anonymous, The Holy Bible).
3 Gen. 1.3.
4 John 1.1.
5 Gen. 1.16-17.
6 Gen. 2.19-20.

It can be reasonably assumed that after the deluge that destroyed human kind, leaving only Noah and his three sons and their wives, that they all spoke the same language.[1] The Tower of Babel[2] story gives an account of the confusion of tongues among men due to their sinful pride in attempting to build a tower to reach heaven.

Adam was created spontaneously from the Earth as an adult, so language also was placed in him fully developed and functional from his first breath. In the broadest terms, these Old Testament stories allow us to surmise that biblically, language is recognized as a human cognitive skill that is innate; it is in us at birth because God put it there. However, Adam's experience of language, as well as Eve's, was presumably different from that of their sons Cain and Abel. The sons of Adam learned language like all descending humans did. They acquired it from life experiences with their parents, developmentally, over a two year period of listening which stimulated their innate language abilities.

Ancient Greek religion and mythology was a complex of generally agreed upon traditions manifested locally and particularized to a population of worshipers centered around a shrine or temple. The Athena of Sparta was not quite the Athena of Athens, neither in worship nor in story. Therefore, there are many different traditions concerning the material origin of man and of language.

The original, non-Greek speaking inhabitants of Greece were known as the Pelasgians. Some of their mythological traditions survived the Indo-European Mycenaean and Doric invasions and were absorbed into Greek mythology. When the second century A.D. travel writer Pausanias described Arcadia, the mountainous, landlocked region of the Peloponnesus, he told of Pelasgus, the first human king, and quoted the poet Asius. "The godlike Pelasgus on the wooded mountains black *earth* gave up, that the race of mortals might exist." [3] Earth was a goddess second in all creation only to Chaos and out of herself she created man, almost plant like. This echoes Genesis in the materials of human creation but in the biblical tradition, God formed Adam out of dust. However, this dust is in no way equated to his own divine self or being. It is an extension of his word.

In Homer, when Hera is speaking to Aphrodite and borrowing her girdle in order to lull Zeus in love, she mentions man's material origins indirectly when she says, "...Oceanus, from whom the gods are sprung...," [4]Ultimately,

---

1 Gen. 8.18.
2 Gen. 11.1-9.
3 Pausanias. *Pausanias Description of Greece with an English Translation* by W.H.S. Jones, Litt.D., and H.A. Ormerod, M.A., in 4 Volumes. Cambridge, MA, Harvard University Press; London, William Heinemann Ltd. 1918. Book 8, Chapter 1, Section 4.
4 Hom. Iliad 22.223.

gods and men form one family.[1] Oceanus was the ocean that the ancient Greeks believed encircled the world like a vast river. The pre-Socratic philosopher Thales would echo Homer and make water the primal element, the material origin of all living things.

The best known tale of man's material origin in Greek mythology comes from the poetry of Hesiod,[2] the dour Boeotian farmer, and the *Library and Epitome* of Pseudo-Apollodorus,[3] whose true identity remains shrouded in mystery. These are our original sources of the Promethean creation of man and theft of fire. Prometheus and his brother Titan Epimetheus sided with the Olympians in their war against the Titans. Upon victory, Zeus did not condemn them to be chained in Tartarus alongside of their rebellious brothers and sisters. It was Prometheus who molded the first man out of water and earth.[4] Pausanias mentioned a shrine in Panopeus where two large stones once stood. These were shown to travelers and proclaimed to smell like the skin of a man.[5] It was said that from these two stones Prometheus fashioned the first men. At the first-ever sacrifice to the gods by humans, Prometheus deceived Zeus into accepting the bones and fat of the oxen instead of the rich meaty portions. Incensed at this treachery, Zeus withheld fire — which Prometheus then stole and gave to man. The vengeance of Zeus was twofold. The king of the gods pinned Prometheus upon the highest crag of the Caucasus Mountains. A vulture was to devour his liver each day and each night it would grow back. The torment was to last forever. As punishment for man, Zeus bequeathed to him Pandora, All Endowed, as his companion in life. Pandora was created by Hephaestus. The lame smith god hammered a deceitful mind and a shameless heart into her. Hermes, conductor of departed souls to the land of the dead, the herald of Olympus and the god of thieves, gave Pandora her lying tongue. It was Pandora who opened the box of evils and unleashed them upon humanity. She put her hunger and curiosity above her fear and awe of authority, much as did Eve concerning the fruit of the tree of good and evil. The only thing that mitigated Pandora's crime was the release of hope trailing the woes.

---

1 Hesiod. *Works and Day.* 107-108.

2 Hesiod. *Works and Days.* 59-69.

3 Pseudo-Apollodorus. The Library, with an English Translation by Sir James George Frazer, F.B.A., F.R.S. in 2 Volumes. Cambridge, MA, Harvard University Press; London, William Heinemann Ltd. 1921. Includes Frazer's notes. http://www.perseus.tufts.edu/hopper/text?doc=Perseus:text:1999.01.0022:text=Library:book=1:chapter=7&highlight=pandora

4 Psuedo-Apollodorus. 1.7.

5 Pausanias. *Pausanias Description of Greece with an English Translation* by W.H.S. Jones, Litt.D., and H.A. Ormerod, M.A., in 4 Volumes. Cambridge, MA, Harvard University Press; London, William Heinemann Ltd. 1918. Book 10, Chapter 4, Section 4.

Prometheus's son was Deucalion, a Noah like figure in Greek mythology.[1] He and his wife were the only survivors of a worldwide flood sent by Zeus to destroy wicked humanity. Upon recession of the waters, Deucalion and his wife threw stones over their shoulders and these became the race of humans who inhabit Earth. Hermes later confused their tongues and divided people into separate nations. This divine confusion was in punishment for human wickedness, which, according to mythological sources, always seems to return given time once a golden age is attained by humans.

We cannot leave Greek mythological tales of humanity's material origins and the origin of language without mentioning Hesiod's Five Ages of Man.[2] It is a sort of reverse evolutionary scheme. The first race of men was golden, and times were ideal and people innocent. Extinction gave rise to a race of silver, not quite so developed or so good. Next came the increasingly worse brazen race, followed by the race of demi-gods who sailed to Colchis for the Golden Fleece and who fought at Troy. Extinction of these gave rise to the race of iron, that is, the humans of our present wicked day and age.

Language for the Greeks was a gift of the gods. It was the Muses, especially Calliope, the muse of epic poetry, who inspired men to speak clearly and sing well. Clear speaking was the reward for good behavior and showed the favor of the gods.

In both the Biblical and Greek traditions, which form the basis of Western spirituality, there is an intuition that all life originated in the ocean. Human beings were created by a divinity out of the very soil of Earth. Hesiod even seems to intimate that original man sprang from the ash tree. Women are held accountable in both traditions for humanity's estrangement from divinity. There is a progression of humanity as a species, a devolution from original innocence to increasing wickedness. Each race suffers complete or partial extinction to make way for the next. The inheritors are one rung lower on the moral scale. Floods wiping out humanity are common to both traditions, with only the good surviving to repopulate the Earth. In the Greek tradition, gods and men procreate together. The mythology is replete with half divine humans. Hercules, product of Zeus upon a mortal woman, and Achilles, product of the mortal King Peleus upon the immortal sea nymph Thetis. The biblical God creates but does not procreate with his human creations. Mary's pregnancy with Jesus, Son of God, was a miracle without the slightest tinge of carnality. Both Yahweh and Zeus are considered the Father of Man. Where Zeus must copulate in the flesh or rain down in a shower of gold, Yahweh need only speak. Language is created simultaneously in the biblical Adam by God and is bestowed as a gift upon man by the mythological Hermes.

---

1 Psuedo-Apollodorus. 1.7.
2 Hesiod. Works and Days, 109-201.

The first small family of man in both traditions all spoke the same language but later it was confused by divine decree because of the increase of sinful behavior.

The Vedic traditions of India are a good source for comparison. The variety and complexity of ancient Greek religion and mythology is increased exponentially when considering all that the Hindus have to say about the material origins of humanity and of language in their myths of the hero.

The *Rig Veda* is the oldest religious text still in use today. It is a prayer book, a source of incantations and spells, and a story book compiled from many sources. It was assembled over long periods of time beginning as early as 1700BC in the Indus Valley. There is refreshing honesty in Book 10, Chapter 29, of the Nasadiya Sukta, The Creation Hymn.[1]

> Out of darkness and chaos came the great power of warmth which set the ball rolling but...
> Who verily knows and who can here declare it, whence it was born and whence comes this creation?
> The Gods are later than this world's production. Who knows then whence it first came into being?
> He, the first origin of this creation, whether he formed it all or did not form it,
> Whose eye controls this world in highest heaven, he verily knows it, or perhaps he knows not.

Here, the first origin of creation was known as Poms or Man. He was sacrificed by the gods by the power of their verbal command. From his parts came the sun, the moon and the Earth. The first man was Manu, a descendant of the creator Brahma. Manu's name is associated with the Sanskrit verb to think and the English nouns human and man. By performing the first sacrifice to the gods, man evolved into a higher, more spiritual being, a Rishi or sage. Manu is a Noah-like character in that he was the sole survivor of a worldwide flood. After the waters receded, he poured oblations of butter and milk into a river and a woman emerged called Ina. Manu married her and she became the mother of humanity.

Hindu tradition has a goddess of speech. Her name is Saraswati and she is identified with the Saraswati River. In icons, she has four arms. In her hands she holds a book, the written word; a lute, the sung word; prayer beads, the inspired word; and a water pot, the fluid word. She is a goddess of arts and sciences. Her festival is the first day of spring. In the *Rig Veda*, she is identified as Vac. Vac is also *speech* in Sanskrit. Saraswati is acknowledged as the mother of the *Vedas*. She says in Book 10.125,[2] "I, verily, myself announce

1 Lanman, Charles R. *The Sacred Books and Early Literature of the East.* Vol. IX: India and Brahmanism, *Rig Veda*, Book X-Hymn 129, Verses 6-9, 1917. p. 48.
2 Ibid. Book 10, Hymn 125, Verse 5 of the Nasadiya Sukta. p. 46.

and utter the word that Gods and men alike shall welcome. I make the man I love exceedingly mighty, make him a sage, a rishi, and a Brahman." Language lifts women and men from their lesser status and unites them to divinity.

In Norse mythology, the Poetic Eddas[1] reveal that the Earth was created by the body of the primordial being Ymir. He is like Poms of the Vedic tradition. From his flesh came the gods Vili, Ve and Odin. Chapter nine of the Prose Eddas[2] have the three gods walking along a beach where they come upon two trees. From these, they create the first two humans, Ask and Embla. Ask has been etymologically related to the ash tree. Odin the All Father gave language to the primal parents. Later, after hanging on the cross for nine days, Odin revealed the runes that allow men to write down their thoughts and traditions and pass them down faithfully to their descendants.

Ancient Chinese mythology[3] presents no unified body of beliefs concerning the material origins of man and language. Pre-Taoist traditions claim that from formless chaos, the universal power of *qi* divided into *yin* and *yang*. It coalesced into a cosmic egg out of which was born Pengu. The original man was hairy and primitive. Upon his death, his body parts became the celestial phenomenon, his eyes the sun and the moon and his blood the waters of rivers and seas. From clay, the goddess Nuwa, half snake and half human, was credited with creating the first human being who spoke spontaneously upon creation. Cangjie is the Chinese deity or culture hero credited with inventing writing, but this came much later.

The Popol Vuh[4] is the book of creation of the Quiché Maya who flourished in pre-conquest southern Mexico, Guatemala and Honduras. In the beginning, all was sea and sky. Sovereign Plumed Serpent and the three in one god Heart of Sky thought together about creation. "For the forming of the earth they said, 'Earth.'" First came the animals but when they were bidden to speak by the gods, they could only squawk and cry out. For their lack of language, "...their flesh was brought low: they served, they were eaten, they were killed-the animals on the face of the earth."

The first race of men was made of mud but only spoke nonsensically. These first men were a disappointment to the gods and dissolved in the rains sent against them. The next race of men was carved from wood by Grandmother of Day and Grandmother of Light. They were in looks and speech like men of today but "accomplished nothing before their Maker." The beasts of the

1 Bellows, Henry Adams *The Poetic Edda*. 1936.. Vol. I, Lays of the Gods, Voluspo, The Wise Woman's Prophesy, Verses 3-4. p. 4. www.sacred-texts.com.
2 Sturlusson, Snorri. *The Prose Edda*. Gylfanning. p. 20-21. www.sacred-texts.com.
3 Walls, Jan and Yvonne Walls (translators and editors), *Classical Chinese Myth*. Hong Kong, Joint Publishing Company, 1984. p. 135.
4 Tedlock, Dennis. *Popol Vuh: The Definitive Edition of the Mayan Book of Life and Glories of Gods and Kings*. Touchstone Rockefeller Center, 1230 Avenue of the Americas, New York, NY 10023. 1996.

wild and their own tools and cooking utensils turned against them and tore them apart. Lastly, they were inundated by a flood. Monkeys in the forest are the last vestige of these men of wood. Much later in time, after the Hero Twins defeated the Lords of Death in the ball game in Xibalba, man was molded out of white and yellow corn and other food staples such as cacao by the goddess Xmucane. Water became human blood. The water she used to rinse her hands became human fat. "No woman gave birth to them, nor were they begotten by the builder, sculptor, Bearer, Begetter. By sacrifice alone, by genius alone they were made, they were modeled by the Maker, Modeler, Bearer, Begetter, Sovereign Plumed Serpent. And when they came to fruition, they came out human: They talked and made words." Man was made of corn and created a speaker from his first breath.

The Inca of South America created an empire that rivaled Rome for the amount of territory it controlled. A primary source of Inca mythology is *The Royal Commentaries of the Inca*. It was written in the next generation after the Spanish conquest. The author was the son of a conquistador and an Inca princess, Inca Garcilaso de la Vega. He relates that Viracocha, the Old Man of the Sky, Lord Instructor of the World, created a dark world of stone giants. They were disobedient and they were destroyed in a massive flood. In the second creation, men were fashioned of clay. They were given clothes, language, songs, skills, and crops. Men were ordered to sink back into the earth and reappear in the territories where they would make their lives. These men were brutish, basically living like wild animals until Inti, Our Father the Sun sent a son and a daughter to teach men how to live.[1]

We have gone around the world in both time and space, concentrating our efforts upon the high civilizations which left written records. Materially, people are acknowledged to be made of the same stuff as of all other creation; from earth, from animals, from the gods themselves. Language was a bestowal from the gods. Let us extend our search to pre-literate peoples and cultures, to the myths of the hunter-foragers. Even among the ancient civilizations, they are assumed to represent the oldest human lifeway upon the planet.

---

1 Van Over, Raymond. *Sun Stories: Creation Myths from around the World*. New American Library, Inc.1633 Broadway, New York, NY 10019, 1980. p. 112-116.

Back When All the Animals Were People

In the mid-nineteenth century, a fever for folklore hit Europe and America. The Brothers Grimm in Germany discovered profound linguistic ties between the languages that stretched from India to Ireland and beyond. It was the height of the colonial era. The days when the sun never set upon the British Empire. Travelers of every hue ventured out into the remote regions of the world where recitations of the myth of the hero were daily occurrences. These adventurers were explorers, soldiers, surveyors, government workers, big game hunters, linguists, missionaries, doctors, ethnographers and their wives. Typically at night around the camp fire, they listened to storytellers in their employ. Through their guides and interpreters, they scribbled down the tales that they heard in hand-crafted, leather bound notebooks. Sometimes these seekers for tales interviewed native prisoners. More often than not, the storytellers were just regular men in their society, not specialists, not necessarily particularly renowned for traditional lore among their own people. The versions committed to the adventurer's notes were more summaries of, rather than faithful transcriptions, of these tales. Language was always a barrier. Customs were misunderstood and taken out of context. Bawdy incidences were deleted or disguised in Latin footnotes in order to remain true to science, but also, to refrain from offending 19th century Western concepts of modesty. There was an underlying drive to hammer these tales upon the anvil of ancient Greece and Rome so as to make them more familiar to modern taste. The German linguist Wilhelm Bleek published some of his examples of Bushmen folklore in the *Cape Town Gazette* in 1875. The general public read them enthusiastically. Andrew Lang, a Scots journalist in the era of the Sherlock Holmes stories, was a regular contributor of articles with folkloric themes to the *Daily News* and *Morning Post* and *Longman's Review*. He was at the heart of an enduring controversy with Indo-Europeanist Max Müller that raged in the press concerning Solar Mythology, a theory that linked the origin of mythological characters to heavenly bodies like stars and planets.

There are two inescapable observations to be made concerning human material and linguistic origins when comparing the myths of the hero of the hunter-forager societies that were collected by these adventurous souls. The first observation is that the hunter-forager version of "Once upon a time," goes something like "Back when all the animals were people." Hunter-foragers believed in the close familial relations between themselves and all life on Earth, plants, animals, even rocks and stars. The life sciences are united by the theory of evolution. All life branches from a single source[1] by means of the mechanisms of natural selection,[2] heredity, [3]mutation[4] and symbiosis.[5]The difference between the two ways of looking at things is more one of precision than opposition.

The second observation contains no small amount of irony. Modern physics posits that the atoms that comprise the material being of all living creatures were cooked in the center of stars in a vast evolutionary process of nuclear fission and fusion and exploding supernovae.[6]Ashes to ashes and dust to dust, both terrestrially and cosmically.

Both the intuitive and the rational approaches to the question of human origins have arrived at similar conclusions. Humans are materially one with the Earth and family with the animals upon it. Only civilized, historical humans claim a spontaneous, unique creation for themselves. This belief sets humanity apart from the rest of life on Earth. It endows each individual with a special fate upon dying but it is a fate available only to members of humanity. It isolates us from the living world. It sanctions the manner of our use of natural resources.

By analogy, rational and intuitive approaches to the acquisition of knowledge both point to the same basic truth. That underneath the surface facts, related in each field by their own particular means, the rational and the intuitive both express the same thing as a beginning premise of reality. All is One somehow. Here science and religion can gaze upon each other

---

1 Darwin, Charles. *Transmutation of Species, Notebook B.* 1837. p. 36. He wrote "I think," above his first evolutionary tree hypothesizing that all living forms evolved from a single ultimate ancestor.
2 Darwin, Charles. *The Origin of Species by Means of Natural Selection.* John Murray, London, England. 1859. p. 5.
3 Bowler, Peter J. *Evolution: The History of an Idea.* Berkeley: University of California Press. 2003.
4 Long, M., et al. *The Origin of New Genes: Glimpses From the Young and Old.* Nat. Rev. Genet. November 2003. pp.865–75.
5 Ryan, Frank. *Darwin's Blind Spot.* Houghton Mifflin Company, New York, NY. 2002. p. 15.
6 Sagan, Carl. *Cosmos.* Ballantine Books, New York, NY 10019. 1980.

as siblings of one mother. Blending them is vital to clear, comprehensive thinking. Therefore, I propose to combine the intuitive and the rational approaches to guide my research into the myth of the hero pattern and express my findings most often by means of analogy. By such means, I will lead you, dear reader, to that vista where you can see for yourself that vast promised forest in the distance. We will not be able to go any closer but at least we'll see the outline. A place to briefly rest until someone else comes along with a way onward.

Is not the proper outline of a mystery the highest point of view to which a layman can attain? And who is better to undertake such a task than a layman devoted to books? Storytelling is the layman art par excellence. Storytelling levels all other human talents. Storytelling is a tribal clubhouse whose only entrance fee is empathy with a voice. Stories are the meeting ground of all hungry minds. Stories are battlegrounds of politics and compromise. Myth is so general in humans, anyone with an honest hunger in his or her mind for it is qualified to think and write about it. In story and the myth of the hero, there are many unknown women and men who are masters.

There comes a blindness upon too close observation with a single, clear lens. It is the blindness required of exacting precision. Arjuna only has eyes for the bulls eye dead center on the straw target. However, he misses the bird flying by. The myth of the hero best reveals itself through a jewel of many facets rather than a single clear lens. You have to stand back at the proper distance from the painting in order to see the myth of the hero pop out of the background. Tread too close and it recedes into hiding again and vanishes from sight.

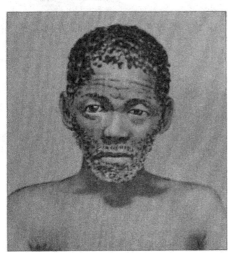

A brief look at some myths from around the world will confirm that in the hunter-forager mind, humans and animals shared common material origins and behavioral characteristics and formed a single family.

The Bushmen lived in the traditional hunter-forager lifeway in the Kalahari Desert of Southwest Africa. Few if any still live in the Old Way. They hunted the eland and the giraffe. Their cave paintings indicate that they have done so for at least thirteen thousand years. This is surely far short of their actual span of existence.[1] The Bushmen constitute the oldest continuous human culture on Earth. Their gene pool contains the greatest variety within it of any other human race. Their faces show traces of all races, Negroid, Mongoloid and Caucasoid. They are the Parent People. The Bushmen believed that in the beginning, all the people were animals. The fire of creation was wielded by *Koaxa* the Creator to brand the animals, changing them into this and that species. From the moment of their transformation by fire, the Bushmen claim that the animals stopped being people and took up their lives as clawed, horned and winged creatures.[2]

The Pygmies of the Ituri Forest of Central Africa hunt and fish every creature imaginable in their environment. They even take down elephants singlehandedly with a short stabbing spear from leafy ambush alongside game trails. From Pygmy mythology comes the most ancient version of the Garden of Eden story. In Pygmy mythical time, all animals were on an even footing with humans and could speak.[3]

The Semang are Negrito hunter-foragers who live in the remaining tropical forests on the Malay Peninsula in Southeast Asia. Marginalized by Buddhist and Islamic majorities and dwindling inexorably, some Semang still hunt in the forest in order to supplement their horticulture. These days, if they wear anything on their feet,

1 Garlake, Peter. *The Hunter's Vision: The Prehistoric Art of Zimbabwe*. British Museum Publications, London, England. 1995. p. 17.
2 Biesele, Megan. *Women Like Meat*. Indiana University Press, 601 N. Morton Street, Bloomington, Indiana 47404 1993. pp. 21, 115.
3 Turnbull, Colin, M. *The Forest People*. Touchstone Books, Simon and Schuster, Rockefeller Center, 1230 Avenue of the Americas, New York, NY 10020, 1968. p. 17.
Pulford, Mary, H. *Peoples of the Ituri*. Harcourt Brace Custom Publishers, 8th Floor, Orlando, Florida 32887, 1993. p. 19.

it might well be plastic flip flops. Kari, the god who shakes lightning from a gigantic stone flower, created the cosmos. His breath is the wind. It was another celestial god, Ple, associated with trees, flowers, winds and diseases, who actually created the Earth and the people on it out of clay and water. Kari gave them their souls which had hung on a tree in paradise. With the death of the body, those same souls would return to the same tree upon the wings of a bird. Animals, all things in general, had souls. Animals often metamorphose out of lower creatures. Their appearance is due to burns suffered in a fire.

The Semang believe that there was a conversation between the first parents and a baboon. The first woman saw that the other animals had children and wanted her own but did not know how to go about getting them. Baboon was kind enough to set her straight and soon she conceived two boys and two girls with her husband.

The problem with all genealogies is that even if one could be traced all the way back to its ultimate roots, it would seem to terminate in incest.[1] Natural selection originates all life on Earth in a single cell. Both approaches account for the diversity of, better than the creation of, branching, interrelating life.

The Andaman Islanders, who live on a tropical archipelago in the middle of the Indian Ocean, hunt dugong at sea and komodo dragons on the land. To this day, some continue their traditional lifeway under the protection of the Indian government. Few outside visitors are allowed to visit their remaining islands. Their creator, the spider *Biliku-Tarai*, also gave birth to birds, cicadas and prawns, as well as the sun, moon, rain, thunder, lightning, winds, and storms. Another mythological character, *Tomo*, upset his wife's canoe. She transformed into a crab and their grandchildren became lizards.[2]

Among the kangaroo hunting Murinbata tribe of the Northern Territory of Australia, a time is spoken of called the *Kardoorair*, which means "at first all things were men."[3]

1 Evans, Ivor H.N. *Studies in Religion, Folk-lore, & Custom in British Borneo and the Malay Peninsula.* Cambridge University Press, 1923. Bibliolife P.O. Box 21206, Charleston, SC 29413. pp. 143-199.
2 Radcliffe-Brown A.R. *The Andaman Islanders.* The Free Press, New York, New York 1922. pp. 150, 196.
3 Robinson, Roland. *Aboriginal Myths and Legends.* Sun Books Pty Ltd Melbourne, Victoria, Australia 1966. p. 31.

Hunter-foragers believed that humans were materially and cognitively related to the animals with whom they shared the Earth and upon whom they acknowledged dependence for their being, their wisdom and their very survival.

The Inuit, commonly known as the Eskimos, live in the Arctic Circle, harpoon seals through ice holes and even take on polar bears with their ancient weapons. They name the Mother of Animals Sedna, who, as a victim of bride capture, was thrown overboard because she complained so loudly on the voyage home with her new husband. Clinging to the gunwale of the boat and begging for mercy, she had her fingers chopped off. These severed digits sank into the ocean and metamorphosed into the seals and the walruses that nourished the Inuit.[1]

The Chumash lived on the Central Coast of California. They hunted whales at sea and bear in the mountains that rise above modern day Santa Barbara. They met the Spanish Franciscan fathers who colonized California in the 18th century and they served as the impressed labor force that constructed the Catholic mission that stands there to this day. Before being

1 Bierhorst, John. *The Mythology of North America.* William Morris and Company Inc. 105 Madison Avenue, New York, NY 10016 1985. pp. 62-63.

forced at gunpoint to convert to Christianity, the Chumash believed that all animals were related, that the bear was the elder sibling of all creatures, that all men were brothers, that Mother Earth was one, and that the world was God.[1]

The Selknam lived at the tip of Patagonia in South America and were guanaco hunters and harpooners of seal. By the 1950s, the last native speaker of their language had perished. They were famous for their physical hardiness. They lived nearly naked in icy, windswept conditions and greeted an astounded, well bundled Charles Darwin when he landed there on his voyage as the naturalist on the H.M.S. Beagle in 1831. He mistakenly claimed that these people lacked a deity. For the Selknam, the creator *Kenós* transformed people who grew old into animals, birds, rocks, mountains, winds, clouds and stars.[2]

These societies were separated, not only by thousands of miles, but also by thousands of years. Their stories confirm that the notion that humans are materially one with the rest of creation is very deep and ancient within us. Science confirms this mythological intuition empirically. It is possible that the notion of "in the beginning, all the animals were people," had a historical place of origin, probably pre-migration Africa and diffused through time across mountain range, desert and sea, spread by roving bands of hunters, storyteller to storyteller. This is perhaps beyond proving. It is a tantalizing concept. Stories leave scant physical evidence in their wake. Yet they leave something. The odds against independent invention in each society are astronomically huge. So what accounts for the striking similarity of this mythological motif across such gulfs of time and space if cultural diffusion and independent invention are dubious possibilities?

1 Blackburn, Thomas C. *December's Child-A Book of Chumash Oral Narratives.* University of California Press, Berkeley, California, 1975. pp. 102-103.
2 Wilbert, Johannes. *Folk Literature of the Selknam Indians.* University of California, Los Angeles, California, 1975. p. 24.

THEORIES OF MIND

Past scholars of myth have rooted the universality of mythological motifs in the common psychology of all humans, whether they live as hunter-foragers or as citizens of a consuming global civilization of science and technology. People interested in how the human mind works have hypothesized various mental structures that organize the manifest reality of the senses into some semblance of coherence. These mental structures are intangible. Theoretically they exist in the realms of pure thought. It was suspected from the first that they were somehow tied to the body but it was beyond the scope of the science of the day to demonstrate the connections empirically. The inkling that instincts fell under this heading was long suspected by such writers as Schopenhauer, Nietzsche, Freud and Jung. However it remained beyond proof, until the brand new science of epigenetics demonstrated how the environment initiates the expression of individual genes, and therefore behavior such as speech.

The first mental construct of note was Plato's theory of forms[1] which finds expression in many of his dialogues. In *Meno*, the discovery or recollection of knowledge as latent in the soul. In *Phaedo*, knowledge of the Forms inherent in the soul before birth. *The Republic, Book III* has the Allegory of the Cave: The struggle to understand the forms behind reality is likened to prisoners chained in a cave with a fire at their backs. They can only guess at the true nature of the origin of the shadowy shapes flickering on the wall before their imprisoned eyes.

---

1 Plato's theory of forms: *Meno* 71-81, 85-86; discovery/recollection of knowledge latent in the soul: *Phaedo* 73-80: Knowledge of Forms inherent in the soul before birth: *The Republic, Book III*. Allegory of the Cave: The struggle to understand forms behind reality like men in cave guessing at the true nature of the origin of shadows in firelight. Universals understood by mind and not perceived by senses: *Theaetetus* 184-186.

In *Theaetetus*, universals are understood by the mind and not perceived by the senses. Plato's theory of forms has numerous modern variations and nuances. The basic notion is that there is an unseen super-reality that supports and guides the perceived world. Whether the forms existed as a physical location above the Earth or within each human mind is controversial.

Adolf Bastian, the 19th century German ethnologist, wrote of the "psychic unity of man." He theorized that there were a number of select, inherent ideas in the minds of all humans that were the same across all cultures, climes and times. These elemental ideas found localized expression in individual cultures and environments.[1] An example of this is the notion of the human spirit. Most of Bastian's views on psychic unity were echoed by the groundbreaking English anthropologist Edward B. Tylor in the 1870s.

Sigmund Freud, the father of psychoanalysis, theorized a three part division of the human mind into the id, the super-ego and the ego. The id refers to the more animal-like, instinctual, autonomic areas of thinking. The super-ego "takes on the influence of those who have stepped into the place of parents; educators, teachers, people chosen as ideal models." It is the conscience of the individual, the unseen guide for behavior and perhaps the repository of "culture" in the human mind.[2] The ego is the executive of the mind, balancing the often conflicting demands of the other two parts.

Freud's student Carl Jung wrote about archetypes that are innate, universal prototypical ideas or psychological organs, analogous to physical ones. Archetypes are morphological structures that evolved in the human mind in response to the demands of life on planet Earth.[3] The Hero as champion and rescuer is one of Jung's archetypes.

Neither Freud nor Jung attempted to physically pinpoint their theoretical constructs in the brain. Id, ego, super-ego and archetypes were features of human thinking, not necessarily of human anatomy. However, they were likened to organs of the mind and were believed to be passed generation to generation.

From cognitive psychology and the work of F.C. Bartlett comes Schema Theory. Organizing structures in the mind incorporate input by associating it with information that is already part of the network. We are constantly reorganizing and restructuring our schema in order to accommodate new input.[4]

---

1 Tylor, Edward B. *"Professor Adolf Bastian."* Man 5. 1905. pp.138-143. Elementargedanken-Elementary thoughts.
2 Freud, Sigmund. *New Introductory Lectures* W. W. Norton & Company, 500 Fifth Avenue New York, New York 10110. 1990. p. 95-96.
3 Boeree, C. George. *Carl Jung.* Http//www.ship.edu/edu-cgboeree/jung.html.
4 Bartlett, F.C. *Remembering.* University of Cambridge, NewYork, NY 10011. 1995. pp. 199-200.

Noam Chomsky, a linguist at M.I.T., published *Syntactic Structures*[1] in 1957. Any given sentence in any given language has a deep structure in the mind. The mental operations of add, delete, move and replace transform the deep structure. These transformations form the basis for the surface structure which comes out of the mouth as speech. In the 1960s, he presented The Language Acquisition Device (LAD) as a hypothetical mental organ to account for human babies' innate capacity for language acquisition.

Lastly, there is the 1978 paper, "Does the chimpanzee have a theory of mind?" by Premack and Woodruff.[2] A theory of mind is the ability of an individual to attribute the same basic emotions and cognition that he or she possesses to others of their own kind. This also comes with the ability to recognize when they are different from self. Theory of mind makes possible empathy, altruism, deception and storytelling.

All of these notions could contribute to an explanation about how the mythological motif of "in the beginning, all the people were animals" could reside as an organized structure in the human mind. However, none of them can explain how the motif got there in the first place. Nor do they attempt to tie their psychic apparatuses to neurological functions and structures in the brain, nor to the life experiences of human hunter-foragers that serve as the ultimate pattern upon which these structures evolved.

The myth of the hero can be likened to an inheritable mental structure or a psychic apparatus. Its origins can be fruitfully traced to animal behavior and ultimately to the brain. The brain and all behavior are products of the interplay of the environment, the Earth and the individual. Nature and nurture can no longer be separated in our thinking about behavior. Humans are part of the family of life on Earth. All of what is human, both physically and cognitively, had extensive history in animality long before the hominids arose in East Africa some four million years ago. Hominids synthesized all skills and capabilities into one generalized upright bipedal package. The myth of the hero is Earth's imprint upon human cognition. Capacity for storytelling is what finally separates humanity from its animal origins. Storytelling is just as much a feature of human biology as of its culture. Comparing the reasons that hunter-foragers speak with the reasons that primates vocalize almost predicts the myth of the hero in human leisure speech behavior as an emergent feature. The perspective by which this hypothesis will be explored is by turns evolutionary, structural, functional, empirical and materialistic. It will treat storytelling behavior as coming out of

1 Chomsky, Noam. *Syntactic Structure*. Mouton de Gruyter, London, New York,1957, 2002.
2 Premack, David and Guy Woodruff. *Does the chimpanzee have a theory of mind?* Behavioral and Brain Sciences, Volume 1, Issue 4, Dec 1978. Cambridge University Press. pp. 515-526.

human biology and evolutionary history. Storytelling, and the accompanying mythological motifs, is in our genes and is reinforced by our daily activities. Natural history and myth seem to have arrived at the same place concerning human origins. The main difference is how.

Are science and spirit mutually repellent, like magnetic north and south poles? Or is another analogy more apt? Chlorine is poisonous and sodium reacts violently in water. However, combine these distinct elements in a 1:1 ratio and they form an ionic compound with the chemical formula of NaCl. Sodium chloride is table salt, an essential mineral in human nutrition. It takes a careful blend of science and spirit to comprehend and appreciate the myth of the hero and its origin in our physical being. The logic results in a surprise to our understanding of ourselves as spiritual creatures.

Does blending the objective with the subjective only distort both perspectives? Is this endeavor like oil and vinegar, where they only combine by vigorous shaking and separate naturally once calm returns? Can there be a scientific perspective for the mind that is not a complete refutation of the spirit of the heart? A mediation of opposites that yields a new vantage point and a new focus? The myth of the hero is the perfect terrain upon which to mingle light from both science and spirit. The last three sections confirm that rational science and intuitive myth arrived at analogous conclusions concerning human material origins and familial relations with all life on earth. This justifies further exploration, if only to disprove any significance to it beyond mere coincidence.

In studying the myth of the hero, the question hints at one of the central discontents of modern civilization. Religion, where the mind is thought of as an organ of perception, might be considered as a search for spirit from the top down. Science, where the mind is the computer of the five senses, might be considered as a search for spirit from the ground up. They are merely different methods of inquiry. Prayer above and experiment below. Both disciplines arrive at recognizably analogous understandings of humanity. But if science and spirit are talking about the same thing, why should they be at such odds? How can any adult achieve full actuation head and heart apart? Publically schooled citizens are the inheritors of a broad but divisive education. Can an individual taxpayer ever achieve happiness viewing science and spirit as two diametrically opposed paths?

Universal

When Vasco da Gama and Christopher Columbus set sail upon their epic voyages, they found human beings had already settled all of the lands to which they laid claim for their respective kings. The only discoveries that they actually made were the people who had already gotten there way ahead of the "discoverers." Those hither to unknown peoples were as ancient as any known back in Europe. In many cases, modern research has revealed them to be even more ancient. All of these so-called "discovered" people in "unknown" lands spoke human languages. All of these people told stories and had myths of the hero in their oral literatures.

In *La Relación of Fray Ramón Pané*,[1] we meet the first European missionary in the New World to learn a native language. It is one of the first true ethnographies from the New World. He records, "I write only of the Indians of the island of Hispañola for I know nothing about the other islands and have never seen them. These Indians also know whence they came and where the sun and moon had their beginning, and how the sea was made, and of the place to which the dead go. They believe that the dead people appear on the roads to one who walks alone, but when many go together, the dead do not appear. All this they were taught by their forebears, for they cannot read or count above ten." Father Pané's work revealed that the people whom Columbus brought to light upon the world historical stage had already been in possession of a rich and ancient mythology long before the Spaniards arrived. The striking parallels between Taino myths and stories out of the Christian Bible were evident from the first reading.

Father Bartholomé de las Casas was the first colonial official to hold the post of Protector of the Indians for the Spanish monarchy. He suggested that, based

---

1 Pane, Ramón. *La relación of Fray Ramón Pane.* http://faculty.smu.edu/bakewell/bakewell/texts/panerelacion.html.

upon the fact that the inhabitants had such a rich mythology, they must have souls, live spiritual lives and be fully human even though their race could not be traced back to a line of descent from any one of Noah's sons who are presented as the ancestors of the three races acknowledged in the book of *Genesis* in the Hebrew Bible. He penned one of the saddest testaments to come out of the Americas. " [I]nto and among these gentle sheep, endowed by their Maker and Creator with all the qualities aforesaid, did creep the Spaniards, who no sooner had knowledge of these people than they became like fierce wolves and tigers and lions who have gone many days without food or nourishment. And no other thing have they done for forty years until this day, and still today see fit to do, but dismember, slay, perturb, afflict, torment, and destroy the Indians by all manner of cruelty new and divers and most singular manners such as never before seen or read or heard of some few of which shall be recounted below, and they do this to such a degree that on the Island of Hispañola, of the above three millions souls that we once saw, today there be no more than two hundred of those native people remaining."[1]Recognition of full humanity and spirituality did little to stem the complete subjugation of the Taino people or their resulting genocide at the hands of the gold seekers. The brigands at least had to grant that they were exploiting fellow children of God who were storytellers with myths of the hero just like themselves.

People love stories and myths from exotic places. This too, seems very old in human history and is a universal. Long before Europe fell in love with Marco Polo and his tales of the Far East, Herodotus, the ancient Greek writer, who has been dubbed, alternatively as both the Father of History, and the Father of Lies, recorded the Egyptian tale of Rhampsanitus in his history of the Persian invasion. This particular story has nothing to do with the war but it remains one of the most delightful and memorable parts of the *Histories of Herodotus* and is a set piece in all courses devoted to the study of it.[2]

A universal is a behavior, pattern or institution that is common to all human cultures. The myth of the hero is a universal of human culture. It always has been. This is confirmed in historical and literary sources from civilizations around the globe down the ages. It is also confirmed in the ethnographic record of every primitive people that has ever been studied by anthropologists. The myth of the hero is a complex structure. It makes sense to break it down into parts. Myth has long been seen as history in fantastic guise.

---

1 De las Casas, Bishop don Fray Bartolomé. *A Short Account of the Destruction of the Indies*. Written 1542, published 1552. Introduction. http://nationalhumanitiescenter. org/pds/amerbegin/contact/text7/casas_destruction.pdf.
2 Herodotus. *The Histories*. Book II, chapters 121–124.

History

The word myth comes down to modern English from the ancient Greek; *muthos*, word, something spoken, a speech act. It is first encountered in Homer's *Odyssey*.[1] In the home of Odysseus, the bard Phemio has been called upon by the suitors to sing of the return of the Greeks from the Trojan War. Penelope, the long suffering wife of Odysseus, descends the stairs from her chambers and calls a halt to the song. She claims that it breaks her heart to be reminded of her husband lost for so many years. Her son Telemachus, in his first act as a man, rebukes his mother, saying "μῦθος δ᾿ἄνδρεσσι μελήσει πᾶσι," or "speech is man's concern." *Muthos* — combined with another Greek word, *logos*, which also means word, but with the added connotation of the study of — gives us our word "mythology."

The first action in the Bible is, "And God *said*..."[2] This recognition of the importance of speech in relation to creation was later echoed in the Book of John,[3] "In the beginning was the *word*..." "Saga" comes from Old Norse and shares the same root as "say" in English. In Icelandic, "saga" is a story, a narrative, a history, something said. It is amazing how much modern scholarship on myth strays completely from this fundamental fact.

The word "hero" also comes from ancient Greek *heros*. It passes almost unchanged from Latin to Old French to English. It too is first encountered in Homer in the opening lines of the *Iliad*, "πολλὰς δ᾿ ἰφθίμους ψυχὰς Ἄϊδι προΐαψεν ἡρώων." Due to the anger of Achilles, "many strong souls of heroes were sent to Hades."[4] This sense of the hero has remained virtually unchanged through time

---

1 Homer. *Odyssey*, Book 1:358.
2 Gen. 1:1.
3 John. 1:1.
4 *Iliad*, Book 1:3-4.

and space and language. It refers to a man or woman bravely facing danger by violent means, a rescuer, a champion. This is the narrowest definition of the word. What follows will broaden the significance and reveal the true context and ubiquity of the term hero, which, like myth, has eroded under modern usage.

At the beginning of the 21st century, myth as an everyday word has fallen in stature to mean a lie, a bizarre, false belief or a fable for children. *Myth Busters*, a popular television program, is devoted to exploring commonly held beliefs by means of scientific method. Among other things, the show has debunked the assertion that helium-filled footballs fly further than those filled with air and has confirmed that Coca Cola is, in fact, a great chrome brightener. It is lamentable that a term of such scope as myth has seemingly been so degenerated in common usage. Yet myth has captivated some of the most brilliant minds in history and generated shelves of scholarly works. Myth,[1] like Orion the Hunter, is a constellation of many stars and viewing angles.

Euhemerus was an ancient Greek writer who flourished shortly after the death of Alexander the Great in 323 BC. He was the court mythographer of Cassander I of Macedon. His chief work was a romance called *A Sacred History*,[2] set in a utopian world. Sadly, the work is lost and only survives in fragments and commentaries. The first-person narrator is cast away upon a fantastical island off of the Arabian Peninsula. He discovers a golden pillar that recorded all the births and deaths of the gods. He claimed that Zeus, the king of the Greek gods, had originally been a mortal ruler whose tomb could be found on the island of Crete. It still bore his name. All gods were once human rulers. The lives of kings, benefactors and culture heroes became exaggerated and embellished by oral tradition until these humans were transformed into deities.

Euhemerus is remembered as well as he is today chiefly due to the fact that he was often quoted by the early church fathers in their defense of Christianity against paganism. Lacantius, an advisor to Constantine, the first Christian emperor of the Roman Empire, accused Euhemerus of atheism. Other early church thinkers such as Eusebius, Clement of Alexandria, Tertullian, Firmicus Matemus and Augustine all mention Euhemerus' belief that the ancient gods were originally human and therefore, inferior to the Christian

---

1 Meletinsky, Eleazer. *The Poetics of Myth.* Routledge, New York NY 10001 1998. A general overview of the most influential scholarship concerning myth from Plato to Levy-Strauss. For a review more specifically aimed at the myth of the hero, see Robert A. Segal's introduction to his work *In Quest of the Hero*. Princeton University Press, 41 William Street, Princeton, NJ 08540. 1990.
2 Diodorus v.41.4–46, vi.1.

God, whose origin was a divine mystery.[1] Euhemerism has come to mean an historical interpretation of myth. Myth was viewed as garbled, manipulated, poorly remembered history. Heroes were historical figures amplified with divine qualities.[2] Perhaps the clearest example of man become god can be found in the career of Hercules. As a son of Zeus and a mortal woman, he was of divine origin but lived a fully human life between adventures. Upon his agonizing death, betrayed by the woman he loved, Hercules walked up Mount Olympus and joined the gods in eternity without actually dying. As a minor deity, hero shrines devoted to his worship were erected all across the Greek speaking world. Need we mention that the Emperor Augustus was decreed to be a god by official proclamation of the Roman senate upon his death? Or that his grandson Caligula forced the Senate to recognize that he was a living god before he fell to the assassins' daggers?

There are glimmers of euhemerism in the *Histories of Herodotus*.[3] Io, a human priestess of Argo, was transformed by Zeus into a goddess. He was grateful to Io for nursing his illegitimate son Dionysios. She had shielded the baby from the jealousy of Hera, the god king's sister and cuckold wife. The myth rationalizes the genealogy of Perseus, the founder of the kingdom of Mycene of Trojan War fame. Herodotus himself believed that Homer's *Iliad* was based upon an actual historical conflict which took place about 400 years before his time.

The ancient Greeks took their mythology as seriously as modern Americans take their history. Peisistratos was the tyrant of Athens from 546 to 527 BC. He founded the Panathenaic Festival, a rival to the Olympic Games. He was responsible for compiling the first written editions of the *Iliad* and the *Odyssey*.[4] However, Peisistratos was also accused of tampering with the texts in order to solidify Athenian claims to jurisdiction of the island of Salamis against its rival city-state Megara. Some claim that the tyrant only meant to bolster the relatively small part that the Athenians played in Homer's account of the Trojan War. This fraud, along with the rise of Greek science, both mark myth's decline in the West as the prestige vehicle for expressing human truth. Yet myth still somehow haunts the minds of modern, skeptical people.

A version of euhemerism was advanced by the Italian Renaissance historian Giambattista Vico. It has a taste of evolution and modern psychology to it. He held that mythology represented the infancy and adolescence of

---

1 De Angelis, Franco Benjamin Garstad. *Euhemerus in Context*, Classical Antiquity, Vol. 25, No. 2, Oct 2006, p. 212

2 Spyridakis, S. The Classical Journal, Vol. 63, No. 8, May, 1968, *Zeus Is Dead: Euhemerus and Crete* pp. 337-340.

3 Herodotus. *Histories* I.1, Myth of Io. *Histories* 2.118, Trojan War.

4 Finley, M.I. *The World of Odysseus*. Penguin Books Ltd., 27 Wrights Lane, London w8 5tz, England. 1954. pp. 37-39.

historical thinking. "The first men, the children as it were of the human race, not being able to form intelligible class concepts of things, had a natural need to create poetic (mythological) characters..."[1] Myth and heroes of myth were products of non-rational, infantile reasoning processes which could only resort to poetic, metaphorical, allegorical methods to express higher thought in the times before abstract vocabulary evolved and enabled humans to express themselves cogently, empirically, and scientifically.

In modern times, euhemerism has been revived in the writings of Thomas Bulfinch. Since its publication in the 1850s, *Bulfinch's Mythology* has been one of the most popular works published in the United States. For one hundred years, it was the standard American authority on the myths of the Greeks and the Romans and is still in print in our day. Bulfinch advanced an historical interpretation of the origins of myth, "...tends to cherish in our minds the idea of the source from which we sprung. We are entitled to our full share in the glories and recollections of the land of our forefathers."[2]

Lewis Spence was a Scottish journalist who flourished in the first half of the last century. He had a passion for anthropology and folklore and saw the influence of ancient Egypt in cultures from all around the world. In 1921, he published *An Introduction to Mythology*. In this work, Spence declared that myth was "history in disguise."[3]

It is probably impossible to ignore the nagging inkling that mythology is somehow attached to history. Every mythological hero, (so argues common sense,) must have as inspiration, some origin in actuality, in a human being who performed heroic exploits that were commemorated and embellished by oral tradition of grateful descendants. We can allow that notion and still claim that myth has next to nothing to do with history. History is comprised of documents that were written within the living memory of the participants or witnesses of notable, transforming events. No myth can claim such documentation. Documented myth is literature. The most that can be said for the historical approach to myth is that it is too speculative to do much beyond stir up controversy between conflicting viewpoints without the possibility of resolution. Thomas Mann[4] reminds us that history is a body of water that grows deeper the further you let out your fishing line with no possibility of ever sounding bottom.

It can be argued that broadly speaking, any theory of the origin of myth outside of divine inspiration or bestowal is somehow rooted in human

1 Meletinsky, Eleazar. *The Poetics of Myth*. Routlege, 29 West 35th Street, New York, NY, 10001. 1998. p. 6.
2 Bullfinch, Thomas. The Project Gutenberg EBook of *Bulfinch's Mythology*. Author's preface. http://www.gutenberg.org/cache/epub/4928/pg4928-images.html.
3 Spence, Lewis. *An Introduction to Mythology*, Moffat Yard & Company, 1921. p. 42.
4 Mann, Thomas. *Freud and the Future*. Daedalus Vol. 88, No. 2, Myth and Mythmaking , Spring, 1959. pp. 374-378.

behavior, historical, psychological or linguistic. Myth is the past remembered creatively or is a revelation of our inner being or an aspect of our singing voices. Myth is truth beyond mere facts. But myth is ultimately rooted in human day to day behavior, not just the shadowy past creatively recalled. It mediates human relations with the Earth. Myth is both externally bestowed and internally evolving simultaneously.

BESTOWAL, REVELATION, INSPIRATION

A few words are necessary upon this topic and justify a brief digression. While discussing the origins of any human behavior, there is an anticipation set up in the mind of the reader to receive an explanation concerning the transition point where the attained behavior is achieved out of some lower, less complicated form. At what point does candle flame become electric light? To grow up in Western culture is to be taught to seek for bestowals, revelations and inspiration in order to answer questions of cultural origins. The light bulb going off in the brain is the West's version of Sartori, the Zen notion of "sudden awakening." Jason the Argonaut suddenly steals the Golden Fleece and bestows its revivifying powers upon his city of Iolchus. Saul, the persecutor of heretic Christians, becomes Paul, the original proselytizer of the Catholic Church, after a sudden vision of Jesus, (whom he had never personally met or seen), on the road to Damascus. The English Romantic poet Samuel Taylor Coleridge wrote *Kublai Khan* in order to salvage what he could of a rudely interrupted opium dream. It seemed to be inspired from beyond his ken and not be the product of his own speaking mind. American folk icon of the 1960s Bob Dylan says that he does not know where some of his songs like *Blowin' in the Wind* came from. Of course, like all songs, it came from the breath of the daughter of Zeus and Mnemosyne, the Goddess of Memory. Euterpe was the Muse of music and lyric poetry. Ultimately, all inspired words come from her as a gift.

What unites bestowal, revelation and inspiration is that each notion, either explicitly or implicitly, posits a source beyond the mind of the perceiver for the contents of his or her thinking. This experience is commemorated in story and if accepted on faith, remembered and passed on. There is an important question here. How does the witness to bestowal, revelation or inspiration definitively differentiate between his or her own thinking and the mental images that purportedly come from outside the mind as messages from a superhuman being? There are no means of independent verification. All that we can go on is a feeling, a sympathetic resonance, a hunch. However, the Orion Complex will view the myth of the hero as the story, already ancient in our species, that human beings evolved language in order to express. The myth of the hero was realized over a long course of development, not revealed suddenly from a mysterious beyond. No doubt there are punctuated equilibriums and saltations in this evolutionary process, that is, long periods of traditions followed by sudden creative outbursts. But overall, the Orion Complex adopts a gradualist, unifying approach. The expectation for an explanation by bestowal, revelation or inspiration confuses the issue concerning the origins of language and story.

Dates and occasions are impossible to verify with any degree of certainty, let alone singling out brilliant individuals. We see what was in the ancient past and we see what is today and there is a lot missing in between. Establishing links is tricky and evidence is most often indirect. We can only hope to achieve an *en media res* understanding.

WHY THE ORION COMPLEX?

It is time for me to justify my use of the term "the Orion Complex." It appears frequently in the thoughts presented above with only context to serve as a definition. Even to my own ear, it sounds a bit pretentious. I am sympathetic to those perceptive readers who would liken it to Freud's Oedipus Complex and wonder if I am trying steal a bit of thunder for my own writings from this cultural meme of tremendous scope and distribution and lend, along with its echo, a bit of gravitas to my own efforts. No doubt. However, allow me to outline my rationale behind my use of this term, the Orion Complex. Please forgive the personal nature of some of the writing that follows in this section. Then again, I beg the reader's indulgence as a layman and not as an expert communicating to fellow specialists. It might humbly request to be regarded as an informal (and unfunded) piece of field work.

One summer, I determined to visit the ancient Maya metropolis of Tikal. Preparation for this exciting prospect led me to Freidel, Schele and Parker's book *Maya Cosmos*. However, I was stopped dead in my tracks with this sentence. "The sky has become important for us in a way we never anticipated."[1]

Maya Cosmos was going to discuss the movement of the heavenly bodies across the sky as the Mayas understood it and how they ordered their lives accordingly. I had a middling knowledge of Western astronomy and worried that I would not be able to follow the book. I did not really understand the movements of the sun, the moon and the stars in relation to the plot of ground upon which I stood

---

1 Freidel, David and Linda Schele and Joy Parker. *Maya Cosmos: Three Thousand Years on the Shaman's Path*. HarperCollins Publishers, Inc. 10 East Third Street, New York NY 10022. 1993. p. 9.

and looked up at the heavens. I determined to make up for this shortcoming before I plunged ahead with my reading.

I bought a star chart, but I did not bother with a telescope. The Maya priests who gazed at the sky from atop their temples did not use telescopes. They were naked eye astronomers who were interested in planets and constellations and how their seasonal movements across the sky related to rising and setting points on the horizon. Their math was so good that they could track individual stars, planets and constellations as they rose and set on the horizon going backward or forward in time. Their storytellers took the terrain features and memorized the outlines and silhouettes with stories. For each temple ground, their engineers and architects knew exactly where the planet Venus rose and set on the horizon. Their calendar was precise enough to predict the date it would first appear after a seasonal absence. They planted their crops accordingly. Their astronomy was so precise that their architects could build massive temples of hewn stone with their walls and altars in perfect alignment with the rising and setting points on the horizon of particular stars on specific dates. I determined to build my own horizon observation circle. From this spot on Earth, I would follow the heavens slowly moving overhead and triangulate star and horizon point with my circle of stones with me at the center.

Luckily I had a dear old friend with a hundred acres of land at the headwaters of the Santa Rosa Creek. This was back up in the spring green and summer golden hills that rise above Cambria where the pines meet the sea, just south of Big Sur on the Central Coast of California. I could drive the one lane winding road alongside the oak lined creek and be there from home in forty minutes.

Greg called his land Madrona after the tree in the same family as the manzanita. The shiny leaves are green, the papery bark is red and the branches are twisted and awry. He did not live at Madrona but he had erected a yurt and it served as a weekend getaway for family and friends. North of the yurt on some flat land with a 360° view of the chaparral-covered hills on the horizon, I built my observation circle right in front of a beautiful stand of Madrones to the west.

My plan was simple. I wanted to understand how the sky moved in relation to the piece of ground upon which I stood and looked up. I took a piece of rope and measured it to my height. I tied one end of it to a spike and drove it into the ground. The other end of the rope I tied to another spike. I pulled it taut and inscribed a perfect circle in the hard packed dirt of about twelve feet in diameter. This method of drawing a circle was reputedly invented by Daedalus,[1] the grand architect of Greek mythology who designed

---

1 Pseudo-Apollodorus. *Library and Epitome.* E.1.

---

the labyrinth for Minos, the wealthy king of Crete. It took all of Daedalus'
ingenuity to escape from his possessive patron. He fashioned wings of wax
and feathers and flew away over the sea. However, freedom cost him Icarus,
his only son.

I pulled up the spike that I had driven into the center of the circle and
placed a compass over the hole. Now the search for stones began. Madrona
is full of reddish chert. Old-timers claim that it should never be used for
fireplaces because the heat releases poisonous mercury. I placed a head-sized
boulder of it at each cardinal direction.

I stood in the center of the circle and looked around at my budding
medicine wheel. It produced an odd reaction in me. I knew that if death were
to take me at that moment, the circle that I had just inscribed in the dirt
represented where my head would rest after toppling. I had never had such
a concise experience of my personal space, of all the territory on Earth to
which I could rightly lay claim at any given moment of life. It was humbling.
It made me think of Greg, dying so slowly of dignity-robbing cancer.

It was growing dark and the stars were starting to come out. I shook off
my mood and lost myself in the complexities of the star chart. I hungered for
a focus out of the chaos of my life. The sky became that focus. The map is not
the territory? On paper, this is correct. But the sky itself is the ultimate map
and it is also the territory. This awareness must have been what pressed the
ancients to gaze up at the night sky in the first place. They knew instinctively
that it was their only chance to locate themselves in the vastness.

Just as humans cannot look up at clouds, or at paint splashed
spontaneously on a canvas, or at an uneven horizon line without imagining
shapes and figures and characters, we cannot look up at the sweep of
brightest stars without working them into constellations. At this juncture, I
only knew two of them for sure; the Big Dipper and Orion, the Hunter. As it
turned out, these two were all that I needed to get started.

I turned north and found the Big Dipper. I followed the two bright stars
that form the leading edge of the bowl to where they lined up with Polaris,
the Pole Star, the North Star. In relation to the center, I marked its location
on the circle with another rock. It was just a bit to the left of magnetic north.
I drew a mental line down from Polaris to where it intersected the distant
horizon somewhere out on hills of Camp Roberts. I memorized the shape of
the skyline at that point. Day or night, without a compass, I knew how to
find true north from this particular point at Madrona. I marked the spot on
the horizon. It would never move, because Polaris never moved. It hovered in
a stationary position over the top of the world above the North Pole. All the
other stars spun around it.

Once true north had been distinguished from magnetic north, the other directions were simple to reckon. Right face, east. Right face, south. Right face, west. One last 90 degree turn brought me full circle looking north once more. I aligned the marker stones on the circumference of the circle with the center where I stood and with distant points out on the horizon; east with a nondescript ridge of chaparral; south with a distinct rock pinnacle; west with an oak tree that towered above a deep valley; and north with a slight dip in the faraway tree line.

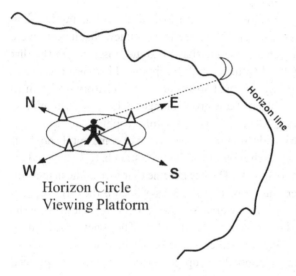

Horizon Circle
Viewing Platform

I got a hibachi out of my car and built a small fire to warm my hands. I studied the star chart until the wee hours of the morning. I learned many constellations and high magnitude stars and how they all lay in relation to each other and how to use one to find another. I learned to appreciate the slow, predictable roll of stars and planets moving east to west across the sky. Before it got dark, I could anticipate where the stars of the grand winter triangle would come out; first Capella to the northeast, then Deneb to the northwest, and finally Vega lower across the sky toward sundown. The moon seemed to be above or below the path of the sun. I could never make up my mind if it traveled faster or slower in relation to the background stars. It was a melody of winds to gaze up at the heavens. The slow spinning spot of Earth upon which I sat facing southeast became my sky ride.

With observation and experience, the map of the sky started to come together in my head. I spent many a night sitting in the center of my circle gazing up, my dog Pirate resting his chin on my feet and keeping them warm. Orion, the Hunter, the best known constellation of them all, held particular fascination for me. He stuck out so clearly with two of the brightest stars in the sky as part of his formation; Rigel as his left foot and Betelgeuse as his right shoulder. His club and his shield extended out in front of him facing the horns of Taurus the Bull just one constellation to the west. The three stars of his belt angling up to the right.

His father was a mystery. Some called Orion[1] the son of the sea god Poseidon. Some say he came into this life in this way. Zeus, Hermes and Poseidon visited Hyrieus, the king of Boeotia. The king feted the gods in accordance to the laws of hospitality. He slaughtered a bull and roasted it and fed his guests. When the grateful gods asked Hyrieus what he would like in return for his generosity, the king begged the gods to give him a son. Zeus ordered the bull's hide to be placed before them and the gods urinated on it. Hyrieus was ordered to bury it and dig it up nine months later. Orion the Earthborn emerged from this womb of soil and grew to be a giant capable of wading across the sea. He became the greatest hunter of all time.

Once he visited the isle of Chios and in his drunkenness, he forced himself on Merope, the daughter of King Oenopion. In a rage, Oenopion had Orion's eyes put out. The blind giant stumbled to the isle Lemnos where Hephaestus had his forge. Orion begged the lame smith of the gods to help him. Hephaestus gave Orion his servant Cedalion to be his eyes. Riding upon the giant's shoulders, the boy guided Orion east to the palace of Helios. There the sun god restored Orion's sight.[2]

However, Orion's troubles were far from over. His journeys took him to the isle of Crete where he hunted with the goddess Artemis. His blood up from the chase, Orion joyfully swore that he could kill every beast upon the Earth. Gaia, the Earth Mother, was alarmed. She sent a giant scorpion after Orion to punish his audacious enthusiasm. The beast slew the overweening hunter and Zeus set both of their images among the stars[3] as the constellations Orion and Scorpius, opposite each other with the entire sky to keep them apart.

There is another story about Orion's death. The goddess Artemis was tricked by her jealous brother Apollo into attempting to shoot a distant target bobbing on the waves. Artemis let fly and killed Orion while he was out taking a morning swim. In sorrow, for some claimed that he was her secret lover, Artemis begged Zeus to memorialize the hunter. In honor of his daughter's sorrow, the king of gods placed Orion in the sky as the best known constellation of Western civilization.

The Nama Bushmen tell a story about the same stars that form Orion. Their story also associates the constellation with the hunt. The constellation that we call the Pleiades sent her husband, the star Aldebaran, to hunt the three zebras, the three stars of Orion's belt, for dinner that night. "If thou

---

1 Graves, Robert. *The Greek Myths*. Volume I. Penguin Books Ltd. Great Britain. 1953. pp.151-153.
2 Pseudo-Apollodorus 1.4.3
3 Ibid.

dost not shoot, thou darest not come home." The hapless husband shot his only arrow and missed. The constellation Leo the lion stood on the other side and menaced the zebras, so the hunter could not retrieve his arrow. He could not return home because of the wives' curse. The forlorn hunter sat outside of the camp all alone in the cold night shivering. The Pleiades boasted to the other hunters in camp, "You cannot compare yourselves to us and be our equals. We defy our own husband to come home because he has not killed game."[1]

The Maya made a constellation of some of Orion's stars. Alnitak, Saiph and Rigel form a triangle that are said to be the three hearthstones of the typical cooking fire. The Great Nebula M42 smolders within the fire ring of stars.[2]

His first wife was Side or Pomegranate. Because she vied with Hera for beauty, the jealous queen of the gods threw her into Hades. Orion is associated with the pomegranate because he appears in the night sky around harvest time in autumn.[3]

For Hesiod, when Orion was midway in the heavens at dawn, it was time to harvest the grapes and make wine. And when Orion set, it was time to plough the land.[4] He also cautioned against sea voyages when Orion was rising or setting because it was associated with storms. Polybius tells of a Roman fleet that ignored this advice and was destroyed off the southern coast of Sicily for sailing during this time of the year.[5]

The Greek historian Plutarch associated Orion with the Egyptian god Horus, the falcon headed god of the sky, war and hunting. His festival was associated with the winter solstice when Orion was prominent in the sky.[6]

Both Scorpius and Orion are to be found along the Milky Way. This bright ribbon of stardust is an edgewise view of our galaxy. It takes a moonless night far away from city lights to really appreciate it. Orion and Scorpius are situated directly opposite to each other on the horizon at the two places where the east-west ecliptic and the roughly north-south Milky Way intersect. When one constellation is going down in the west, the other is coming up in the east. When you watch Scorpius sink in the western ocean at sunset, you are looking toward the center of the galaxy. When you

1 Schmidt, Sigrid. *South African |Xam Bushman Traditions and Their Relations to Further Khoisan Folklore.* Rüdiger Köppe Verlag, Köln 2013. p. 34.
2 Milbrath, Susan. *Star Gods of the Maya: Astronomy in Art, Folklore, and Calenders.* University of Texas Press, Austin TX 78713-7819. p. 39.
3 Pseudo-Apollodorus. *Library,* 1.4.106.
4 Hesiod. *Works and Days.* 609-621.
5 Polybius. *Histories,* 1.37. Evelyn S. Shuckburgh. translator. London, New York. Macmillan. 1889. Reprint Bloomington 1962.
6 Plutarch. *Moralia.* Plut. De Iside 21. Translation by. Frank Cole Babbitt. Cambridge, MA. Harvard University Press. London. William Heinemann Ltd. 1936. 5.

turn around to the east and watch Orion rise, you are looking out and away from the center of the Milky Way into deep, intergalactic space.

The top star of Orion's sloping belt is called Mintaka. It is the first star of the belt to rise on the eastern horizon and the first to fall on the western. It lies directly on the celestial equator. Its position out in space is directly above the equator of the Earth like the Pole Star is directly above the North Pole. If you extended the equator of the Earth out into space, Mintaka would be on this plane.

One twilight, while facing south, I watched the stars come out in the looming night. Orion had risen up from the eastern horizon to its zenith position on the celestial meridian and pointed toward due south. It was ready to begin its long slow descent to the western horizon. I faced true east and raised my right hand to 1:00 and pointed at Mintaka due south. Then I raised my left hand to 10:30 and pointed to the Pole Star due north. Left hand down to heart, heart out to right hand. Polaris down to center of the Earth, center of the Earth out to Mintaka. Connect the three points and they form a 90 degree angle.

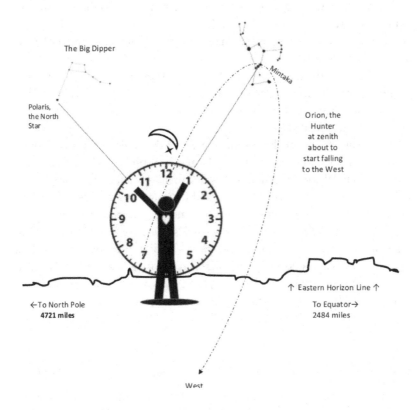

The Big Dipper

Polaris, the North Star

Mintaka

Orion, the Hunter at zenith about to start falling to the West

↑ Eastern Horizon Line ↑

←To North Pole
4721 miles

To Equator→
2484 miles

West

I had a hunch. I went to Greg's tool shed and fetched a carpenter's square. I stuck it in the ground in the center of my circle and pointed the blade, the long end, toward the North Pole and the tongue, the short end, toward Mintaka. They formed a perfect 90 degree right angle in relation to each other when their lines intersected at the center of the Earth. The carpenter's square confirmed the configuration of my arms.

If I walked until the Pole Star was directly overhead, I would be at the North Pole. I could stand there and watch the whole day pass without moving my head side to side. Just gazing straight ahead due east for 24 hours would present the whole sky to my eyes. A day long spin would bring me back to the same section of sky that I started with the night before this static vigil at the top of the world.

If I walked until Mintaka was directly overhead, I would be standing on the equator in South America. The stars would sweep past me overhead as if they were painted on the inside of a barrel.

The Pole Star was lower in the sky from my location. That meant it would be a longer walk to the point where it was directly overhead at the top of the world. Mintaka was higher up in the sky. That meant it would be a shorter walk until it was directly overhead at La Mitad del Mundo in Ecuador where you can stand with your right foot in the northern hemisphere and with your left foot in the southern.

This clearly demonstrated the line of latitude[1] upon which Cambria, California, was located, at 35° 57' North. Just a little more than a third of the way up the globe from the middle. Orion's position at zenith in relation to the North Star revealed this.

However, it was not the sky moving. All of the stellar bodies were fixed in place, as if they were on the inside of a gigantic sphere with Earth floating in the center. All apparent motion was due to my spot of ground spinning in a circle while it advanced day by day in orbit around the sun. Even the statue of Liberty in all of her majestic calm and grandeur, apparently rock steady above New York Harbor, spins on the Earth's axis 25,000 miles in 24 hours. It simultaneously advances one day in its yearly rotation around the Sun[2] at a thousand miles a second. Only sheer size and gravity give some stability to it. To be a child of Earth is to spiral through the stars, whether you are speeding down the highway or standing a vigil in the wild just looking up.

---

1 The east-west (right-left) lines on the map. Longitude are north-south (up-down) lines.

2 Cain, Fraser. *How Fast Does the Earth Rotate?* Universe Today: space astronomy news, 2009. http://www.universetoday.com/26623/how-fast-does-the-earth-rotate/

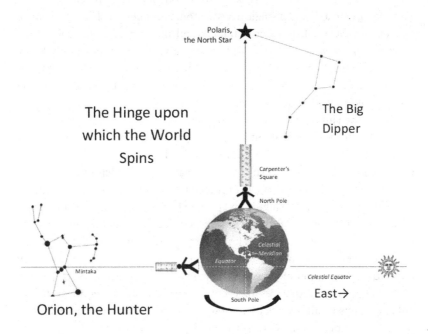

The Hinge upon which the World Spins

The Big Dipper

Polaris, the North Star

Carpenter's Square

North Pole

Celestial Meridian

Equator

Mintaka

Celestial Equator

East→

South Pole

Orion, the Hunter

One last conundrum of the sky plagued me. From the point of ground upon which I stood to the center of the earth was some 4000 miles. The carpenter's square pointed as true at the surface where I was as it did in the diagram, which was theoretically true with the center of the earth. From me to earth's core was a trifling distance compared to the immense distances of Polaris and Mintaka from my spot of earth. Their light takes years to reach my sight. My naked eye was not keen enough to sense the error. 4000 miles was a huge distance to me in body and mind, but it was nothing compared to interstellar distances.

I laughed out loud. Most of this could have been figured out with a good map and a few simple calculations. Then I grew very solemn, humbled by lovely, sparkling vastness. Understanding the relation of my spot of ground with Polaris and Mintaka abstractly did not portray it freely to my mind's eye. My eyes needed to confirm my imagination. The 90 degree relation of the North Star with the Earth's center and the star of Mintaka unveiled the invisible stand upon which the whole world sphere spun on its daily spin. Weather permitting; it was there plainly in the night sky any time I cared to look up. I would probably never get a better or more sweeping view of my particular location on the Earth's surface with a single glance, unless I went out in space. It was all I could possibly take in at once with my naked eye and though it seemed big, I also realized how little of it that I was actually looking at. Astronomers are looking so far out into the universe that the imperfection in a lens of a single carbon atom is enough to obscure an entire galaxy. No matter what I came to understand about the sky, the whole wide world with everyone on it was still lost vis-à-vis the vastness. I only knew my galactic neighborhood better and though it stretched for light years, it remained a marvel how small it all still was, against the all. I needed nothing but my naked eyes to confirm this.

Orion the Hunter had been a good guide. I had been stewing on what the myth of the hero revealed about human origins and our place on Earth since I studied Anthropology at U.C.S.D. None of the theories concerning the origin of and significance of the myth of the hero satisfied me. I felt like something obvious was being overlooked. I continued to read on the subject long after I graduated while I raised a family and pursued a career as a classroom teacher. I enjoyed reading folktales to my kids at bedtime. I thought about the myth of the hero every day in passing. Hints of it popped up in the oddest of places. I wondered how being hunter-foragers every step of the way out of animality affected the evolution of speech in humans. Did the cognitive capacity to relate narratives, (sequences of events), have adaptive functions beyond enhancing leisure after work hours? I was convinced that the lives of hunter-foragers held deep insights into the myth of the hero but I did not know where to begin. The number of potential perspectives was vast. However, the time was not yet right to take up another project. I had too many other pressing concerns with family and work and a long poem that I was writing.

I could follow *Maya Cosmos* now and it revealed the true nature of the Maya Cross. It was a representation in stone of the two places in the sky where the ecliptic, the line which is the path of the sun, moon, planets and constellations of the zodiac cross the Milky Way at right angles. Toward Scorpius and the center of the galaxy lay the entry to the land of the dead. Toward Orion, out away from the center of the galaxy into deep space, lay the place of creation. I traveled to Guatemala and studied Spanish in San Pedro on the shores of Lago Atitlán I visited nearby Urutlán, the ancient capital of the Quiché Maya. There temples were aligned with the rising of stars in the constellation of Orion upon the horizon. However, after I got back, my marriage failed. Then Greg died of biliary duct cancer.

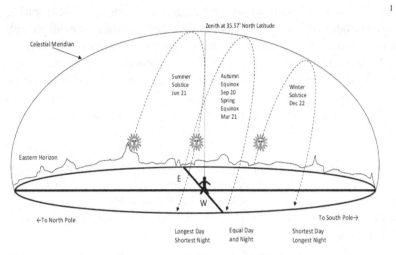

Zenith at 35.57° North Latitude

Celestial Meridian

Summer
Solstice
Jun 21

Autumn
Equinox
Sep 20
Spring
Equinox
Mar 21

Winter
Solstice
Dec 22

Eastern Horizon

E

W

←To North Pole

To South Pole→

Longest Day
Shortest Night

Equal Day
and Night

Shortest Day
Longest Night

A Year of Sunrises

(After a drawing by P. Dunham, Aveni, 1980, fig. 23)

Out of the blue, I met Annika. From the first moment that I saw her, I never doubted my feelings. We knew pretty quickly where we were headed but planned on waiting until all the family on both sides were comfortable with the idea of our second try at marriage. However, life has a way pursuing its own agenda.

Annika's sister Veronica was a victim of childhood diabetes. Both of her kidneys were failing her, and she was waiting on the donor list. In the interim, she was on dialysis. When I had known Annika for about six months, Veronica suddenly suffered congestive heart failure and underwent emergency quintuple by-pass surgery. Treatment went very well but it bumped her off of the donor list to get a new kidney. Veronica had nowhere else to turn. She asked her big sister Annika to donate one of hers and the dear, brave woman agreed without the slightest hesitation.

When Annika told me of these developments, I thought we should get married right away so that she would be on my health insurance and we would not have to worry about any pre-existing conditions later on. To my great joy, she agreed. We held a small private ceremony out on her mother's land and celebrated a June wedding.

---

1 Milbrath, Susan. *Star Gods of the Maya: Astronomy in Art, Folklore and Calendars.* University of Texas Press. Austin TX 78713-7819. p. 45.

The following summer, we all went to U.C. San Francisco for the procedure. The sisters were a perfect match. It went as well as it possibly could. The doctors, staff and surroundings were positively awe inspiring. We came out of it believing that we had stepped into the best of all possible futures. Both of the sisters fully recovered and are doing fine to this day.

What more loving proof of the fundamental oneness of the cosmos could there be than Annika's gift of life to her sister? The time had come for me to write this book. I am not a folklorist, anthropologist, primatologist or geneticist. I am a poet with an interest in these subjects as they fit into the larger mosaic of life. All of these disciplines have their say on the myth of the hero. Like many people, I am startled by the implications of ancient and modern knowledge for my personal life. I yearn for reconciliation between science and spirit. It takes a balance of both perspectives in order to negotiate the daily ups and downs for the long run. For a single life. For a society. For a world. Are we on the verge of a spiritual revolution or a recovery? Or a brand new commitment to discovery?

The Orion Complex, and its verbal manifestation as the myth of the hero, is the clearest statement of which humans are capable that we all live in a mysterious, ever changing world where everything is one and every speck of life on Earth is our kin. It shows us that for hunter-foragers, hunger is a surer guide to truth than satiety. Where a human sees only death, a spirit intuits metamorphosis. No wonder that the Earth is a goddess in traditions all over the globe. The Earth is the origin, the sustenance, and the destination of every single person. The constellation Orion is well known and easy to make out in the night sky of late winter and early spring at sunset in northern latitudes. On New Year's Eve, Orion is high up around its zenith position due south at midnight. The stars Polaris and Mintaka and the center of the Earth form the mighty hinge upon which the whole world spins. The career of this grand figure of myth is a hunter's story. Understanding the relationship between Polaris above the North Pole and Mintaka at zenith above the equator locates each person on the globe in terms of latitude with a single sweep of the eye. A complex is a complicated assemblage. The sky had become very important to me as well and in ways that I could never have anticipated. Not only does any given piece of Earth upon which I stand slowly twist, grind and shake under my very feet by tectonic forces, it also hurtles through space like a sky ride now that I know how to appreciate the apparent movement of the heavens. The sky ride taught me that my eyes are wrong and that I need my imagination to correct them. It is for these reasons that I chose The Orion Complex to be the guiding spirit in this work devoted to the myth of the hero.

MYTH AND THE GREAT MINDS

What follows is an attempt to pay homage to how rich and diverse a field of thought that myth presents to the traveler. However, it is beyond the scope of this work to attempt a comprehensive survey of all the available scholarship. As ever, the filter of these vast, tantalizing resources will be the myth of the hero, the Orion Complex rendered verbally. The great minds that follow did not dismiss myth as a lie or a false belief, for the most part. All of these scholars intuited that there were tremendous truths hidden under the phantasmagoria of the tales that many modern people have dismissed as mere entertaining fables for children.

When considered side by side, these approaches to myth demonstrate an astonishing diversity and range. Each has a literature with a lifetime of reading material. Language, poetry, music, theology, law, astronomy, history, classics, anthropology, psychology, philosophy and logic all view myth as their special purview. All of these fields have been enriched by the study of myth and the general human imagination expanded greatly by their efforts. The arts ancient and modern are full of myth. If anything unites these disparate viewpoints, it would be the belief that myth could be explained as an aspect of symbolic thinking.

Plato was the friend and disciple of Socrates who flourished in Athens circa 420 B.C. There are many myths in Plato's writing; the legend of Atlantis from *Timaeus*, the origin of love from the *Symposium* and the parable of the cave from the *Republic* to name just three but concerning myth itself, he is fairly mum. For Plato, myth has an oracular quality. The stories seem to be bestowals from or a channeling from the deity itself. Plato also cautioned young people from taking the stories about the gods and heroes literally.

Plato's student Aristotle thought humans had an instinct for imitation. Good poetry provoked an instinctual reaction of wonder and catharsis. He saw myth, epic and dramas as "representations of life," in his *Poetics*. He used "mythos" as we would plot, or the order of incidences. In *Metaphysics*, he likens myth to philosophy in that it is an exercise in wonder. However, he was also very scornful of Hesiod when the dour farmer made the silly claim that immortal gods drink ambrosia like mortals drink wine. It is hard to say how much distinction that Plato and Aristotle drew between poetry and myth, but it is safe to say it is less than we do in our day because the two were so intertwined to the Greeks.

The 19th century Romantics viewed myth as symbolic, metaphorical, and allegorical, with little direct relation to concrete reality. Like all art, "myth" and the "hero" were exercises in aesthetics, or traditions based upon local theories of beauty. Above all, myths were individual expressions of artists. For the German Romantic philosopher F.W. von Schilling,[1] myth had a theogonic, revelatory aspect and transcended history because it came before history. Myth was pure poetry and spontaneous imagination of a lonely, individual artist. A myth is the universe in "majestic disguise." Myth is the raw material of art. Mythopoetics can be used for individual, creative mythology. It is the instrument by means of which the divine, the absolute can contemplate itself. Symbolism is the underlying principle of mythology. This is the essential feature of Freud, Jung, Cassirer and Levi-Stauss's approach to the study of myth. Myth symbolizes eternal principles of human life. However, myth is first, last and foremost, the lonely work of an individual artist.

In the early 19th century, linguistic studies of European languages occurred and word etymologies were compared. Scholars like the Brothers Grimm in Germany extended their comparative linguistic research beyond linguistics into the fields of folklore and mythology. They discovered profound similarities in theme and plot in stories from India to Europe just as they had for word origins and grammatical structures. Scholarship suggested ties between present day language families that extended back in time to a pre-historical past. An Indo-European homeland of extreme antiquity was speculated to be located somewhere on the steppes of southern Russia. In that theoretical region, the ancestor of Sanskrit, Persian, Greek, Latin, and Norse was spoken. For reasons lost to history, the Indo-Europeans had spread from India to Ireland a thousand years before the life of Christ.

Max Müller, the foremost Indo-Europeanist of his day, edited *The Sacred Books of the East*.[2] He inscribed a wonderful dedication to this series. "There never was a false god, nor was there ever really a false religion, unless you

---

1 Schilling, von, F.W. *Historical-Critical Introduction to the Philosophy of Mythology*. State University of New York Press , 2008.
2 Müller, Max. *The Sacred Books of the East*. Parke, Austin, and Lipscomb, Inc. New York, NY 1917.

call a child a false man." He viewed myth as a "disease of language." Myth made use of concrete images to allude metaphorically to abstract ideas. He thought that all myths transformed stars and planets into mythological beings. "Zeus" and "pater," Latin for "father," blended and became "Jupiter." Müller was one of the long line of scholars who viewed myth as an artifact of faulty logic, however delightful. In spite of his famous pejorative definition, he never explored myth as speech behavior. The truth of the mystery had to be uncovered out of the depths of symbolism in spite of the true mystery being hidden in plain sight.

With the expansion of the British Empire in the 19th century, a wealth of ethnographic knowledge flooded the kingdom as her majesty's government administered numerous cultures and ethnic groups. Some of the first ethnographically informed research on mythology was written by Victorian scholars in England. Edward B. Tylor published his groundbreaking anthropological classic *Primitive Culture* in 1871.[1] It starts, "Culture or Civilization, taken in its wide ethnographic sense, is that complex whole which includes knowledge, belief, art, morals, law, custom, and any other capabilities and habits acquired by man as a member of society." Anthropology was a sort of "science of history." Society was rule-governed, environmentally influenced, developmental and evolutionary. He recognized that myths of the hero followed a pattern found in many places in the world. Central to Tylor's thinking was an echo of Bastian's "psychic unity of man." Primitive traditions exist as "survivals" in modern, civilized cultures. Such traditions and mythology reflect rational thought, shaped by local historical conditions. Myth originated, not in nature, but in animism, or the realization of the soul in each human, rock, river and tree. Ironically, it was Thales, the Father of scientific thinking who also said, "All things are full of gods."[2] Primitive humans realized their soul by the experience of dreams, near death encounters, actual death of loved ones, out of body experiences and hallucinations induced by illness or intoxicants. No irrational or childlike reasoning was attributed to primitive thinking. It was just incorrect factually, a sort of pre-scientific attempt at explaining natural phenomena. Tylor wrote of the linear, progressive cultural evolution from primitive hunter-foragers to Victorian gentlemen almost as if this proved the inevitability of rational logic and scientific thinking and its natural sway over "lower" forms of thinking.

Friedrich Nietzsche, the most poetic and isolated of all the German philosophers, published *The Birth of Tragedy Out of the Spirit of Music* in 1872.[3]

1 Tylor, Edward B. *Primitive Culture*, New York NY: Harper & Row. 1958 (1871).
2 Burnett, John. *Early Greek Philosophy*. Meridian Books. New York NY, 4th edition, 1960. p.
3 Nietzsche, Friedrich. *The Birth of Tragedy Out of the Spirit of Music*. The Portable Nietzsche, translated by Walter Kaufman. Penguin Books, Ltd. 27 Wrights

Greek tragedy, based almost entirely upon myth, arose out of a mediation of the oppositions of the rational Apollonian and the ecstatic Dionysian qualities of ancient Greek religion. Measured rationality was balanced by chaotic, instinctual irrationality. Both qualities were needed in a human life. A man must know how to build walls and equally how to tear them down, the wisdom to know when each is expedient and the courage to try to do whatever is necessary. Myths and heroes reflected this dynamic tension. Oedipus relentlessly pushed for the truth even though this discovery led to his own downfall.[1] Myth was opposed to history but not in a qualitative manner. Myth reflected man's becoming something greater than his original self, an eternal return on the one hand, a grand overreaching on the other.

Franz Boas was the foremost proponent of American ethnography of 19th century. He saw anthropology as a race against time. He encouraged his students to get out into the field and collect as much information and folklore as possible from pre-literate peoples and leave the theorizing to future generations of anthropologists. Primitive cultures were vanishing under the flood tides of Western imperialism and industrial progress, as were their traditions and myths. Myth was, "...*the free play of imagination operating with everyday experiences...*[2] Boas understood that primitive thinking viewed the differences between humans and animals differently than modern, civilized cultures do. He also appreciated myth's capacity to explain natural phenomena in an emotionally satisfying manner. Humans needed to validate everyday experience by means of relating it to a mythic, revered past.[3]

William Robertson Smith, a Scottish scholar of comparative religions, published his *Lectures on the Religion of the Semites* in 1889. He maintained that myth was linked to and subservient to ritual. He sought the origin of ritual in animal sacrifice.[4] By identifying self-evident parallels and comparing by analogy, he demonstrated his point. His work was very influential on Freud and Frazer, among others.

The notion that myth was the verbal part of ritual was taken up by the British classicist Sir James George Frazer in his monumental work, *The*

Lane, London w8 5tz, England, 1977. American anthropologist Ruth Benedict would apply Nietzsche's Apollonian-Dionysian divisions of Greek culture as a tool to distinguish entire cultures as either restrained Apollonian or abandoned Dionysian in *Patterns of Culture*. Pueblo Indian culture was restrained and Apollonian while Plains Indians were abandoned and Dionysian.
1 Sophocles. *Oedipus Tyrannis*. Edited and translated by Hugh Lloyd Jones, The Loeb Classical Library, Harvard University Press, Cambridge, MA, 1994.
2 Boas, Franz. *The Mind of Primitive Man*. Heath & Co. Washington D.C., 1938. p. 611.
3 Meletinsky, Eleazar. *The Poetics of Myth*. Routlege, 29 West 35th Street, New York, NY, 10001. 1998. p. 19.
4 Robertson Smith, William. *Lectures on the Religion of the Semites. Fundamental Institutions. First Series.* Adam & Charles Black, London, England. 1889.

Golden Bough,[1] arguably one of the most influential books of the 20th century. From every corner of the globe, Frazer drew ethnographic details in support of his views concerning the dying god and his rebirth. By analogy, he argued that the institution of the king grew out of this belief. Kings are divine representatives on Earth. He provided literally hundreds of examples of kings who were held by their subjects to be responsible in their very person for the fecundity of the Earth and the harvest and who must be periodically sacrificed in order to be reborn, much as the yearly seasonal cycle goes through its periods of death, gestation and rebirth.

While acknowledging the positive role that they play in human life, Frazer saw magic and mythological thinking as products of faulty reasoning. For example, a key element of the philosophy of magic; like cures like. Events imitated in miniature by the celebrants hopefully produce similar results on the grand scale out in life. The Blackfeet Buffalo dance play acts the killing of the prey animal. Primitives appealed to impersonal, natural forces, not supernatural beings, which came along later in human thinking. Frazer was a dynamist, not an animist.

Frazer was the foremost proponent of the myth and ritual school. His influence upon subsequent lines of research into myth and the hero cannot be overstated. He was the guiding light to a generation of scholars such as Jane Harrison,[2] Francis Cornford,[3] Arthur Cook,[4] and Robert Graves.[5] Bronislaw Malinowski[6] gave up mathematics and physics in order to study anthropology after reading *The Golden Bough*.

However, Frazer seemed to have had small interest in the actual content of myths, which he considered to be the verbal part of rituals that had degenerated and lingered down the days after the rituals themselves had been forgotten. This harkens back to Max Müller's "disease of language." He never considered the origin of rituals, only their localized, historical manifestations and the underlying patterns. Like the other scholars considered above, it never occurred to Frazer to explore the circumstances of myth as a speech act beyond mentioning its verbal connection with ritual. Frazer's main strength is that he sought to tie myth to human behavior, but he did not tarry long down that path. He did not explore nor prove the connection between myth and ritual. He merely assumed that it was so self-evident that all that he had to do was to draw attention to the fact and publish every piece

1 Frazer, James George. *The Golden Bough. A Study in Magic and Religion.* 3rd ed. Macmillan Press, New York, NY, 1926.
2 Harrison, Jane. *Prolegomena to the Study of Greek Religion*, 1903; *Themis*, 1912.
3 Cornford, Francis. *From Religion to Philosophy*, 1913.
4 Cook, Arthur. *Zeus*, 1914.
5 Graves, Robert. *The Greek Myths*. Penguin. 1955; *The White Goddess*. London: Faber & Faber, 1948.
6 Malinowski, Bronislaw. *Myth in Primitive Psychology*, 1926.

of corroborating evidence that he could find from every corner of the globe until the *Golden Bough* grew into a virtual encyclopedia of twelve volumes.

Myth and ritual have a similar function in society for Bronislaw Malinowski. He was a Polish anthropologist of the English classical school. He followed Frazer by viewing myth as the verbal remnant of ritual. From his studies of the Trobriand Islanders of the southeastern Pacific, he concluded that myth and ritual maintain tradition and function to unite society and the individual to supernatural forces and beings. The mythic past is the model for the future.[1]

Emile Durkheim was a French sociologist whose interest in religion and myth rested more upon their effects upon the collective, rather than upon the individual consciousness. He put no great store in myth's power to explain natural phenomena. He held that it founded, organized and maintained a society. He posited a more localized view of religious origins, rather than a universal one. He explored totemism, where primitive people, by means of the imagination, transformed a plant or an animal into an organizing, legitimizing force for a particular clan or lineage's traditions and social structures. A "survival" of this kind in modern American society might be the mascots around which high schools align themselves, for instance, the Coast Union Broncos of Cambria, California. Durkheim saw no flawed, pre-scientific logic in the process. He viewed totemic thinking as a means by which to order reality into such oppositions as the sacred and the profane. Taboo was the main social regulator. Religion was based upon impersonal forces such as *mana*, a Polynesian word that signifies the non-anthropomorphic power or force that is to be found in all people and animals, winds and waters, plants and rocks and all so-called inanimate objects. Myths were examples of pre-abstract thinking, due more to a dearth of abstract vocabulary in primitive people's languages than to a childlike mentality. Durkheim maintained that primitive people's consciousness appeared unable to separate itself from the surrounding world. More will be said upon this heading in what follows.[2]

Durkheim's protégé Lucian Lévy-Bruhl[3] was interested in primitive mentality. He believed that it differed in profound ways from Western, scientific thinking. He based his findings upon cultural and not physiological evidence. By means of mystic participation, the primitive mind does not distinguish clearly between the natural and the supernatural worlds. Seeing beyond the hard lines that separate the observer and the observed results in a unified vision of the universe. This vision is a collective consciousness that transcends mere human thinking and experience and includes

---

1 Malinowski, Bronislaw. *Myth in Primitive Psychology*, 1926.
2 Durkheim, Emile. *The Elementary Forms of the Religious Life*. Oxford University Press, 2008.
3 Lévy-Bruhl, Lucian. *Primitive Mentality*. George Allen & Unwin. London, 1923.

---

all phenomena. The history of human thought led evolutionarily and historically from an infancy of primitive thinking represented by myth to the supreme achievement of scientific thinking, quantum theory. Primitive, mythological thinking often violates a maxim of Aristotelian logic that an object cannot be two things at one time. An example of this is the *characotel* of the Tzutujil Maya who live on the shores of Lago Atitlán in the Highlands of Guatemala. The *characotel* is a human with the ability to become an animal and can simultaneously manifest both forms at once if the practitioner is knowledgeable enough. For Levy-Bruhl, primitive tolerance of inconsistency, as evidenced by the plethora of variations of a single tale within a society, was an indicator of specious logic.[1]

For the German philosopher Ernst Cassirer, mythological thinking is a symbolic blending of cause and effect, the nature of which would alarm David Hume, the skeptic Scottish philosopher, who cautioned against making easy assumptions, of confusing collation with actual correlation. In the myth making mind, such correlations flourish between external reality and internal thinking. The substance of a thing and its characteristics meld until a radical unification occurs between all perceived, distinct objects. This creates a cosmos, a universe and a feeling that all life is connected and one. Dividing lines are not clear between dreaming and waking, life and death. Any and all change is a species of metamorphosis. Myth is a kind of grand intuition about life and humanity's place in it. Ultimately, humans are not distinguishable from their surroundings and superhuman beings become anthropomorphized and mere humans become heroes. Every single thing is some kind of metaphor for every other thing.[2]

Sigmund Freud resorted to Greek myth in order to explain his views concerning the human psyche. Drawing from *Oedipus the King,* Sophocles' play of mystery, patricide and incest, he used a story to explain a story. Freud transformed the myth into a theoretical psychic structure of the mind he called the Oedipus Complex. This described the psycho-sexual drama that threatens to tear apart every nuclear family. It centered upon the male child's jealousy of the father for the attention of the mother and the guilt associated with this disturbing emotion in the unconscious mind. The female child's jealousy of the mother for the father was dubbed the Electra Complex after another character out of Greek myth, Agamemnon's unhappy daughter.

Freud created a myth of his own to explain this controversial dynamic. It reads like a critique of the mammalian mating pattern.[3] An alpha male, dominating as many females as possible, spends most of his time protecting

1 Petrich, Perla, editor. *Literatura Oral de los Pueblos del Lago Atitlán.* Casa de Estudios de los Pueblos de Lago Atitlán, CAEL, Guatemala, C.A. 1996. p. 122.
2 Cassirer, Ernst. *Essay on Man,* 1944. *The Myth of the State,* 1946.
3 Freud, Sigmund. *Totem and Taboo.* Norton and Co. New York NY 1950.

his harem from his own pubescent sons coming into their sexuality. Forced to live on the periphery of the family group, the sons' growing frustrations lead them one day to rise up against their *pater familias*, slay him and replace him in an almost Frazerian ritual sacrifice of the king. Overcome with remorse, they eat the slain patriarch in a mute attempt to preserve in their physical beings the intricate object of their love and hate. This grisly primal act is the foundational episode not only of totemic religion, but also of fully human society. The realization of guilt and shame and their repression was the mental spark that led humans into becoming the beings that they are today.

Freud saw many examples of the Oedipus Complex in Greek myth. The Titan Cronus castrated his father Uranus.[1]Theseus conveniently forgot the promise that he had made to his father Aegeus, the king of Athens. When the young hero sailed back from Crete after penetrating the labyrinth and killing the Minotaur and finding his way back out with the aid of Ariadne's thread, he did not change his sails from black to white. As Aegeus stood on the cliffs and watched Theseus' ship sail in under black sails, he thought his son was dead. In grief, he threw himself to his death in the waters below. Theseus was welcomed back to Athens as king and his mental lapse has been questioned forever after.

The father of psychoanalysis saw dream as a very individualistic use of symbol. He thought that any similarity to myth was far less important to understanding an individual dream than was a thorough understanding of the psycho-sexual history of the dreamer. Dream was not the source of myth although dream might employ mythological motifs in the expression of the individual dreamer's fantasies of wish fulfillment. Freud was interested in individual, not collective psychology.

Where Freud was a doctor treating patients, his former pupil and disciple Carl Jung was a mystic and a teacher as well. He was interested in the unconscious mind like his former mentor had been, but viewed this theoretical mental construct as more than a repository for pent up guilt and sexual fantasies. There was a deeper layer to the unconscious mind of each individual. There was also a collective unconsciousness, a notion that was an elaboration of the common 19th century one posited by such ethnologists as Bastian and Tylor concerning the fundamental "psychic unity of man." Jung's archetypes have been compared to mythological motifs, Plato's forms, Kant's *a priori* ideas and behaviorists' models. Archetypes are structures of the unconscious mind out of which the myths flow. Like language, a latent capacity with which every human is born, archetypes are inherited similarly

---

1 Graves, Robert. *The Greek Myths.* Volume I. Penguin Books. Great Britain 1950. pp. 37-39.

to how height and eye color are. *The existence of archetypes was beyond the reach of scientific analysis to reveal physically in the brain.* These mental structures guide and shape human worldviews but contain no specific content themselves.

Archetypes have been likened to the generalized structure of crystals considered in abstract, while a quartz crystal held in the hand would be an example of an actual myth. The archetypes are like the numerals 0 to 9, and the combinations like 911 and 1969 are the myths. The Hero is one of Jung's archetypes. The Anima/Animus complex refers to the female in the male and the male in the female aspects of human personality. The Shadow is comprised of repressed weaknesses, shortcomings or instincts. The Shadow is personified as the Trickster in primitive mythology. The Spirit or the Wise Old Man or Woman is yet another archetype working behind the scenes of individual human consciousness.

Jung credited dreams as being sources of myths. Dreams were individual expressions of personal myth that were in turn expressions of the collective unconscious. In the dreams of his patients, he saw mythological motifs played out. He was struck by how many times the *mandala*, the concentrically circular diagrams found in the ritual sand paintings of such diverse cultures as the Buddhists of Tibet and the Navajo Indians of the American southwest, showed up in the drawings that his patients made in order to illustrate their dreams. Though causality was impossible to establish, the surprising, apparent similarities between dreams and myths revealed their synchronicity, their unexplainable but undeniable connection.

Finally, Jung held that the consciousness revealed in the logic and reasoning of primitive humanity seemed hardly able to distinguish between subject and object, self and surroundings, fish and fowl. From the Jungian slant, the mystic participation of Lévy-Bruhl was a species of projection, an infusing of perspectives and emotions from the self into other people and things.[1]

Georges Dumézil was a French comparative philologist and Indo-European scholar. His main contribution to the study of myth concerned the three part division of Indo-European society into warrior-priest-farmer. He saw these divisions played out in social functions: politics-religion-economics and demonstrated it in the mythologies from India to Ireland.[2]

As an example, consider the form, function and meaning of the charioteer across the vast Indo-European landscape. In ancient India, according to the *Laws of Manu*, the charioteer was of the *suta* caste, which also included bards such as those who sang the Hindu epic poems, the *Mahabharata* and the *Ramayana*. The charioteer was a non-combatant, whose job was not only

---

1 Jung, Carl. *Man and His Symbols.* Dell, 1968.
2 Dumézil, Georges. *Mitra Varuna: An Essay on Two Indo-European Representatives of Sovereignty.* Zone Press, 1990.

---

to steer his lord's war horses, but also to survive and be a reliable primary historical source for his conduct. In his role as charioteer, he guided his lord's fate in battle, and in his role as the bard, he guided his lord's fate in human memory. This is why Arjuna wanted Krishna to drive his chariot in the battle of Kurukshetra. Krishna was a king in his own right. Given the choice between Krishna's army or having Krishna as his charioteer, Arjuna chose Krishna who ultimately, upon the field of battle, is revealed as God.[1] In the ancient Irish epic of *Táin Bó Cúalgne*, Cu Chulain's non-combative charioteer is named Laeg mac Riangabra. He often functions as a primary source concerning the Ulster hero's deeds in battle. In these two far flung traditions, the same role has the same functions in society and in myth.[2]

The French ethnologist Claude Lévi-Strauss was inspired by structural linguistics. He viewed language and the myth of the hero primarily as means of transmitting information. He was heavily influenced by the French linguist Saussure's notion of the "signified," as opposed to the "signifier," and the differences between *langue* (language) and *parole* (speech). Myth has been around in human history way longer than philosophical or scientific thinking. Myths were ways people thought about themselves in the world, about destiny, life, death and morality.

In his research, Lévi-Strauss drew heavily from the myths of the South American Indians.[3] He viewed myth as symbolic and metaphorical but was less interested in myth's psychological aspects as he was in its logic. He believed that the "anatomy of the mind" was revealed in the mediation of oppositions such as nature and culture. It is by means of such binary oppositions that the mind conceptualizes and organizes the daily perceptions of reality. Myth is a creative exercise in logic. It is capable of rendering the perceptions of such diverse objects as the sun, fire and meat into the binary oppositions of raw and cooked, rotten and fresh. This kind of logic transforms a series of mediations into a myth concerning the origin of cooking.

Primitive, mythological thinking, in spite of its ready appeal to the gross senses and the concreteness of its vocabulary and images, is fully capable of classifying objects and phenomena into coherent, locally meaningful categories. It can generalize and analyze, and is therefore, every bit as logical as scientific reasoning, even if the facts of myth are in error. Primitive thinking is indeed different, but not because primitive people were mentally infantile compared to modern, scientifically educated people. Primitive people lived closer to nature and this predisposed their thinking toward the universal, the collective and the unconscious.

---

1 Miller, Dean A. *The Epic Hero*. JHU Press. 2000. pp. 105-106.
2 Kinsella, Thomas. *Tain Bo Coulaigh*. Oxford University Press, 1969.
3 Lévi-Strauss, Claude. *The Raw and the Cooked*. University of Chicago Press, 1983.

Mytho-logic is structurally fluid and not static. Every myth is conceived of as a metaphor for every other myth in whole or in part. Mythology, taken as a body, seems to be an ocean of story with myriad entry points. Every discrete feature is logically connected to every other feature if the logic can be followed. Myths are not in the main concerned with conclusions or morals. Each myth is an argument that is immediately countered by another myth with a different series of transformations, which in turn, provokes another myth. The entire corpus of South American mythology might be likened to a hall of mirrors with each individual myth reflecting the others in a series of mediated structural oppositions and rule governed transformations. And though he cannot demonstrate it empirically, he believes that this logic is imprinted in the human brain, universal and inherited at birth. Lévi-Strauss's work has been criticized as being an exercise in hyper-formalism. Perhaps this is because he even resorts to algebraic notation to demonstrate connections and mediate oppositions. Whatever else that myth might be, it is the ultimate machine for destroying time. He made an interesting observation. There is no hard and fast distinction between the mind of the anthropologist explaining the myths and the myths explaining the mind of the anthropologist.

Where Lévi-Strauss was concerned with the structure of logic and thought in myth, the Russian linguist and folklorist Vladimir Propp[1] explored the syntax of narrative and sought to demonstrate in Russian fairy tales their irreducible structural elements and their order. In other words, he explored plot logic and sequence. Of all people, Lévi-Strauss accused him of excessive formalism.

Propp outlined a sequence of thirty-one functions found, all or in part, in Russian fairy tales. It begins with Abstention, in which the hero leaves home, followed by Interdiction, in which the hero is warned off of some place or behavior. The Violation of the Interdiction, in which the hero breaks the rule, gets the story rolling through all the adventures until it concludes happily ever after at a wedding. Propp's sequence might be called the building blocks approach, but for all the aspects of myth and fairy tale that it leaves out, it is a highly accurate description of the basic form.

The attempt to grasp myth and reveal its ultimate secrets has inspired a diversity of approaches. Myth is nothing so much as a protean matrix upon which to hang an interpretation. It has been viewed as revelation of the divine, garbled history, pre-scientific explanation of phenomena, dream inspired fantasy, and the verbal remnant of abandoned ritual. Myth is a means by which humans established traditions and organized their societies. It is a revelation of the unconscious human mind. It is a species of logic, sometimes

---

1 Propp, Vladimir. *The Morphology of the Folktale*. University of Texas, 1968.

childlike and irrational, that reveals human thinking in the early stages of its development. Contrarily, excepting its fanciful use of facts, myth is a system of logic not fundamentally different than scientific reasoning. However, none of the above theories spend much time exploring myth as a speech act, and beyond ritual, make much reference to storytelling as human behavior, that is, as an act that can be observed. All act as if myth could be likened to a species of symbolic art that could be explained as a "closed" system complete with its own rule structure. As will be seen, treating myth in this manner always leads to a dead end and a search for a more encompassing perspective to incorporate the anomalies that always pop up.

There are two aspects of these interpretations that bear further exploration; the seeming inability of primitive thinking to distinguish subject and object, and the use of concrete images and vocabulary to create abstract concepts. These notions are the subjects of the next two sections.

INSTANTANEITY AND MYTH

Scholars of mythology as diverse as Vico, Cassirer, Jung, Lévy-Bruhl and Lévi-Strauss have all remarked upon the philosophical aversion, even the inability in hunter-forager consciousness to distinguish between subject and object, self and surroundings. This aversion is due to its fundamental understanding that the universe is a single, unified, living entity. In Vico, Cassirer and Lévy-Bruhl especially, there lurks the sense that there had to be a fundamental, qualitative difference in primitive logic and their own civilized thinking processes. These scholars were fine-tuned to draw exacting distinctions between objects and between objects and people. They were keenly aware of the dangers of anthropomorphizing. It is perhaps not surprising that these well-dressed Europeans had some difficulty in admitting that the half-naked savages about whom they had developed such fascination stood upon the same mental plane as their own. All of these writers were products of societies steeped in science and civilization. Due to their education and religion, they believed themselves to be somewhat above the processes of nature and that they stood at the end point of evolutionary and historical development. They could admire the nobility of savages in a nostalgic, Rousseauian sense, but the ghost of Hobbes also lurked in their thinking and they could not quite bring themselves to acknowledge half-naked primitives as mental and psychological equals. To deem this attitude racism is perhaps too harsh. It certainly reflects these scholars' ethnocentrism. Lévy-Bruhl was struck by the fact that in some Australian Aborigine languages, there were only color words for black and white. Many scholars wondered if this demonstrated some lower level of "savage" perception and cognition.

This led to many theories of linguistic relativity such as the Whorf-Sapir hypothesis.[1]People recall colors better if their language has a specific term for it, but the basic cognitive perception of colors has been demonstrated to be the same for all human groups examined even if there is a lack of color vocabulary in the test subject's language.[2]

It is true that in hunter-forager philosophy and worldview, a fundamental, radical unity of all creatures and objects is supposed. Chief Seattle of the Suquamish tribe stated it most plainly. "We are part of the Earth and it is part of us. The perfumed flowers are our sisters; the deer, the horse, the great eagle, these are our brothers. The rocky crests, the juices in the meadows, the body heat of the pony, and man --- all belong to the same family."[3] This is not so different than the astrophysicist Carl Sagan's famous notion that human bodies are made of star stuff, of heavier elements cooked in the nuclei of stars evolving and exploding in novae, and reforming elsewhere into new stars and planets and life forms such as *Homo sapiens*. Hunter-forager mythologies reveal that humans are created of divinely shaped earth like all the other animals. This is true in Aborigine myth[4] and it is true of the Judeo-Christian tradition of Western civilization where science purportedly reigns supreme.[5]

However, modern humans have a hard time of properly placing themselves in their natural surroundings. It is ironic that Western civilization, in spite of its own origin myth and its science, has dreamed up a special status for humans in this world that is somehow above and beyond nature. Only humans have a special fate upon dying. We cannot help but find ourselves *in* this world but we have evolved a hazy, romantic fallacy that we humans are not quite *of* this world. We deem ourselves spiritual strangers and each human life lived is a mysterious sojourn upon this planet. We cannot quite accept, neither where our religion, nor where our science places us amid our surroundings.

It is a further irony that quantum physics, the scientific theory that drives our economy and our secular worldview, has arrived at a notion concerning the origins of the universe and of humanity that resonates harmoniously with that of hunter-forager consciousness. The Big Bang Theory, the natural explanation of a universe that has been observed to be expanding the faster the further out we look upon the stars, supposes that if this expansion were traced backward in time, all matter would be condensed by gravitational

---

1 Whorf, Benjamin Lee. *Language, Thought and Reality*. M.I.T. Press, 1964.
2 Berlin, Brent and Paul Kay. *Basic Color Terms: Their Universality and Evolution.* Center for the Study of Language, 1999.
3 Seattle, Chief. *Chief Seattle's Thoughts.* http://www.kyphilom.com/www/seattle. html.
4 Robinson, Roland. *Aboriginal Myths and Legends*. Sun Books Pty Ltd Melbourne, Victoria, Australia 1966.
5 Genesis 1-3.

forces into a singularity smaller than the head of a pin. This singularity is theorized to be beyond the laws of physics. Under these crunched conditions, the existence of most sub-atomic particles would have been impossible. The larger atomic elements and molecules that comprise the building blocks of matter in the visible universe could not exist. The singularity is an example of radical unity almost surpassing imagination.[6]

In our day and age, when Einstein's limit of the speed of light is being challenged, the notion of instantaneity[7] has risen to the level of well-reasoned hypothesis and is the subject of serious experimentation. Is every particle in the universe connected to each and every other particle? Can altering the spin of one electron instantaneously affect the spin of another one in phase with it though it is separated by a distance of several kilometers? Did no speed-of-light time lag occur between the alteration of the first and the measurement of change in the second? It would seem that primitive, mythological consciousness and modern, scientific reasoning have once again arrived at analogous conclusions. Intuition and rationality have confirmed each other in casting humanity in an epic play upon a completely integrated, vast stage where origin, interaction and destination are ultimately, however mysteriously, one. Hunter-forager consciousness based upon intuition does not appear to be such a thing of childlike thinking or irrationality after all.

6 Hawkings, Steven. *A Brief History of Time.* Bantam Dell Books New York NY 10012, 1995.
7 Aczel, Amir D. *Entanglement.* Wiley, New York, NY 2002.

How Myths "Think"

Assembling concrete images by means of leisure speech and juxtaposing them playfully is how myth expresses abstract concepts. One of the most cogent examples of mythological thinking comes from an episode out of the creation myth of the *Kumeyaay* (Diegueño) Indians of San Diego, California. It is called *How Knowledge Came to the People*.[1] A few choice words conjure up an indelible emblem in the mind's eye that is almost geometric in its precision and profound in its symbolism.

The people planned a ceremony, and built a large enclosure of brush. Then they sent a messenger to bring the great serpent Umaí-huhlyá-wit from the ocean. He came and coiled himself in the enclosure; but he could not get his entire length inside. On the third morning, when he had coiled as much of his body as the enclosure would contain, the people set fire to it and burned him. His body exploded and scattered. Inside his body was all knowledge, comprising songs, magic secrets, ceremonies, languages and customs. Thus these were scattered over the land and different people acquired different languages and customs.

The brush enclosure is human culture. The great serpent is nature. Analogies abound such as:

Enclosure:Culture::Serpent:Nature;

Enclosure:Serpent::Culture:Nature;

Enclosure:Nature::Serpent:Culture.

---

1 Bierhorst, John, editor. *The Red Swan: The Myths and Tales of the American Indians.* Farrar, Straus and Giroux. New York, NY. 1976. p. 66. I was privileged to hear several different snippets and versions of this story from *Kumeyaay* friends while growing up in San Diego; from Michael Garrett and his mother Fern Southcott and her great uncles Charley and George Ponchetti of the Mesa Grande Reservation in the Laguna Mountains.

Fire, a fundamental energy of the universe, is harnessed by the audacity and imagination of man. It mediates these sets of oppositions and synthesizes them into human culture. The similarities and the differences between humans are explained. The family of humanity is alluded to. The sheer size of the Serpent:Nature half of the analogy cannot be contained inside the smaller Enclosure:Culture half. This juxtaposition establishes which of the two is dominant with a simplicity that a child can comprehend. Nature, the larger of the two, is the origin of humanity. Conversely, no mere work of humanity is capable of containing nature. The sacred and the profane are established. The profane requirement of every animal, that of having to kill in order to live, is sacralized. Slaughter is transformed into sacrifice, or else the humans who set the serpent ablaze were guilty of a wicked, crazed and inhospitable act. The circle of the brush enclosure and the spiral of the coiling serpent are the basic shapes of creation and of life. They are also the most easily imagined symbols of the thinking mind and the shaping hand. The serpent is a creature that comes out of the Earth and renews itself by periodically sloughing its skin. It is a symbol of the origin of life and of cyclic regeneration.

Much, much more could be discussed concerning this gem of a creation myth. The phallic serpent and the vaginal enclosure allude to sexuality. There is a possible Christian influence. The plot is a Tower of Babel like explanation for the origin of different languages. This myth was collected long after the *Kumeyaay* had been forcibly converted to Catholicism. The three times that the serpent coiled himself inside the brush enclosure could allude to the Holy Trinity, or the three days between Christ's death on the cross and his resurrection. The moon is gone from the sky for three days a month. In many cultures, the serpent and the moon are linked as symbols of regeneration and eternal return. Both undergo predictable cycles of phases. Both always return after an absence.

The logic of myth is not an exercise in infantile thinking or a "disease of language." By means of juxtaposing concrete images such as the serpent and the enclosure, myth is capable of expressing abstract concepts. Nature is preponderant over humanity and the ultimate source of our culture. Myth can express this abstraction, even though the languages spoken by hunter-forager societies for the most part lacked abstract, general category words. Abstract notions and vocabulary provide modern humans with a shorthand method to discuss big ideas. Hunter-foragers had to be more artful in order to do so. We bequeath jaw breaking words to our children that are hard to spell and are alien to our everyday conversation. Hunter-foragers left behind heart bracing mythology that cannot die even though languages change and disappear in the sweep of time.

THE BONES OF THE MYTH OF THE HERO

The comparative study of the myth of the hero is an exercise in content analysis.[1] Many myths are read, recurring incidents are cataloged and grouped under appropriate headings. Results are tabulated and an underlying pattern emerges.

Edward B. Tylor, the English anthropologist, was the first writer to recognize the myth of the hero pattern. "The treatment of similar myths from different regions, by arranging them in large compared groups, makes it possible to trace in mythology the operation of imaginative processes recurring with the evident regularity of mental law. And thus stories of which a single instance would have been a mere isolated curiosity, take their place among well-marked and content structures of the human mind."[2]

Three writers employed this empirical method of sifting myths of the hero from many cultures and came up with surprisingly similar results. The bones of the myth of the hero revealed themselves in von Hahn's exposure-return formula in 1876,[3] Otto Rank's Freudian interpretation in 1909[4] and Lord Raglan's myth-

---

1 Neuendorf, Kimberly A. (2002, p.10) offers a six-part definition of content analysis: "Content analysis is a summarizing, quantitative analysis of messages that relies on the scientific method including attention to objectivity, intersubjectivity, a priori design, reliability, validity, generalizability, replicability, and hypothesis testing) and is not limited as to the types of variables that may be measured or the context in which the messages are created or presented." Neuendorf, Kimberly A.: *The Content Analysis Guidebook Online* (2002): http://academic.csuohio.edu/kneuendorf/content/.
2 Tylor, Edward B. *Primitive Culture*. Vol. I, Torchbooks, 1958. p. 282.
3 Von Hahn, Johan Georg. *Sagawissenschaftliche Studien*. Jena: Mauke. 1876.
4 Rank, Otto. *The Myth of the Birth of the Hero*. In Quest of the Hero ed. Robert A. Segal. Princeton University Press, 1990. pp. 1-86.

ritual approach in 1934.[1] Raglan claimed no knowledge of Rank's efforts. Von Hahn's work went largely unappreciated and his work is best known in English from the work of an anonymous scholar who applied his pattern to Celtic myth.[2] The hero patterns of these writers were arrived at more or less independently.

The Myth of the Hero Pattern

Hahn	Rank	Raglan	
01. Illegitimate birth	01. Distinguished parents	01. Mother a royal virgin	**Raglan-Birth rites**
02. Mother a princess	02. Father a king	02. Father a king	Rank-Birth experience
03. Father a god	03. Difficult conception	03. Father related to mother	Van Gennep- Preliminary(Separation)
04. Prophesy of ascendance	04. Prophesy against birth, parricide	04. Unusual conception	Campbell-Departure
05. Abandoned	05. Surrendered to water, a box	05. Reputed son of god	Aristotle-Beginning
06. Suckled by animals	06. Saved by animals, lowly people	06. Attempted murder by father	Hunter-gatherers-Leave taking
07. Raised by animals	07. Suckled by animals, lowly woman	07. Spirited away	
08. High spirited	08. ———	08. Reared by foster parents	
09. Seeks service abroad	09. Grows up	09. No details of childhood	**Raglan-Intiation rites**
10. Triumphant homecoming	10. Finds distinguished parents	10. Goes to future kingdom	Rank-Becoming adult
11. Slays original persecutors, sets mother free	11. Takes revenge on father	11. Victory over king, monster	Van Gennep-Liminal(Initiation)
			Campbell-Initiation
			Aristotle-Middle
			Hunter-gatherers-Hunting
12. Founds cities	12. Acknowledged by people	12. Marries princess	
13. Extraordinary death	13. Achieves ranks and honors	13. Becomes king	
14. Reviled due to incest	14. ———	14. Reigns uneventfully	**Raglan-Funerary rites**
15. Slain by vengeful servant	15. ———	15. Prescribes laws	Rank-Adulthood
16. Murders younger brother	16. ———	16. Loses favor	Van Gennep-Postliminary(Reintegration)
17. ———	17. ———	17. Driven from throne	Campbell-Return
18. ———	18. ———	18. Mysterious death	Aristotle-End
19. ———	19. ———	19. At top of hill	Hunter-gatherers-Homecoming
20. ———	20. ———	20. His children do not succeed him	
21. ———	21. ———	21. Not buried	
22. ———	22. ———	22. One or more sepulchers	

---

1 Raglan, Lord. *The Hero*. Dover Publications, Inc. Mineola, NY 11501.(1956) 2003.
2 Anonymous. *The Aryan Expulsion-and-Return Formula in The Folk and Hero Tales of the Celts*. Lightning Source UK Ltd. Milton Keynes UK.

They show differences laid side by side, especially in the number of incidents they employ; sixteen for von

Hahn and twenty-two for Raglan. Rank does not specifically enumerate them. Von Hahn's and Raglan's schemes take the hero from birth to death, Rank's trails off at adulthood, kingship and marriage. Laying the three schemes out side by side[1] reveals many commonalities and contrasts. All three patterns can be reconciled generally. They lend themselves to a grouping of their individual incidents under three similar phases, Leavetaking–Adventure–Homecoming.

---

1 Raglan Lord. *The Hero.* p. 138.

The Family Drama

The German psychoanalyst Otto Rank was a disciple of Freud at the time in which he wrote *The Myth of the Birth of the Hero* in 1909. He notes the presence of "a baffling similarity, or, in part, a literal correspondence,"[1] of myths separated by time and space and claims that one of the foremost areas of research in mythology should be an explanation for the "extensive analogies in the fundamental outline of mythological tales."[2]

What accounts for the universality of the myth of the hero pattern? By what means does it transcend history, culture, level of civilization, geographical location and chronology? It still remains a phenomenon that is largely unaccounted for today. There is a stubborn particle-wave duality to the question, largely determined by how the observer chooses to look at it. Either there was an original breeding population of human mythmakers who all shared the same elemental ideas before they spread out of Africa across the planet, or the myths were products of independent invention and spread by diffusion, that is, by human migration coming into contact with other groups. Diffusion presupposes bilingualism. The contact would have to be at more than a casual level because the cultural artifact exchanged, a story, is so complex. There are vast mountains, oceans and deserts to cross in the deeps of time, as well as cultural differences to be reconciled.

Were there cultural centers out of which myths flowed? Rank believed that India and not Babylonia was the birthplace of many myths which radiated out into the world on the tongues of travelers. The incredible spread in time and space

---

1 Rank, Otto. *The Myth of the Birth of the Hero.* In Quest of the Hero, ed. Robert A. Segal, Princeton University Press, Princeton NJ 08540. p. 3.
2 Ibid.

make independent invention and diffusion harder to credit, plus the fact that these notions are only very roughly verifiable through archaeology, if at all. Diffusion ultimately just does not smell right to account for the astounding parallels across time and space. As Rank says, "Even granting the migration of all myths, *the origin of the first myth would still have to be explained.*"[1]And he is not going to waste his time speculating about what the first myth might have been. He thinks it is a better bet that the universality of the myth of the hero is to be sought out psychologically, "in the very general traits of the human psyche."[2] This is Rank's leap of faith and it is a fruitful assumption.

There seems to be, for instance, an intimate relationship between dream and myth. Dream features very greatly in psychoanalytic literature. The parallels between the two encourage reasoning by analogy in terms of content and form, although Rank draws no specific examples of dream and myth to compare side by side. Dream and myth both disregard the limitations of physical reality. Transformation and metamorphosis are commonplace in both. Father figures appear as gods and ogres, mother figures as alluring sex objects and cannibal witches.

Dreams do not manifest the myth of the hero pattern of Leavetaking–Adventure–Homecoming openly. There is often the sensation of leaving the known and the comfortable in dreams. Adventure dominates our sleeping minds in REM periods. There is much comfort at arrival or anguish at being cut off the second that we arrive at a safe place. Often the order of events is jumbled when analyzed in relation to the historical events that inspired the dream. But Freud's summary of psychoanalysis is useful here. He claimed that patients ended up on his couch because of home life and work life. The myth of the hero is all about leaving home, achieving something and bringing it home to be shared. The sequence of the myth of the hero pattern is manifested as a shattered structure in the background of dreams.

It is easy to follow Rank's interesting reasoning here. He, like Freud, has a very flexible approach to symbols. Big can really be small, hot can be cold, men can be women and monsters can be fathers, depending on the dream work done by the dreamers in response to the events of the day. Sometimes a cigar is only a cigar unless, for the purposes of explanation, it is not. Rank anticipates Jung's approach to dream and myth with his theory of archetypes. Dreams are assembled out of ancient, universally understood symbolism and "myth is a dream of the masses."[3] Dream and myth address the same issues in human life. Dream is individual myth and myth is public dream that has become stereotypical with retelling.

1 Ibid. p. 5.
2 Ibid. p. 6.
3 Ibid. p. 7.

The exposure of the hero at birth, the foundational experience of all subsequent anxiety in life, demonstrates Rank's ability to manipulate symbols. Many heroes are set adrift on rivers, often in boxes. The water of the river is the amniotic fluid and the box is the womb. There is a reversal of actions at work, similar to those found in the attitudes of neurotics toward their fathers. The guilt over wishing to kill the father is assuaged by the creative justification that, if he only could, the father would kill the child first. This complex of emotions sanctions the hostility of the child toward the father in dream, myth and neurosis. The childish dreamer-mythmaker-neurotic wants to kill the father but in his guilt, justifies and inverts his hostility by portraying the father as wanting to kill him. Self-defense and creative alibi. Therefore, in story, the father pins the baby's ankles together and leaves instructions that he be exposed upon the mountain or thrown into a river. (But it is really the hostility of the baby that the myth is expressing?)

Rank had to address "Solar Mythology," because of its popularity in his day and age but he echoes Franz Boas when he writes, "*The mythologic evolution certainly begins on terrestrial soil, in so far as experiences must first be gathered in the immediate surroundings before they can be projected into the heavenly universe.*"[1]

He ultimately sums up his rooting of myth in psychology by claiming that the human imagination is the ultimate source of myth. He makes no attempt to define imagination or tie it to reality beyond stating that it is at its most active in childhood and diminishes with age *a la* Wordsworth's *Intimations of Immortality*: "It is not now as it hath been of yore." Rank presents his thesis by "analogizing the ego of the child with the myth of the hero."[2] He acknowledges the repellant emotions that the Oedipus Complex stirs up in average people by its claims that adolescents harbor incestuous sexual desires and murderous impulses toward their parents. However, the facts are too compelling to ignore. And in the myths of hunter-foragers, as we will see in the examples presented below, doing in dad in order to do mom is quite common. As a doctor dealing with patients, Rank finds compelling parallels between elemental features of the myth of the hero and the delusions of persecution and grandeur in the case histories of psychotic individuals, paranoiacs and schizotypal behavior in general. However, he does not provide specific examples to expand upon and clarify his assumption, any more than he did with dream.

The myth of the hero is a psychic structure of the mind, like the Oedipus Complex. These psychic structures explain much even though their existence is hard to prove apart from the phenomena that they purport to explain. They can only be studied indirectly by their effects, in this case, the myths.

---

1 Ibid. p. 7.
2 Ibid. p. 70.

They are just as much scientific assumptions as they are scientific theories. A lot of disparate facts are unified into a coherent theory if the Oedipus Complex and the myth of the hero are assumed to be true. However, it is futile to attribute physical reality to them or to presume to locate them in the anatomy or physiology of the brain. That was in Rank's day. The genetics and neuroscience of our day and age has something new to add to this subject.

Rank is both correct and repellant when he claims that the source of the human faculty of imagination, manifested in dream and myth, as well as in neurosis, must be sought for in the daily reality and surroundings of the dreamer and the mythmaker, and the neurotic. It is distressing to link what is most grand in the human imagination to that which is most desperate and ill-conceived. In *Totem and Taboo*,[1]Rank's mentor Sigmund Freud notes the similarities between taboo in Aborigine culture and compulsion disease in neurotics, *although he admits that any similarities might be superficial.*[2] The ground upon which the parallel is most fruitful is to be found in ambivalence, the capacity to feel two distinct ways about the same person or object. This is most evident in the primitive's emotional relation with his totem animal, which he must not kill and eat (but does once a year ceremonially to commemorate the relationship) and the compulsive neurotic's emotional relation with the object which he or she is both terrified of and cannot refrain from touching in a malady known as *le délire de toucher*.

Freud, and his pupil Rank, would approve of Golding's attempt in *Lord of the Flies*[3] to trace the defects of society back to the defects of individual human nature. The seed crystal ultimately provides the shape of the more complex structure. But let us be reminded that Freud himself noted that any correspondence might well be superficial between neurosis, totem and taboo. Neurosis is private and individual, taboo is social and collective. Neurosis is self-created by emotional reaction to personal experience. Taboo is acquired by enculturation and socialization. A child learns it from his care-givers. A neurosis isolates the individual from his loved ones. A taboo, though factually suspect, integrates that individual into a broader society. When a neurotic violates his personal taboo, he believes his loved ones to be harmed. When a primitive violates a totemic taboo, he himself is harmed. In this view, both the primitive and the neurotic are guilty of "mistaking an ideal connection for a real one." Neurosis demonstrates "far-reaching" correspondences with art, religion and philosophy. At the same time, neurosis seems to be a distortion, even a caricature of them.

1 Freud, Sigmund. *Totem and Taboo*. Norton and Co. New York NY 1950.
2 Ibid. p. 30.
3 Golding, William. Lord of the Flies. Penguin Publishing Group. New York, NY. 1999. Afterword.

Freud compared a Maori chief with a female patient. The Chief: "For a similar reason a Maori chief would not blow on a fire with his mouth, for his sacred breath would communicate its sanctity to the fire, which would pass it on to the meat in the pot, which would pass it on to the man who ate the meat which was in the pot, which stood on the fire, which was breathed by the chief; so that the eater, infected by the chief's breath conveyed through these intermediaries, would surely die."[1] The Female Patient: "My patient demanded that a utensil which her husband had purchased and brought home should be removed lest it make the place where she lives impossible. For she has heard that this object was bought in a store which is situated, let us say, in Stag Street. But the word 'stag' is the name of a friend now in a distant city, whom she had known in her youth under her maiden name and whom she now finds 'impossible', that is taboo. The object bought in Vienna is just as taboo as this friend with whom she does not want to come into contact."[2]

Modern people would generally consider the Maori belief to be a mere superstition. The linking of such disconnected phenomena is fabulous to modern thinking. However, in a burst of naïve rationalism, a scientific mind could imagine a blast of breath, with all the air and trace chemicals broken down into sub-atomic particles by the heat and at least one particle quantum tunneling though the pot and into the meat and eaten by someone, and in the digestive process, it triggers cancer. Can a human direct such a particle to such an end by an act of sheer will? Are these linkages too venturesome? Perhaps they are more outlandish in the proof than in the speculation. The function of such belief among the Maori is easy to grasp. It is a demonstration of supernatural power with the purpose of arousing fear and coercing submission to the chief's political power. Such beliefs are manipulations of credulity, if one has a cynical turn of mind regarding the individual pursuit of power.

Modern people would generally consider Freud's Female Patient to have mental health issues. There is little natural in her associations. They might make sense within, but not beyond, her own personal experience and thinking processes. Where her associations make some sense, they are trivial, based upon mere homophony, which trigger painful memories of her past and result in an outlandish connection between an old hatred and a new gift. To be fair to her, the feminine role in late 19th century Vienna might have made it necessary to resort to madness in order to rebel and win some control of her life from stifling male dominance which would keep her sitting pretty in closed rooms all day long until summoned to bed. In such a climate of gender inequality, even a loving husband could drive an intelligent woman to distraction.

---

1 Freud, Sigmund. *Totem and Taboo*. p. 31.
2 Ibid. p.32.

The Maori belief is a plank in the social support for political and religious authority of the chiefdom. It is public. It is shared. It can even be tested. An individual who could survive eating food cooked upon a fire fanned by the breath of a chief would be considered to be a power in his or her own right. The Female Patient's descent into neurosis is private. Her mental anguish can only be revealed by her stories, which are "take it or leave it" experiences for the listener. These associations cannot be shared automatically, but must be explained. It is in the explanation where the deepest madness lies.

It is important to keep in mind that linking primitive customs to mental health is to apply group behavior standards to individual behavior.[1] It is well that Freud reminds us in the beginning of his thoughts on this subject that "The similarities between taboo and compulsion disease may be purely superficial, holding good only for the manifestations of both without extending into their deeper characteristics."[2] However well-reasoned his assertions, it is understandable that religiously minded people rebel against comparing their devotions with superficial correspondences with neurosis and schizotypal behavior. It is precisely the superficiality of the correspondences that make the wide sweep of their declaration so insulting. It is no more *a propos* than calling a hammer a murder weapon merely because it can be used incorrectly in such a manner. More than a correspondence, perhaps it is better to call such attempts at linkage a juxtaposition. Freud was very aware of the damage his so-called insight could produce. "We must beware of introducing the contempt for what is merely thought or wished which characterizes our sober world where there are only material values, into the world of primitive man and the neurotic, which is full of inner riches only."[3] He might have believed that he was only drawing a useful parallel when he compared taboo to neurosis. While Freud may not have coined the term taboo, he is responsible for its current usage in modern discourse. It provided him and us with a useful "abstract" term, a shorthand if you will, that facilitated discussion of broader abstractions. The unintended consequence of this correspondence was to float the notion in the general public that religious behavior is on a par with mental illness. Visions, hearing voices are regularly referred to in the media as schizotypal behavior. How unintended Freud's efforts were are also suspect. He later wrote *The Future of an Illusion*[4] in which he proclaimed that reason would lead to religion's demise and be replaced with scientific rationality. He was ever the first to draw notice to over-valuing thought, the Omnipotence of Thought[5], as one of his patients dubbed it. Contending that mere reason is enough to dissuade

---

1 Ibid. p. 30.
2 Ibid. p. 30.
3 Ibid. p. 139.
4 Freud, Sigmund. *The Future of an Illusion*. W.W. Norton & Co. New York, NY. (1927).1989.
5 Freud, Sigmund. *Totem and Taboo*. p. 77-79.

humans from seeking spirit was a mysterious blind spot in someone so involved in the workings of the mind. In response to the deepest yearnings that humans have, he could only offer that modern man must submit to death "in a spirit of recognition."[1]This is perhaps the champion piece of naïve rationalism "of all the words of tongue or pen..."[2]

The title of Rank's work is misleading. In fact, he deals very little with the actual experience of being born. He devotes no time to explaining how the adventure of birth ties in to the development of the adult.

The womb is where your heart first started beating, your eyes first opened, your tongue first tasted, your ears first heard and your hands first grasped. The womb is where your brain first sparked to mind ready for deadly, beautiful, symbolic, dualistic life upon birth. The womb is a human being's first home and the pattern upon which all subsequent homes are experienced emotionally. Birth starts with buffeting and rejection and a desperate forced escape through the narrows. This is your first experience of terror. There is a radical, shocking rearrangement of all your senses. You are smacked on the rear in order to stimulate you to sear your lungs with air. A finger is forced down your throat to clear your air passage. This is your first violation by a stranger. Your first response is a cry. With it, you announce your own arrival into the world to all within earshot. It is also a plea for food. This cry is the seed of all subsequent speech. Your first act, even before the cord is cut, is to crawl toward your mother's breast. Your first act in life is a search for food. Because you are human, loving hands will help you find what you are searching for. Your first need was satisfied with a cry. It was your first lesson in hope and prayer. Every successful birth is a movement from primary, autonomic source of sustenance to a new, separate, external one that can only be achieved by laboring through a strange new world. The stereotypical birth narrative reveals a three part structure.

Womb:birth::home:leavetaking
Breast:search::game:hunting-foraging
Nipple:suck::meat:eat

Your transition from womb to breast is the seed crystal existential origin of Earth's daily minimum requirement of all living creatures. You must be able to move to get what you need to survive. The birth experience is the first myth of the hero. However, it happens to us before we can verbalize it. So we forget the pain, the shock and the terror. The new connection blinds us to our animality. When we come of age as hunter-forager adults, the three part pattern of Leavetaking–Adventure–Homecoming is reinforced in response to a daily recurring stimulus; hunger. When our endeavors securing

1 Ibid. p. 82.
2 Whittier, John Greenleaf. "Of all the words of tongue and pen, The saddest these- it might have been."

sustenance are verbalized, it reflects the myth of the hero pattern. The hunter-forager daily round is the existential reality upon which the human leisure imagination, symbolized by means of speech, becomes the myth of the hero.

LORD RAGLAN AND VAN GENNEP

FitzRoy Somerset, 4th Baron Raglan, was the great grandson of Lord Raglan of Crimean War fame. He was an independent folklorist with a military background. He had done a tour of duty in the Sudan at the beginning of his career where he became interested in anthropology and folklore.

Lord Raglan was aware of the three part division of his scheme of the myth of the hero. "The first point to be noted is that the incidents fall definitely into three groups: those connected with the hero's birth, those connected with his accession to the throne and those connected with his death. They thus correspond to the three principal *rites de passage* — that is to say, the rites of birth, at initiation (into adulthood) and at death."[1] For Raglan, "myth is really a narrative linked with a rite." The god is the hero of the ritual and the hero of the myth is the god.

Raglan had read the German-born French folklorist Arnold Van Gennep and quoted him as a source. In his linking of myth to ritual, he does not elaborate upon the linkages in detail. Van Gennep did with rituals what Raglan did with myths. He examined their order and content empirically. He eliminated any form of supernaturalism from his thinking and sought a rational explanation for religious behavior as expressed in rites and ceremonies. He wanted to trace historical origins and by comparative analysis, establish functional relationships. He considered his work as an aspect of taxonomy and sought general laws from empirical observations without resorting to metaphysical speculation.[2]

Rituals were associated with the life crises of birth, puberty, adulthood, marriage, and death. Rites of passage centered upon these crises. They functioned

---

1 Raglan, Lord. *The Hero*. p. 186.
2 Gennep, Arnold. *The Rites of Passage*. The University of Chicago Press. Chicago IL 60637, (1909) 1960.

as mechanisms that incorporated an individual into a new social status within his or her group. They helped the individual understand and accept his or her evolving role in society. They helped the society understand and accept the individual in his or her new role and status.

Van Gennep's schema broke rituals down along two axes. Animistic rites were devoted to personal superhuman beings like gods. Dynamistic rites were devoted to impersonal superhuman powers like the Pacific Islander concept of *mana*.

Animistic and dynamistic rites each shared three distinctions. 1) Sympathetic rites versus rites of contagion.

Sympathetic rites were based upon the reciprocity of like on like or opposite on opposite. They imitate in miniature the effect desired to be replicated out in nature full scale. The Bushman who paints an image in a cave of his spear piercing an eland does so in the hopes that it assures his upcoming hunt will be successful. We interpret his sure, graceful lines in this manner because primitive hunters who survived into the age of anthropology and were studied in the field, claimed that this was the same reason that they painted images deep in caves. They were doing just like their ancient ancestors did.[1]

Rites of contagion deal with the creation of or avoidance of magic substances that are believed to produce desired effects. The West African belief that pregnant women should not eat mulberries to avoid disfiguring the baby is an example. Mulberries in this case are some kind of witchcraft substance.

2) Positive rites versus negative rites. Positive rites translate desires into actions, often imitative. In baseball, on deck players waiting their turn at bat swing the bat timed to the pitch thrown to the batter who is actually "up." Negative rites are basically taboos, behaviors to avoid. Do not walk under ladders.

3) Direct versus indirect rites. Direct rites produce effects immediately. Curses and spells fall into this category. Indirect rites produce effects at one remove in time. Vows and prayers that set in motion desired effects by means of an appeal to or manipulation of animistic or dynamistic forces are examples.

Using Van Gennep's schema, any given rite can be classified by relating it to four categories. Crossing your fingers for the next batter to strike out is dynamistic (it is not actually a prayer to the God of our Fathers); contagious (it is basically a gesture associated with luck, in this case bad, with the hope that it will rub off on the batter); positive (the batter will swing and miss the

1 Orpen, Joseph. *Mythology of the Maluti Bushmen*. The Cape Monthly Magazine, South Africa, May, 1874.

pitch or let a strike go by); and direct (it has got to happen faster than the time it takes for the pitch to get to the strike zone).

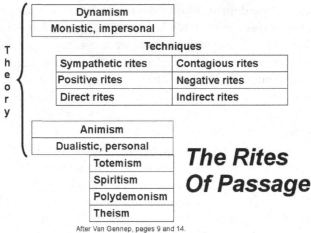

After Van Gennep, pages 9 and 14.

Van Gennep broke individual rites into three stages; 1) Preliminary or Separation; 2) Liminary or Initiation; and 3) Postliminary or Integration. In the preliminary stage of Aborigine initiation rites, the boy is summoned to the ceremonial grounds by the sound of the bull roarers. A group of disguised men come and kidnap him from where he is cowering among the women. The liminal stage of the ceremony is the circumcision rite that now marks him as an adult man. The postliminary rites are those which welcome the initiate back into society and recognize him in his new role and status. Van Gennep also associated complete ceremonies with individual stages of his schema. Funerary rites were rites of separation. Marriage rites were rites of incorporation. Adult initiations were liminal, transitional rites.

Without recognizing the internal dynamics of rituals and comparing them to the internal dynamics of myth, Raglan also links his groupings of incidents in myths to complete rites. The resemblance of parts is related to wholes. Birth, incidents 1-8, is related to rites of separation. Ascension to the throne, incidents 9-13, is related to rites of transition. Death, incidents 14-22, is related to funerary rites.

Raglan did not believe that myths could be tied to history, or that myths were pre-scientific explanations of natural phenomena. His ridicule could be sharp. Likening myth to garbled history is a point of view that could reduce the Norman Conquest to a tale of man who jumped a pond in order to marry a rich woman by force. Solar Mythology also fell under his scorn. "The siege of Troy is but a repetition of the siege of the East by the solar powers that every evening is robbed of their brightest treasures in the west."[1] But if he was aware that many myths and folktales from primitive cultures claim an etiological function for themselves in their texts, he chose to ignore it.

Though he linked myths to rites most strenuously, he seems to fail in this endeavor by his own standards. Berating Classical scholars as romantics for flamboyant, inexact reasoning by analogy in contrast to scientists who reason patiently and empirically, Raglan wrote, "If a process cannot actually be proved to occur, it is surely the duty of those who postulate it to give some reason for believing in its occurrence."[2] Raglan disdains reasoning by analogy but this is exactly what he does in linking myth to ritual. In a bow to Frazer, he claims that the foundational rites upon which the myth of the hero hang are the ones devoted to the institution of the ritual king, the god's representative on Earth. His sacred marriage with the goddess in the person of the chief priestess of the temple. The association of his moral and physical state to the fecundity of the land. The ritual king's seasonal sacrifice and rebirth. But Raglan makes no attempt to examine his claim in any kind of systematic detail and rests his case by appeals to authorities like Hooke, Frazer and Harrison. If myths, by analogy, originate in rites, he is mum on the origin of rites. So is Van Gennep.

To search animal behavior in order to shed light upon ritual was never so much as mentioned in either Raglan or Van Gennep's writings. However, animal behavior is full of ritual. Rituals lead to changes in status in humans and in animals. Bowerbirds strut and bow instinctively when courting. Chimpanzees spontaneously dance in rainstorms. Once more, the depths out of which full blown human rituals evolved are plain to see at a lower stage of development in animal behavior. In bowerbirds, marriage and in chimpanzees; joy? Awe? Will to power?

Konrad Lorentz in *On Aggression* made the argument that certain ritualized behavior in animals was not learned but manifested out of their instincts. All animal rituals were assumed to be redirections of the basic instinctual drive of aggression. He cites Huxley's study of the Crested Grebe and claimed that certain behaviors had lost their original intention and therefore, became ritualized and symbolic. The mating dance evolved from the aggressive response. In other words, one behavior came to symbolize, illicit and respond to another kind of behavior, even in ducks. Lorentz believed that human behavior and culture had a similar development though the process remains obscure.[3] Perhaps because the genetics and neurology of his day as yet lacked the tools and procedures to make such bold linkages empirically demonstrable. Ritual can be linked to animal origins but that

1 Raglan, Lord. *The Hero*. p. 92.
2 Ibid. p. 91.
3 Lorentz, Konrad. *On Aggression*. Bantam Books. New York, NY, 10017, 1966. p 55.

does not make it the true source of the myth of the hero. It is here asserted that grand, dramatic rituals and rites of passage are the children of the myth of the hero, not vice versa, and that both have a common source that is deep in human neurology and daily experience. Ritual is the extension of the myth of the hero into the realms of the performing arts, not the origin of it. The best that can be said of the myth-ritual school is that it attempts to root the myth of the hero in human behavior. The problem is that it is the wrong human behavior.

Raglan's scheme dovetails well, if not perfectly with Indo-European myths of the hero such as Hercules, Perseus, Romulus, Moses and King Arthur. However, even his paragon Oedipus falls one short in his catalog of twenty-two incidences, while Robin Hood, arguably a figure of some historicity, only gets a score of thirteen. By his own standards, "No belief or practice can be claimed as natural unless it is universal and even the most widespread myths and rites are not that."[1]

It is the contention of this work that the myth of the hero pattern is fully universal and therefore, natural to humankind. If a small group of young humans were planted on a garden planet completely naked and without a single tool, if they survived to leave progeny, these descendants would be singing the myth of the hero around their hearth fires. The conditions of life as the most adaptive animal out in nature would evoke the myth of the hero in their budding culture. All that would have to happen is the recitation of the daily hunt mixed with dreams.

The fit of Raglan's catalog of incidents is even looser when hero myths from hunter-forager societies are examined under its aegis. Most notably absent are incidents 1 through 8 dealing with the troubling circumstances of the birth of the hero, his virgin mother, his divine father, the dread portents of his birth, his exposure and exile to stave off fate, and his fosterage with animals or with social inferiors. Raglan's scheme of the myth of the hero is a reflection of its social function among ancient Indo-Europeans.

The unusual circumstances of the hero's birth lent divine sanction to a class social system which placed individuals by virtue of their father's standing into their lifelong roles as warriors, priests or farmers. The hero's mystic status rests largely upon his miraculous rise to the throne in spite of the unfortunate circumstances of his birth and fosterage. Even when kings, through early misfortune, are exiled among commoners, their natural superiority will lead them from obscurity to their divinely sanctioned place in life. A conservative American meme sheds light upon this notion. If all income were distributed evenly throughout society, within a year, the rich would be rich again and the poor would be poor. There is also

1 Raglan, Lord. *The Hero.* p. 114.

the Horatio Alger meme, the extraordinary boy or girl going from rags to riches. Adventure roots heroes out of obscurity in order to reveal their true natures to the world and adventure rewards them for their efforts. Heroes never come from the common stock. Divine, royal heroes only utilize the common stock as a firmament out of which to rise. The civilized myth of the hero becomes subtle propaganda in favor of a class based social system consisting of a minority of intermarrying ruling families exerting sway over a majority of servile commoners with whom they did not marry. It instills a certain spiritual dread into the natural resentment felt toward superiors in any hierarchy. It helped quell and mitigate negative behavior toward rulers. Hunter-forager societies were egalitarian; therefore, this machinery plays a smaller role in their myths of the hero.

Every incident of Raglan's scheme, considered individually as motifs, can be found in the body of all mythological traditions, but it requires a certain synthesizing to manifest them for they do not always show up as a complete pattern in individual stories as recorded *in our books*. It is important to bear in mind the fact that these patterns were literary based. None of the authors of the myth of the hero patterns had ever collected a tale out in the field, though Rank came closest in that he interviewed patients and heard their individualized myths. These scholars maintained a hierarchy of versions of any given myth. They held to the bias that the version with the highest poetic qualities was also the most reliable factually. None of them emphasized myth as speech behavior, as performance. They saw themselves, especially Raglan, as explorers amid forms long frozen into classical perfection by cultivated appreciation. Myth as speech behavior had no place in their literary ponderings of sacred revelations and the workings of the human mind. The strength of Raglan and Van Gennep is their strict adherence to empirical methods. Their discipline unveiled the clear structures of the rites of passage and the myth of the hero.

Inspired by this approach, the folklorist Alan Dundes examined the life of Jesus as a myth of the hero. He found that it made a tight, if not exact, fit.[1] In an exercise of whimsy, Francis Utley applied the myth of the hero pattern to the life of Abraham Lincoln.[2] Humor is revealing. Raglan's particular pattern fits Lincoln's life perfectly. Utley reasoned as if this fact somewhat undermined the validity of the hero pattern. The whole point of this work is that we must lift the pattern from the pages of books and search for its operation out in life. And this will prove to be a fruitful assumption for what is to come once we achieve the right vantage point.

---

1 Dundes, Alan. *The Hero Pattern and the Life of Jesus.* Protocol of the Twentyfifth Colloquy, 1976.
2 Utley, Francis. *Lincoln Wasn't There or Lord Raglan's Hero.* CEA Chapbook. Supplement to CEA Critic 22, no. 9. Washington, D.C. 1965.

OUR ELDEST STORYTELLERS

In order to test the universality of Lord Raglan's pattern, of which he himself made no such claims, it has to be applied to some myths of the hero taken from outside of the Indo-European tradition. These myths should come from outside of all civilized literary traditions, in general. Ideally, and in order for this endeavor to avoid becoming an inductive nightmare running into volumes and volumes heaping up example after example, we are searching for the most theoretically ancient people, the eldest storytellers, and therefore, the most ancient myths of the hero upon the planet. If the hero pattern is observable at this level, it explains why it radiated to every continent and is found everywhere humans are found. Was the myth of the hero with modern humans from the beginning and every step of the way as they migrated out of Africa, fifty to two hundred thousand years ago? The field of primitive myth is vast. In the selection process, Tylor's words serve as a guide and a caution.

In discussing problems so complex as those of the development of civilization, it is not enough to put forward theories accompanied by a few illustrative examples. The statement of the facts must form the staple of the argument, and the limit of needful detail is only reached when each group so displays its general law, that fresh cases come to range themselves in their proper niches as new instances of an already established rule. Should it seem to any readers that my attempt to reach this limit sometimes leads to the heaping up of too cumbrous detail, I would point out that the theoretical novelty as well as the practical importance of many of the issues raised, make it most unadvisable to stint them of their full evidence. In the course of ten years chiefly spent in these researches, it has been my constant task to select the most instructive ethnological facts from the vast mass on record, and by lopping away unnecessary matter to reduce the data on each problem to what is indispensable for reasonable proof.[1]

This was gospel to Frazer in the Golden Bough. Nevertheless, it evolved from book to an encyclopedia. Something of the opposite is proposed here. There is a wealth of pertinent comparative materials available in our day that was not in Tylor's and Frazer's. To sharpen the focus, we will employ several filters, beginning with genetics, to narrow our search. Our goal ultimately is to present the single drop that will offer up the taste of the sea. At the same time, every effort will be made to highlight the limitations of this perspective.

Hypothetically, our Eldest Storytellers should constitute a distinct ethnicity with strong cultural traditions supporting marriage within the group. Within and amongst their relatively isolated breeding population, they should show the widest genetic diversity. For any selected gene whose connection with anatomy or behavior has been established, our Eldest Storytellers should have more variations of it within their group compared to the number of variations of the same gene found in neighboring groups. In the genealogical trees formed of selected mutations that lead backward to the most recent commonly shared ancestor, the genome which has accumulated the greatest number of variations of that selected gene is hypothesized to be the eldest. Our Eldest Storytellers will hopefully constitute an extended family of descendants of the very first branch of modern humans to arrive in the territory and survive in the same manner as did their ascendants until recent times. As a people and as a lifeway, our Eldest Storytellers will constitute a continuum from the Pleistocene to the present as much as the facts allow us to present them as such.

Our Eldest Storytellers should have traditions that lay claim to autochthonic origins. They will have come up out of the earth in the time of the ancestors at specific locations within their present living territory. They will claim to hunt the same hunting grounds for the same game in the same manner as did their original ancestors and drink from the same water holes as they did since the beginning.

Our Eldest Storytellers will be nomadic hunter-foragers because this lifeway reflects the political, economic, familial and religious experience in which modern people out in nature evolved from lower orders of hominids into their present modern form, heart, body, mind and soul. Hunter-foragers are therefore assumed to be exemplars of humanity's formative lifeway. Standing up on two feet and applying tool making and weapon throwing and running in the pursuit of meat was the path humans took when they branched from their nearest cousin species the chimpanzee some five million years ago.

1

Archeology and rock art will confirm that the territory in which these people were "discovered" will have been continuously occupied by hunter-foragers from the time it was first settled. The limit of carbon-14 dating methods is about fifty thousand years. This basic time period is also noteworthy regarding some other notions considered below as the beginning of a chain of events in the spread of humanity beyond Africa.

To put a reliable date upon any stone artifact is generally mired in some controversy. It is still more contentious with bones. With cultural artifacts such as language and story, often there is just no way to measure age beyond living memory. Scientific disciplines are constantly recalibrating their values of their measuring devices. Hubble's Constant, the mathematics which explains the expansion of the universe, if such be the case, is constantly under revision and has been mired in controversy for decades. Q, one of its most crucial variables, was recently changed from a positive to a negative value. Now astrophysics claims that our universe threatens to tear itself apart under its own outward momentum. The West's twelve month calendar is an artifact of political and religious chicanery where it is not merely in plain error. More important than purportedly exact, but often controversial carbon-14 or potassium argon dates, is the general order of events in broad terms. No controversies surrounding archeological data serve as confounds for the Orion Complex, nor are any controversial archeological theories required to accept its validity. Here, the devil is not in the details. Here, *ancient*, for purposes of brevity, can refer to a time of more than fifty-thousand years ago. Whether modern humans migrated from their original territory one or two hundred thousand years ago is neither here nor there to our considerations, because we can rest assured that with improved methodology will also come renewed controversy and the precise date of this migration will continue to waver between the well-considered extremes of expert opinion. Some crucial dates seem to be getting pushed back further and further into the past, such as evidence of tool use now back to 2.4 million years. However, the theoretical human-chimpanzee split has been moved up closer to present times. Paleontology suggests that the bones indicate twenty million years ago. Molecular biology suggests that comparative DNA indicates the split was as little as five million years ago. Not to dismiss a lot of hard work and excellent thinking that has led to such divergent opinion, but these are debates into which we are unqualified to enter, let alone judge. The general order of events is more germane to our argument than exact dates of their occurrence. When this human-chimpanzee split happened is far less important for our argument than accepting the fact that it happened. Then upright bipedality, tool use and fire. Finally, leaving Africa as a hunter-forager and spreading out across the globe.

Our Eldest Storytellers ideally, should have retained their ancient, original language. This language will be related neither to their neighbors nor to any other known language in the world. If the beginning could be compared to the end, this language might stand as a model for internal linguistic change over time because of its continuous relative isolation from outside influences. Hunter-forager ancestors, passing their own mother tongues parent to child to their hunter-forager descendants for hundreds of thousands of years in the same locale, never once conquered by another culture until the West descended. Our Eldest Storytellers will not have been linguistically overshadowed by the newcomers who marginalized them economically and politically. They will be acknowledged by their neighbors as the first comers to the territory, however grudgingly. It is acknowledged that this is shaky criteria under the best of circumstances. However, not so shaky as to call a halt to the journey.

This is not to say that the descendants of this original group will speak a language that is even remotely recognizable to the original settlers who were their ancestors. Languages spoken in isolation also change internally. Slang comes and goes generationally. From our historical experience of ancient Greek becoming modern Greek, and Latin becoming Italian, it is possible to suggest that once contact is broken between them, two languages which share a common origin could lose all resemblance to one another after ten thousand years. In any given locale, a full cycle of this transformational process has been at work from five to ten times since modern man left Africa.

Even languages spoken in isolation for millennium by people following the same lifeway are known to change dramatically through time. In English the Great Vowel Shift occurred in the 1300s. Up to that era, English vowels were generally pronounced short in the manner of Continental languages. Then over the course of one-hundred and fifty years, don't bite (beet) your sister became don't bite (byte) your sister. There is no generally accepted reason among scholars as to why this dramatic change in pronunciation took place. Comparing Chaucer's rhymes in the 1350s with Shakespeare's in the 1590s gives evidence of this shift but no clue as to why the speakers started pronouncing common vocabulary differently from the manner in which their grandparents did.[1]

In *Totem and Taboo*, Freud mentions a dynamic that keeps vocabulary perennially refreshing itself. A missionary named Dobritzhofer observed the Abipons of Paraguay change the name for jaguar three times during his seven year sojourn among them. People are often named after animals in Abipon culture. Upon death, it is taboo to mention the deceased by name and a circumlocution must be employed if the word is used among the loved ones

---

1 Labov, William. *Principles of Linguistic Change*. Blackwell Publishing. 1994. p. 145.

and acquaintances of the deceased. Death customs constantly recycle and transform vocabulary among the Abipons.[1]

More prosaically, we all remember sitting in a circle in grade school playing the telephone game, Russian Scandal, Chinese Whispers. The first kid whispers something into the next kid's ear. He or she does likewise until it is whispered into each ear around the circle. Even when every attempt is made to remain true to the original message, we are startled and delighted by the mistakes that accumulate with each retelling until the final version is a surprise. Retelling results in distortion. We feel we have achieved some insight into how tricky memory is and how rumors progress.[2]

These examples of the protean, ephemeral, mysterious quality of spontaneous language are always something to bear in mind as we attempt use the stories that follow, the most ancient examples of Lord Raglan's myth of the hero pattern that we can discover, as living fossils or windows upon the ancient past. It is striking that anything, however vague, could survive such processes over such vast stretches of time. However, as we shall see in the pages following, something tangible endures. The myth of the hero pattern.

Our Eldest Storytellers will have survived as hunter-foragers up to the time of modern anthropology and will have been studied by academic professionals who spent years among them and who learned their respective languages and took down their stories with fidelity, devotion, cultural sensitivity and cross-cultural insight.

This will be as close as we can come to discovering our Eldest Storytellers and viewing their stories, their myths of the hero, as living fossils of Pleistocene human narrative thinking. Hunter-forager societies are rich in myth. The primal status of these societies and the stories that they tell make them perfect test subjects to see how Lord Raglan's hero pattern fits. Here primal status should read as more consciously involved in living out in and working with nature, and primitive, as it was originally intended, that is, first, with no pejorative connotation attached.

---

1 Freud, Sigmund. *Totem and Taboo.* p.55-56.
2 Paul, Marla. "Your Memory is like the Telephone Game: Each time you recall an event, your brain distorts it," *Northwestern Now,* Sep. 9, 2012. https://news.northwestern.edu/stories/2012/09/your-memory-is-like-the-telephone-game.

Modern Primitive Equals Pre-historic Past

It is a widely held assumption that the modern primitive is a window upon the pre-historic past. Primitive people and their cultures are assumed to be living fossils like the lobe finned Ceolacanth. This fish was well represented in the fossil record but was thought to have been long extinct. However, a live example was netted in waters off of the coast of South Africa in the 1930s. It was hailed as a living fossil for evolutionary theory that represented a step toward amphibians and reptiles. It also provided insight into and confirmation of the fossil record. When J.M. Orphen, the Chief Magistrate of St. John's Territory, needed interpretation of the rock art that he had found in South Africa in the Maluti Mountains, he consulted Qing, a Bushman hunter in his employ who was completely conversant with the meaning that his ancestors were trying to convey. Qing claimed that Bushmen in his day and age painted the same images for the same reasons, mostly, success in the hunt and rainmaking.[1] Modern people wonder if the artists of the caves of Trois Frères and Lascaux painted for the same reasons. Perhaps the hunter-foragers of ancient France were more like modern Bushmen than their city dwelling descendants of today.

The more "primitive" an artifact or tradition is the further back into time we are peering. This is one of the articles of faith in anthropology. However, caution is in order. All societies bifurcate, branch and accumulate local innovations at differing paces, some faster, some slower. Australopithecines made the same stone tools by the same methods parent to child for hundreds of thousands of years before new techniques were discovered and diffused. Primitive societies

---

1 Orpen, Joseph. *Mythology of the Maluti Bushmen*. The Cape Monthly Magazine, July, 1874. Rhodes University. http://www.ru.ac.za/corylibrary/online/primarysources/mythologyofthemalutibushmen/

can be conservative and slow to change traditions. The Acheulian hand axe,[1] found in most non-rainforest parts of Africa showed very few changes over a span of more than one million years. Primitive people often claim the past as sanction for their present ideas and techniques. They make a tool or tell a story like their ancestors did and are proud of it. In fact, following traditions established by ancestors is often a spiritual duty for hunter-foragers.

However, anthropologists have also documented individually inspired innovation and change in primitive cultures with small populations. On the Small Andaman Island among the Onge, a well-known seer named Enagaghe had a message from the spirits concerning the manner in which hunting trophies were to be displayed. His recitation of the dream and the sanction obtained from its telling initiated a change on this heading in his society dating 1954.[2] There is the widespread acceptance of Beh's song and the giraffe dance among the Ju/'hoansi Bushmen in Namibia. It was first observed by Lorna Marshall in the 1970s. It originated with a new song made up by an elderly woman while she was out alone in the bush. She dreamed that she saw a herd of giraffes running away from an approaching thunderstorm. It has spread to many Bushmen groups and was observed still going strong in the 1990s by Megan Biesele.[3] A. Hoff has observed that the Water-bull has been replaced by the Water-Snake in storytelling among the Nama since contact with and enculturation into Western life.[4]

Hunter-foragers and Hottentot (Khoikhoi) agriculturalists have equally long spans of evolution dating from the time of their branching into separate populations. Back when southwest Africa was wetter, the present day Bushmen ancestors might have had an interlude of several thousand years as subsistence farmers. When drier climatic conditions recreated the Kalahari, they re-specialized as hunter-foragers. Perhaps the most ancient people on Earth had to rediscover the hunter-forager lifeway once the ground changed under their very feet and robbed them of their sedentary livelihood.

Hunter-forager myth is a lens both clear and opaque by which to gaze long range and speculate about human origins. Their myths of the hero were gathered in recent times. They are as far back into the past as modern people can gaze. The data is therefore, necessarily indirect, and of limited accuracy. It is the best that we can do. However, our folkloric gathering of stories and

1 Bordes, Francoise. *The Old Stone Age*. McGraw-Hill Book Company. New York NY, 1968.
2 Cipriani, Lidio. *The Andaman Islanders*. Weidenfeld and Nicolson, 20 New Bond Street, London W1, 1966. p. 76.
3 Biesele, Megan. *Women Like Meat*. The folklore and foraging ideology of the Kalahari Ju/'hoan. Indiana University Press, Bloomington IN 47404, 1993. pp. 67-70.
4 Schmidt, Sigrid. *South African |Xam Bushman Traditions and Their Relationships to Further Khoisan Folklore*, Rüdiger Köppe Velag Köln, Cologne, Germany, 2013. p. 218.

myths has entered a new phase. Global communications reach most places. It is a commonplace in our day and age to travel to the highlands of Guatemala for example, and watch a Mayan woman, dressed in traditional garb sitting at a back strap loom in the doorway of her hut, interrupt her weaving to answer her cell phone. Bushmen myths were immediately suspected of Bantu and European influences by Wilhelm Bleek.[1] Hybridization is the story with DNA as well as with myths of the hero. The original storytellers have almost all died out. We can never be sure again what given story actually came from where. These days, people in the most far-off places hear things from everywhere around the globe instantly. The fear, so eloquently and diligently espoused by Franz Boas, the father of American anthropology, that traditional culture is vanishing, has sadly almost been realized. Perhaps vanished is a bit overstating the difficulty. Perhaps homogenized is a better term. Or globalized. From now on, hybridization is the rule with myths of the hero rather than the exception.

1 Ibid. p. 21.

THE BUSHMEN AS PARENT PEOPLE

What substantiates the claim that the Bushmen of Southwest Africa are the Parent People of mankind? Charles Darwin speculated that Africa was the cradle of humanity. "In each great region of the world the living mammals are closely related to the extinct species of the same region. It is, therefore, probable that Africa was formerly inhabited by extinct apes closely allied to the gorilla and chimpanzee; and as these two species are now man's nearest allies, it is somewhat more probable that our early progenitors lived on the African continent than elsewhere."[1] The oldest archeological evidence for a primate is tiny, tree dwelling *Archicebus achilles*, named for its strange feet and long tail. It was found in 2013 in an ancient lake bed, not in Africa, but in China. The remains date back 55 million years. Origins are ever muddy. Africa might not be the home of primates, but it is the most widely accepted home of hominids and probably the home of modern people too.[2]

In Southwest Africa among the neighboring Hottentots and Bantus, the Bushmen are acknowledged as the ancient ones, the first people before all others on the land. Generally, pastoralist economies will out-compete hunter-forager economies within a shared territory. Pastoralism artificially extends the carrying capacity of the land and can enable, at least in the short term, a larger population to thrive. Cattle herders edge out bow hunters because they hold ground fiercely. They cannot just up stakes and move on to new pasturage in response to hunger.

1 Darwin, Charles. *The Descent of Man*. Chapter 6. On the Affinities and Geneology of Man. D. Appleton & Co. New York NY, 1871. pp. 191-192. Darwin online.org.
2 Gray, Richard. Archicebus Achilles could be humanity's earliest primate cousin. The Telegraph. 05 Jun 2013. http://www.telegraph.co.uk/news/science/science-news/10102084/Archicebus-achilles-could-be-humanitys-earliest-primate-cousin.html.

Since the Bantu migrations from the north started twenty-five hundred years ago, the Bushmen have become more and more marginalized hunter-foragers. They have retreated to, and held out in, the harshest of environments unfit for crops and livestock. Not many live in the Old Way.

How have the bones been used to describe the Bushmen? Raymond Dart was an Australian anatomist and anthropologist. In 1924, he discovered the Taung skull in South Africa. It took time and help to get his interpretation of his find accepted in the Eurocentric academic world, but by the late 1940s, *Australopithecus africanus* was acknowledged as an ancestor of modern man.[1] In 1953, he published *The Predatory Transition from Ape to Man.*[2] Robert Audrey in the 1960s polished Dart's ideas up into the Killer Ape Hypothesis.[3] The long process of hunting down, killing and eating animals evolved apes into human beings. Almost dismissively, the hunter-forager Bushmen were deemed to be the direct human descendants of bone wielding *Australopithecus africanus* like those portrayed at the beginning of Stanley Kubrick's film *2001, A Space Odyssey*. Instead of honoring the Bushmen as the Parent People among *Homo sapiens*, the killer ape hypothesis was used by some groups to justify racism and the "natural" cultural superiority of Europeans. By other groups, it was used to explain criminal behavior as being almost inevitable, the beast being genetically what it is. The editor of the scholarly journal that published Dart's original work claimed that the bones he used as evidence "were only the ancestors of the modern Bushmen and Negroes, and of *nobody else*."[4] Only something so wrong could sound so sure.

In 2005, Dr. Spencer Wells,[5] a geneticist and anthropologist, became the head of The National Geographic Genographic Project. His aim was to map the human genome and establish the place of origin of modern people and date and trace their migrations across land and sea to every corner of the globe. He worked with DNA, the molecular book of life in the shape of a spiral ladder that lives at the heart of every cell in the nucleus. It is the place where, in response to some stimulus from the environment, instructions for protein synthesis are assembled and start their journey to the ribosome for transcription into actual proteins. Then chemical cascade by chemical cascade, a particular behavior is manifested. DNA is the place where the

1 Dart R.A. *Australopithecus africanus: The Man-Ape of South Africa.* Nature, Vol.115, No.2884, 1925. p. 195-9.
2 Dart, R.A. "*The Predatory Transition from Ape to Man.*" International Anthropological and Linguistic Review, 1, 1953. pp. 201–217.
3 Ardrey, Robert. *African Genesis: A Personal Investigation into the Animal Origins and Nature of Man.* New York: Atheneum. 1961. *The Territorial Imperative.* Dell Publishing Co. New York NY 1966.
4 Dart, R.A. "*The Predatory Transition from Ape to Man.*"
5 Wells, Spencer. *The Journey of Man: A Genetic Odyssey.* Princeton University Press, 2002.

heredity of each individual can be traced with advanced techniques, even down to the viral infections suffered over a lifetime. It is such an important issue. Ultimately, any meaningful discussion of the origins of the myth of the hero requires squaring its argument with the insights of current genetics. DNA merits a short digression for purposes of clarification.

DEOXYRIBONUCLEIC ACID

To paraphrase J.P. Donleavy, author of *The Ginger Man*, meet your maker, the mad molecule. "The further from DNA, the further from the truth."[1] If DNA is the ultimate template of life, fitting the empirical details together and conceiving of the structure of DNA is one of the supreme achievements of the human imagination.

The first step toward its discovery took place with the use of basophilic aniline dyes. This was a fundamentally new technique for staining the chromatin material, a weak acid found in the nucleus of a cell as a homogenous tangled mix. Chromosomes were first observed in plant cells by the Swiss botanist Karl Wilhelm von Nägeli in 1842. Next they were seen in worms by the Belgian scientist Edouard Van Beneden. Chromosome behavior, when DNA coiled into Xs and Ys in salamander cells, was later described by German anatomist Walther Fleming, the discoverer of mitosis, or cell division, in 1882. The name chromosome comes from the Greek meaning "color body." It was later coined by another German anatomist, Heinrich von Waldeyer. In the 1880s, Theodor Boveri proved that chromosomes are the vectors of heredity. Chromosomes are made of unbelievably long vines of coiled DNA. DNA itself was first isolated from human pus cells in 1869 and identified as a nucleic acid.

It took another eighty years to work out DNA's constituent atoms, and their various chemical bonds, the angles and the strengths of those bonds, as well as levels of molecular structure. In the spring of 1953, the geometry and the architecture came together for the researchers. Francis Crick and James D. Watson, building upon the indispensable X-ray crystallography of Rosalind

1 Gribbin, John and Jeremy Cherlas. *The First Chimpanzee*. Barnes and Noble Books, 2001. p. 88.

Franklin, unveiled the double helix to the world. It is useful to employ an artful blend of backbones, snakes, ladders and finally zippers in order to imagine their achievement; the structure of DNA, the code of life.

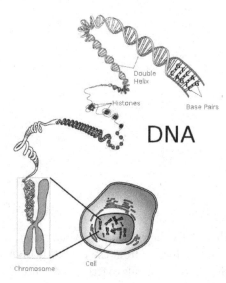

DNA is comprised of a long polymer or sequence of repeating units. By analogy, if this foundational strand is likened to a backbone, each individual vertebra would be a monosaccharide sugar molecule ester bonded to a phosphate group. These repeating sugar-phosphate units are called nucleotides. Sugar is sweet and phosphorus burns white hot and causes flowers to bloom. DNA strands are millions of nucleotides in length. These strands are generally paired in the nucleus of the cell, running in opposite directions, antiparallel like two snakes slithering past each other head to tail. Stretched out, a single human's DNA would extend beyond the solar system.

HOCH₂   O   H   HOCH₂   O   H   2. The Sugars

Ribose   Deoxyribose

3. Phosphate Group

Attached at the sugars and jutting out at right angles to the repeating nucleotides are one of four nucleobases. If the two antiparallel strands can now be likened to the side rails of a ladder and the nucleobases meet in the middle and bond between them like rungs, then the metaphor is almost complete. The structure of DNA is like a ladder twisted tight from top to bottom. It is a spiral of two vines wrapping around each other. There are alternating major and minor grooves running along on the outside every twist and turn of its entire length. DNA does not exist in the nucleus of the cell as a naked molecule. Each living creature's DNA is clothed in external molecules that affect its function with the environment in ways unique to each individual and the environment in which they live.

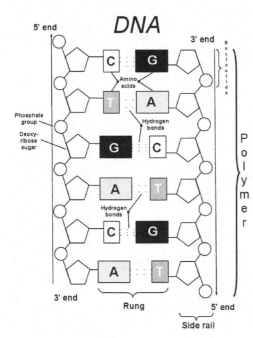

Inside, the nucleobases bond in the middle of the rung. The strengths of these bonds have been experimentally verified. It is well known just how much heat it takes to break them apart and cause the long strands to unravel. This process is called denaturing and it has been used to compare the genomes of humans and chimpanzees.[1]

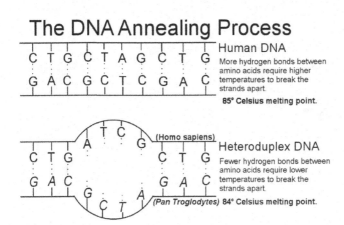

The DNA Annealing Process

C T G C T A G C T G **Human DNA**

G A C G C T C G A C

More hydrogen bonds between amino acids require higher temperatures to break the strands apart.

85° Celsius melting point.

(Homo sapiens)

Heteroduplex DNA

C T G   C T G

G A C   G A C

Fewer hydrogen bonds between amino acids require lower temperatures to break the strands apart.

(Pan Troglodytes) **84° Celsius melting point.**

1 Alberts B, Johnson A, Lewis J, Raff M, Roberts K, Walter P. *Molecular Biology of the Cell*. (6th ed.). Garland. Chapter 4: DNA, Chromosomes and Genomes, 2014. http://learn.genetics.utah.edu/.

Tracking Down the Most Ancient People Known to DNA

Dr. Spencer Wells concentrated his efforts on the Y chromosome. DNA exists in the cellular nucleus as long, writhing stands. Before cellular division, these individual strands coil tightly into characteristically shaped X's. However, one chromosome coils into a Y shape. The Y chromosome is inherited only from the father's side.

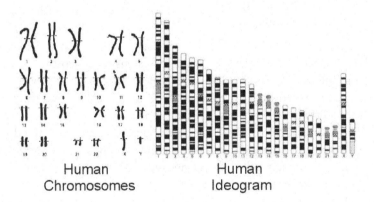

Human
Chromosomes

Human
Ideogram

Proteins, the basic building blocks of life, are made of amino acids. Each amino acid is coded for by three nucleotides. Using a line from Elizabeth Barrett Browning, we can demonstrate how the process of replication works. If *how do I love thee?* is the original, then an exact replication would be *how do I love thee?* The variations *now do I love thee!* and *wow, do I love thee!* represent point mutations. Because there is no great change in meaning, these variations would probably produce small overall effect. There are several ways to code for each amino acid and it is this redundancy which makes variation possible. But if you get *cow, do I love thee!* you have made only one change, but it constitutes a drastic change in meaning, as you would with *how do I love ghee!*

During the replication process, mistakes occur rarely but they do. Some mutations cause no effect. The majority of mutations that cause effects are harmful. However, a few are surprisingly beneficial. A father will pass all types of mutations on the Y chromosome down to his son. Any given mutation can serve as a marker to trace heredity and form genealogical trees that suggest common ancestry, age and migration patterns, among other things.

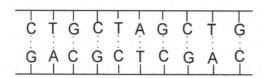

4. **Regular DNA**

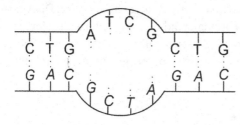

5. **Point Mutation**

Dr. Wells chose the San Bushmen of Namibia to start his research. It would be interesting to hear the thoughts of the Bushmen themselves after they listened to this tall, blue eyed, white skinned man of the race which threatens to sweep them to extinction in the name of inevitable progress. How did they react among themselves to his acknowledging them as the Parent People? From their body of oral tradition, it is plain that Bushmen appreciate irony.

Dr. Wells swabbed the inside of cheeks of hunter-foragers and stored the samples in test tubes. Back in the lab, he ran these through an innovative new sequencing computer called the GenoChip. The complexity of this process has been likened to throwing a Bible, a dictionary and a cookbook into a wood chipper and trying to reassemble the Bible out of the pile of shreds after throwing a couple of buckets of water onto the mess. Literally billions and billions of computations are necessary. This requires computers with incredible speed and memory capacity. To put this into perspective, if a hypothetical human were capable of doing one computation per second and he or she worked twenty-four hours a day for sixty-five years, this person would only get approximately 5.6 million calculations done in an entire lifetime. It would take one-hundred and seventy nine lifetimes to do one billion calculations. And we are talking about doing billions and billions of computations and calculations over the course of months to sort out a genome.

The Bushmen were found to have the largest number of alleles or the greatest genetic variety of certain selected genes on the Y chromosome within its population compared to any other group. For instance, one hundred randomly selected Icelanders would show far less variety in facial features than would one hundred similarly selected Bushmen. Though their population is tiny compared to the worldwide Caucasian population, genetically, there is more variety within the Bushmen because they are an older population or inter-marrying group. Technically speaking, there are more phenotypes within the genotype. The Bushmen form the main trunk of the human family tree. The Caucasians are out on the outer branches. In terms of world population figures, and because the Bushmen are so few, it is a strange tree. The main trunk is as small as a twig and the newest branches are as gigantic as Sequoias.

Bushmen antiquity is evident in their faces for hints of all the major races are already there for all to see; high cheek bones, slanted eyes, wooly hair, flat and hooked noses, thin and ample lips, blue eyes and skin shades ranging from dark to red and light yellow. In the Bushmen, it is easy to see where all humans came from. They are rightly called the Parent People and Dr. Wells' DNA testing confirms this. Was there a Y chromosomal Adam? A single male from whom all humans alive today descend? In theory, there is and according to genealogical trees based upon tracing mutations as markers going generation to generation back to their source, Y chromosomal Adam is believed to have lived from 100,000 to 200,000 years ago in East Africa.

The mitochondria are another source of DNA. The mitochondria are the powerhouses of the cell. It is thought the mitochondrion may once have been a free-floating, single cell creature. It was captured by a larger, eukaryotic cell and, in a case of symbiosis and beneficial mutualism, found a new home and thrived in it. The mitochondria eat complex molecules free floating in the cell's cytoplasm, its inner sea, and digests them. They transform them into ATPs which the host cell uses to fuel its most basic operations such as respiration and active transport of nutrients across the membrane.

The genome of the mitochondria has only 37 genes. It is far easier to map and keep track of. Most important of all, mitochondrial DNA is only inherited from the mother so, like with the Y chromosome, it is possible to create genealogical trees that go back to a single female *Homo sapiens* who lived some 100,000 to 200,000 years ago. She is our most recent common ancestor. All humans alive today count Mitochondrial Eve as their ultimate human grandmother. She is believed also to have lived in East Africa. Mitochondrial

DNA genealogies as well place the Bushmen as the Parent People for the same reasons as do those devoted to the DNA on the Y chromosome. Their population has the greatest accumulation of mutations and varieties of a selected gene within it compared to those of younger, descending groups that branched off of it.

Will the science ever become so exact as to narrow the field down to a single couple that we all can rightly call the grandparents of humanity? That would certainly put the story of Adam and Eve and the Garden of Eden in its proper perspective. If such pinpointing is ever possible, the primal pair would be the manifestations of, and inheritors of, a long evolutionary heritage originating in and emerging out of animality. They would not be fully developed modern people that appeared spontaneously out of ashes and dust at the verbal behest of a superhuman being.

THE GARDEN OF EDEN

Though they may differ in details, both Y chromosomal and mitochondrial DNA studies place the origin of humans in Africa. The Garden of Eden has expanded from East Africa to include the entire continent. Africa is huge. All of North America would fit into the Sahara alone. It is surrounded by sea on all sides and there is only one way to walk out, at the bottleneck, at Sinai up at the northeast corner. After crossing the largest desert in the world to leave Africa, the world beyond would welcome the traveler with more desert to cross on foot in search of water. Africa was vast within its limits. It was a big and complex enough cell for the human hunter-forager lifeway to evolve inside its generous confines over millions of years.

Archeology and rock art suggest that the lands inhabited by the Bushmen in modern times have been occupied continuously by hunter-foragers for the last seventy thousand years.[1] They still speak their original language, which is not related to their neighbors' nor to any other known language in the world. Finally, it is tradition among the Bushmen that they originated by the same operations of God as he used to make the animals. They are as much a part of the landscape as the animals that they hunt.

It was fortunate that the continent of Africa was not an easy place from which to escape in the beginning. The process of hybridization of genes and ideas benefited not only by the continent's variety and vastness, but also by its absolute confines. The world ocean formed a fence around the entire continent, within whose boundaries ideas could bounce back and forth for millions of years. Innovations could accumulate and be shared over time and distance. The

---

1 Garlake, Peter. *The Hunter's Vision: The Prehistoric Art of Zimbabwe*. British Museum Publications, London, England. 1995.

variety and vastness within and the isolation of Africa without fostered the evolution of a large number of different hominid groups. They all lived in diverse ecologies but they all worked on similar problems associated with applying tools in the pursuit of the human hunter-forager lifeway. The oldest human tools from Olduvai Gorge date from 2.4 million years ago. By 1.4 million, the classic pear-shaped Acheulian hand axe was in use all over sub-Saharan Africa. It stayed in use another million years among hominids before *Homo erectus* took it with them when they left Africa. This humble, efficient tool was the result of the cumulative ingenuity and trial and error of tens of thousands of generations of hominids parent to child.[1]

This collective wisdom haled from tens of thousands of localities employing myriad materials. Any apparent isolation of a particular group was only relative. Genes spread because of hybridization at the edges of groups. Hunting boy from upstream happens upon foraging girl from downstream and falls in love. This must be how far back Romeo and Juliet goes. Mating became marriage as language and speech became more precise. So ideas and techniques spread. The human hunter-forager lifeway was literally hammered out by millions of hominids over millions of years from the Cape of Good Hope to the Straits of Gibraltar, and from the Bight of Benin to the Horn of Africa, the storied edges of the great continent of Eden.

The genetics seems to support a pan-Africa Eden where the hunter-forager lifeway was slowly adapted and innovated north, south, east and west, by performance, by stolen glance, by word of mouth.

---

1 Bordes, Francoise. *The Old Stone Age*. McGraw-Hill Book Company. New York NY, 1968.

THE GRAND MIGRATION

Both Y chromosome and mitochondrial methods produce results that suggest that modern people migrated out of Africa roughly 70,000 years ago. Climatically, it was a different world back then. The Sahara was drier and bigger. The River Nile had stopped flowing. The sea levels were lower by about eighty meters. Did the earliest modern people to leave Mother Africa brave the waterless desert sands or did they jump to the Arabian Peninsula by way of the Gates of Grief where Eretria and Yemen almost touch at the end of the Red Sea? Whichever way they went, they encountered hominid forerunners who had migrated out of Africa and gotten there before them; the Neanderthals in Europe and the *Homo erectus* in Asia. Modern people interbred with them. The DNA of all humans outside of Africa have one to four percent Neanderthal inheritance. There is no trace of Neanderthal DNA among Africans. The picture is very complex and ever shifting toward greater complexity with each new discovery.

Mitochondrial DNA analysis has organized certain mutations into hierarchical groups. All humans found outside of Africa fall into the M and N clade. The Bushmen fall into the L, or ascending clade from which M and N ultimately derive, and are part of this group which is found only in Africa. It is another piece of evidence supporting their antiquity and status as the Parent People. Parent to child in the same basic region in relative isolation, the Bushmen are suggested to reach most directly back to this original modern human breeding population, as do the Pygmies of the Ituri Forest of the Congo. This is what the evidence may suggest if not prove at this point.

Paternal and Maternal Lineages

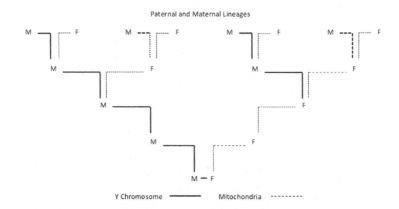

Y Chromosome ——— Mitochondria ‑‑‑‑‑‑‑‑‑

It is fascinating that, while we find the most ancient archeological evidence of modern people in Africa with Omo Man at around 190,000 years ago,[1] it is in Australia over six thousand miles away to the East across a vast ocean, that we find the next oldest, reliable traces of modern people with the discovery of Mongo Man. Though the findings are controversial, Mongo Man is dated back to at least 50,000 years.[2]

In this grand migration of modern people out of Africa, it is important to keep in mind that they were not the first humans to leave the homeland. Did those pioneering hominids who went them before speak? MRIs and latex endocranial casts of Neanderthal skulls[3] suggest that based upon the impressions made of the inside of the skull by the outside of the brain, Broca's and Wernicke's area were developed enough to make speech possible. Broca and Wernicke's areas are located for about ninety percent of humans on the left side of their brains. They mapped out areas devoted to word recognition and memory. The FOXP2 gene, the only gene to date known to be associated with language, differs in Neanderthals in only two places compared with modern people. The paleo-neurology suggests it is a good bet that the humans who left Africa so long ago, before modern humans did, were speakers to some degree.

It is interesting to speculate about the first meeting of modern humans with Neanderthals. Neanderthals had been in Europe for almost two-

1 Fleagle, J., Assefa, Z., Brown, F., Shea, J. *"Paleoanthropology of the Kibish Formation, southern Ethiopia: Introduction"*. Journal of Human Evolution, Sep 2008. 55 (3): 360–365.

2 Bowler JM, Jones R, Allen H, Thorne AG. *"Pleistocene human remains from Australia: a living site and human cremation from Lake Mungo, Western New South Wales."* World Archaeol. 2 (1), 1970. pp. 39–60.

3 Max Plank Gessellschaft. *The brains of Neanderthals and modern humans developed differently.* Nov 08, 2010. https://www.mpg.de/623578/pressRelease201011021

hundred thousand years when it took place. It is reasonable to assume that those same light conditions which would lead to lighter skin in Caucasoid people, would also have been at work upon the Neanderthals. In order to absorb vitamin D more efficiently from less intense sunlight at latitudes north of the tropic of cancer, the skin lightens. Ironically, when modern people first encountered Neanderthals a-hunting hill or dale, it is entirely possible that they were heavily pigmented and the creature that they met, fated for extinction and who was to become a caricature of the brutal cave man in the public imagination, was fair skinned.

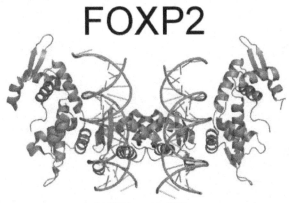

FOXP2 bound to DNA.

Assuming that they had language and speech, did Neanderthals and *Homo erectus* have myths of the hero? We cannot know. Story and myth leave scant traces upon bones and stones. None of the people survived. Their memory is but a ghostly presence in our genes. Whatever legacy of unique story that they may have bequeathed to us lies buried in the myths that have been handed down to and perpetuated by the survivors of the contact, that is, modern humans. Do these cousin hominids ultimately show up in folktale and myth as Polyphemus, Grendel and Goliath? Like fossils of memory in mineralizing words that preserve the shape as bone becomes stone. When science and poetry reach toward each other in one mind, such possibilities are, however tantalizing, not easy to understand or to prove. I call these lovely diversions hopeless Sassettis.

There is scant archeological evidence to support an overland migration from Africa through Arabia and Persia, India and Southeast Asia. The coastlines have changed dramatically as sea levels have risen and flooded probable coastal routes. Back then, Arabia was as lush as equatorial Africa. It has since dried up and hidden all evidence of modern man beneath sand and rubble. Further east in the lands of bamboo, what need to carve bone or knap stone for tools? Bamboo is a versatile, but biodegradable, material. It can serve as pole, spear head or knife depending on the need. How did early modern humans span the 100 kilometers of open ocean that lay between East Timor and Northwestern Australia. We have no archeological record of seagoing craft dated from those times. The best guess is that the original Australians made the passage by bamboo raft.[1]

In order to see how people made it from Africa to Australia, we now need to consider the Negrito people or the Coastal Clan as Dr. Wells has dubbed them. This is the group of people of the M and N clades of mitochondrial DNA who followed the coastline until they reached Australia. It might have taken only a few thousand years, a hundred generations for these coastal nomads to walk all the way Down Under from Africa.

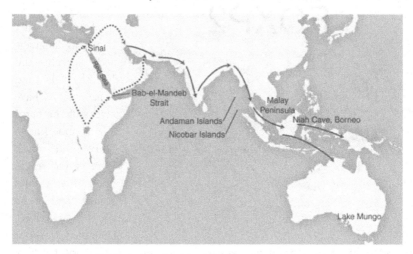

6. **The Grand Migration**

Is there any linguistic evidence for the Negrito-Coastal Clan concept? Bushmen languages have consonantal clicks. These clicks are thought to be artifacts from the hunter-forager lifeway. Clicks do not startle animals being hunted. The original group of modern people who left Africa would seem to have lost the click because there are no click languages found in any residual people along the coastal route. However, Damin,[2] a click language, was used

---

1 Heyerdahl, Thor. *Kon-Tiki: Across the Pacific by Raft,* , Chicago, Rand McNally & Company, 1950.
American Indians in the Pacific: The Theory behind the Kon-Tiki Expedition,, London, George Allen and Unwin, 1952. Also Danielsson, Bengt. *From Raft To Raft: The Account of a Fantastic Raft Voyage from Tahiti to Chile and back to Polynesia,* London, George Allen & Unwin, 1960 for how amazing bamboo rafts can sail the seas. Also https://www.wired.com/2010/01/ancient-seafarers/ Finally Capelloti, P.J. *The Theory of the Archaeological Raft: Motivation, Method and Madness in Experimental Archaeology.* EXARC, 2006. http://exarc.net/issue-2012-1/ea/theory-archaeological-raft-motivation-method-and-madness-experimental-archaeology.
2 Dixon, R. M. W. *The Languages of Australia* , 1980."Damin also has four nasalized clicks - bilabial /m!/, dental /nh!/, apico-alveolar /n!/ and apico-domal /n.!/."

by the elder initiated men of the Lardil and the Yangkaal tribes in Aboriginal Australia. Are the clicks of Damin vestigial organs of diffusion or an example of independent invention?

How long would it take branching and geographical isolation to make two languages of common origin to lose all resemblance to each other? Indo-European and Altaic language families are theorized to comprise the Nostratic macro-family. They had an ancestral homeland in south central Asia. If they shared a common ancestor, it is a long dead language spoken over fifteen thousand years ago. That was when one part of the group stretched west and became the Europeans and the other part stretched east and became the Turkmen and Mongolian tribes. The DNA split and the languages split but not along any precise lines.

Such a complete loss of apparent resemblance between sibling languages might have happened at least once, if not many times, from the time modern man dispersed from Africa. We assume that those hunter-foragers told myths of the hero and that those stories remained roughly intact through many, many turnovers in language and these survive as narrative fossils gathered by anthropologists of a folkloric bent.

The Negritos: The Link between the Bushmen, and the Aborigines

Negrito, or small black person, is a term that the Spanish colonizers of the Philippines called the short, wooly haired, dark skinned hunter-foragers that they encountered in isolated places. Negrito came to have a broader application wherever similar people were encountered in Southeast Asia. Were the Negritos isolated survivors of the grand migration of modern people out of Africa? Had they and their descendants held the territories in which they were "discovered" continuously as hunter-foragers since the Pleistocene before they were marginalized and almost totally absorbed by subsequent waves of Asian agriculturalists? Most Negrito nomadic hunter-foragers speak a language related to their majority neighbors. They have kept to their traditional lifeways in spite of yielding their original language to the newcomers. This seems to be the case of the hunter-forager Batek on the island of Palawan in the Philippines. Their language today belongs to the central Visayan family, a branch of the Austronesian language family that arrived in the Philippines with settlers from Taiwan about 5,000 years ago. Something similar happened to the Semang of Malaysia who these days also speak an Austronesian language.

Word etymology is one of the surest clues of pre-historical ties between far flung peoples. However, linguistic forms seem to have a limited durability across the millennia. The Philippine Negritos speak Austronesian languages.

The Malay Negritos speak Mon-Khmer languages of the Austroasiatic branch. The Andaman Islanders speak a language with no proven connections to any other language spoken anywhere except their small island chain. The connections between the Philippines and Malays seems sure. Connecting those two with the Andaman Islanders is tantalizing but not yet satisfactorily demonstrated. There are other hints to a common Negrito past in the mythology.

The Thunder Complex is a group of distinct and peculiar notions associated with thunder and lightning as the punishers of human breakers of taboo. For mockery of animals, thunder can announce the lightning that transforms the offender into stone. The Thunder Complex is found among the Negritos of the Philippines and the Malay Peninsula. Aspects of it are found among the Andaman Islanders.[1]

Hints of the Thunder Complex can be traced back to Africa. Many of the deities there sit in heaven and throws thunderbolts down on people when they do not live in peace to break taboo. Lightning brings sickness to them. Megan Biesele remarked that among the Bushmen, there are hundreds of "respect words" used in dangerous circumstances such as lions and rain. These "respect words" are circumlocutions similar to kennings found in Viking poetry, where the sea is referred to as the "whale road." Among the Bushmen, lions are often referred to as "moonless nights" and water as "soft throat." Game animals are never to be mocked or spoken about directly. It is believed that hunters change the weather and the lightning by the manner in which they hunt and kill their prey, even down to the words they speak and their tone of voice. Hair among the Bushmen is also associated with clouds and is used as a burnt offering to change the weather. The Semang also do this.

---

1 Blust, Robert. *Terror from the Sky: Unconventional Linguistic Clues from the Negrito Past.* Digital Commons @ Wayne State. Human Biology, Volume 85, Issue 1, Special Issue on Revisiting the "Negrito" Hypothesis, Article 18, 2013.

THE HISTORIC-GEOGRAPHICAL METHOD

A short survey of motifs suggests a folkloric continuum stretches from Africa to Australia. This continuum provides mitigating linguistic evidence in support of the Out of Africa hypothesis and the Coastal Clan hypothesis. It should come as no surprise that far-flung peoples of similar genetic and linguistic origins, living in isolation from each other until recent times, each following the same basic lifeway as their ancestors did and even allowing for differing environments, should continue to tell the same kinds of stories as variations upon a theme. The myths accompanied the genes through all their permutations. Connections, parallels and analogous structures, however transformed by time and the individuation of isolation, still exist like megaliths shrouded in creeping mists. This harkens back to a founding notion of folklore and anthropology. A notion that has lost some stature in academic circles but requires the briefest of mentions here to acknowledge our intellectual origins and our debt to the past.

Later in his career, Radcliffe-Brown lamented that as yet, the social science of anthropology had no universally accepted methodology by its practitioners.[1] He advocated studying the functionality of a cultural practice or artifact within the society it was found. Science for him was the study of relationships, not origins. This was an indirect acknowledgement of the limitations that were coming to the fore concerning the Historic-Geographic Method.

The birth of folklore as an academic study and the Historic-Geographic Method[2] began in Finland. Johan Oskar Immanuel Rancken, 1824–1895, was a

---

1 A. R. Radcliffe-Brown. On Social Structure. *Journal of the Royal Anthropological Institute of Great Britain and Ireland*, 1940. 70(1): 3.
2 Goldberg, Christine. *The Historic-Geographic Method: Past and Future. Journal of Folklore Research*. University of Indiana Press, Vol. 21, No. 1, Apr 1984. pp. 1-18.

history teacher at the Vasa Lyceum. In his youth, he had been inspired by the newly published Finnish epic poem *Kalevala* about the creation of the world and the exploits of the shamanic national hero Vainamoinen. When Rancken was twenty-four years old, he went to teach at the University of Helsinki. Politically, he was sympathetic to budding Finnish nationalism and independence from Russia, as well as the rights of the Swedish-speaking minority. The best and the worst of the uses to which folklore studies have been used politically emanated from the interests of Rancken. He believed all people have a basic right to their own culture and minority rights should be protected. Thus his interest in the minority Swedes living in his country. He also believed in nationalism and independence "when in the course of human events..." Thus his interest in Finnish freedom. Nazi Germany could be cited to illustrate the poor use to which folklore has been put by unscrupulous politicians. Then again, has there ever been a government which has not been guilty of appealing to its national heroes in pursuit of a self-serving cause?

To Rancken, history was the overarching paradigm that united all branches of human knowledge under one aegis, much as in our day, the theory of evolution unifies the sciences. To study the history and evolution of any given phenomenon is to determine its form and the time and place of origin. Rancken passed the torch to the father and son team of Julius and Kaarle Krohn. Comparing versions of the folklore and poetry that comprised the Finnish national epic *Kalevala*, they saw comparison as a means to trace sources back to their origins. Kaarle published *Die folkloristische Arbeitsmethode*[1] in 1926. His aim was to produce a genetic analysis of folkloric topics in order to find their origins and trace their distributions. His goal was to determine the Ur-form, or basic pattern. He defined which parts and which levels that comparison should be conducted. It was practical and realistic. "The purpose of this analytic procedure...is the determination of the Ur-form of any characteristic theme under study as well as the original combination and arrangement of these traits in order to determine the basic form as the pattern form in various areas; from the relationship of the basic form and the pattern form, the routes of diffusion and the development of the tradition in question can be discovered."[2] Krohn confined himself to Asian and European folklore. In other words, he consulted only literary sources for his tales.

Walter Anderson, a German folklorist, published *Handwortenbuch des deutschen Märchen* in 1934. He delineated twenty-one strictly limited

1 Krohn, Julius. Folklore Methodology: Formulated by Julius Krohn and Expanded by Nordic Researchers. Welsch, Roger L., translator, University of Texas Press, Austin, TX, 1981.
2 Wolf-Knuts, Ulrika. *On the history of comparison in folklore studies.* Thick Corpus, Kalevala Institute.
University of Turku, Finland, Folklore Fellows' Summer School, 1999.

phases according to which a folktale should be studied. There were three unconditional principals. All variants of a tale, both printed and oral must be considered. Traits must be compared in an empirical method devoid of pre-conception or whim. Time and place for each tale must be scrupulously recorded. The main line of comparison is geographical for each episode, motif and trait. The aim of all folkloric studies is the writing of a monograph that attempts to determine the original form, the common archetype from which all variants derive, the time and place of origin, including all local redactions and routes of distribution. It is a practical, understandable methodology that dove-tails with common sense. Everything has a history and an evolutionary development. But lacking evidence, it becomes impossible to achieve. It is the ultimate fallibility of the inductive method of which the Scottish philosopher David Hume was so skeptical. Ideally, gathering all available data and allowing the data itself to demonstrate the patterns is the proper way to proceed. The problem with this is that there are always gaps in the record. This is probably what Radcliffe-Brown was alluding to when he lamented the lack of methodology in fieldwork and theory and concerned himself only with how a trait was structured and how it functioned in society.

Indo-European scholars of the 19th and early 20th century bent their efforts toward distilling a primordial culture from which Western languages, patterns of thinking and storytelling were assumed to have developed. Assumptions must be based upon facts, not whims. Andrew Lang declared, "Comparison is the way of doing folklore research." He was interested in "survivals." These were "...ideas which are in our time but not of our time." He criticized many scholars for what he dubbed an "addiction to primordialism."[1]He was himself criticized for making comparisons based upon superficial similarities much as Erich von Daanken is criticized in our day for claims beyond substantiation.[2]

For instance, comparing the carving of the reclining figure of Pacal in Palenque to an ancient astronaut based merely upon similar seating postures.[3] Pacal, an ancient Maya king, appeared in a posture carved upon his sepulcher that was superficially reminiscent of an astronaut strapped into a nose cone. But when we try to interpret Pacal's posture in relation to

---

1 Ibid.
2 Sagan, Carl. Foreword to Story, Ronald, *The Space-gods revealed. A close look at the theories of Erich von Däniken* (2 ed.), Barnes & Noble, 1980. pp. xii-xiii. "That writing as careless as von Däniken's, whose principal thesis is that our ancestors were dummies, should be so popular is a sober commentary on the credulousness and despair of our times. I also hope for the continuing popularity of books like *Chariots of the Gods?* in high school and college logic courses, as object lessons in sloppy thinking. I know of no recent books so riddled with logical and factual errors as the works of von Däniken."
3 Von Daankan, Erich. *Chariots of the Gods.* Berkley Books. 1999. Also "*The Case of the Ancient Astronauts.*" Horizon. 3 August 1978. BBC.

the band of writing along the edge of the stone slab and with the background tree under which he appears to be seated, it is likely that he was not an ancient astronaut but that he was looking up at the sky on the day that he died. At sunset of that day in August of 683 A.D., Venus was up in the western sky and Scorpius rose to the south at the base of the Milky Way arching almost directly overhead to the north.[1] This is the location where the ecliptic crosses the Milky Way. Perhaps Pacal's sepulchral slab represents the king looking up at the Maya Cross. The actual alignment of this ancient king's body was on a north–south line. His knees are drawn up to a 90 degree position reminiscent of the fetal position. In ancient Egypt in the Valley of Kings, the night sky was painted on the ceiling above the sarcophagus of Ramses VI. The Milky Way was mythologized as the goddess Nut giving birth to Ra, the sun.[2]

Did the ancient Maya astronomers understand the mechanism of the Pole Star-Mintaka hinge upon which the sky spun overhead? Both von Daanken's theory and my own are probably impossible to substantiate given our present state of knowledge. At least the latter theory makes a stab at contextualizing the phenomenon within its cultural setting before making more universal statements and comparing it cross-culturally to a completely unverifiable situation based upon whim and self-interest.

The main hope when comparing artifacts[3], customs or myths is that the "superficial" similarity is put in its proper cultural context and function so as to enrich, extend and strengthen the perceived linkages. This must be done if there is any hope to demonstrate common origins between phenomena compared in a meaningful, significant, truly cross-cultural way.

1 This was determined by consulting several astronomy applications which allow a view of the night sky and the configuration of the heavens at precise distant dates in the past. These applications are accurate down to hour and second of the selected date.
2 Wells, Ronald A. *Astronomy in Egypt*: Astronomy before the telescope, Christopher Walker, editor, British Museum Press, London, 1996. pp. 29-35. See also Plate II.
3 Milbrath, Susan. *Star Gods of the Maya: Astronomy in Art, Folklore and Calendars*. University of Texas Press. Austin TX 78713-7819. For the graphic above: Pacal is Plate 10. Hieroglyphs of Venus on p. 187.

Venus

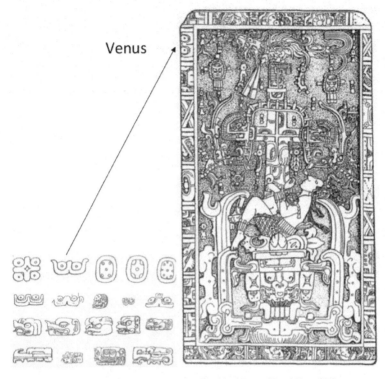

Mayan Hieroglyphs of Venus   Sepulchral Cover of Pacal, King of Palenque

Ancient Astronaut or Ancient Stargazer?

SNAKES AND SWALLOWING

Let us examine two traits that show up in myths from Africa to Australia and some places in between. There is a similarity of motif and function. The purpose is to establish a folkloric continuum in support of the apparent flow of human genes. Ultimately, we will compare myths of the hero, but first let us examine swallowing, throwing and running in the mythology of the Bushmen, the Andaman Islanders, the Semang and the Australian aborigines as auxiliary evidence. First snakes and swallowing.

Snakes, among other mythological functions, are commonly held to be guardian spirits of water holes, springs, billabongs and honey. This concept is understated in a myth collected by Sigrid Schmidt from the Damara in Namibia. A group of children come upon a snake in a waterhole and kill it because as the tale reveals, a snake must be killed. However, the father was furious with his children when he learns of their blunder. His worry is justified. The waterhole dries up and does not flow again until the great rains come.[1] In the Andaman Islands, if someone sees a dark cloud approach and rain is not wanted, the natives threaten Puluga, the storm bringer, by threatening to call up a wara-jobo, a snake that only appears in hot weather during honey season. It is from this snake that the pattern for painting their bodies is taken.[2] Among the Batek Negritos of the Malay peninsula, the naga or giant snake lives in the earth and guards the rivers, which rise and fall at his whim. The snake is the reflection on earth of the celestial rainbow and is a guardian of springs and headwaters. It is certain that

---

1 Schmidt, Sigrid. *Tricksters, Monsters and Clever Girls*. Rüdiger, Köppe, Verlag, Köln, 2001. 58. The Water Snake. pp. 123-124.
2 Radcliffe-Brown, A.R. *The Andaman Islanders*. First Free Press, New York NY, (1922) 1964. p.162. Also, Plates XI, X.

the concept of the naga has been influenced by Hindu beliefs.[1] The concept of a snake guarding a waterhole is ubiquitous in Aboriginal myth. For instance, Wadi-Waral, Rain-falling-down, traveled to Bararibaru soak where Guleyi or Rainbow Snake lived.[2] Further examples from Australia could fill a good sized volume. It is clear that the concept of the guardian snake is very ancient in the storytelling of people.

Being swallowed by a serpent is a primal fear. As such, this notion appears in myths from Africa to Australia. Sigrid Schmidt records a tale that reads like a true-life tragedy. A man orders his reluctant wife to gather a certain berry out in a certain place. At the assigned location, the woman puts her baby down and starts to pick. A python comes and swallows the baby while she is working. When the young mother returns, all that remains is a fat python lying in the sun. She runs for her husband who kills the snake, but he is too late to save the baby's life. Is this the story of an overbearing husband or of a neglectful wife?[3] On North Andaman Island among the Aka-Jeru, there is reputed to be a giant snake out in the depths of the forest called or-ĉubi who killed and swallowed people while they were out gathering honey.[4] The Negritos of the Cheka River on the Malay Peninsula call a lunar eclipse "snake swallow."[5] Tak Chemempes, a shape shifter in the beliefs of Kintak Bong Negritos, once made himself into a crocodile who swallowed the sleeping people who ate the eggs she had laid by the river.[6] However, it is in Australia that the swallowing serpent comes to full fruition as a mythological motif. Strehlow, Spencer and Gillan, Robinson, the Brendts and Geza Roheim all record numerous stories of snakes swallowing people and regurgitating them. The Murngin triangular dance ground for the boy's initiation ceremony is patterned like a giant snake. Boys enter the mouth of the snake, are transformed into adults in the body and exit the anus as initiated men.[7] Swallowing by a snake and regurgitation is symbolic of a transformation, a metamorphosis. It is the central metaphor of initiation into adulthood. There are literally dozens and dozens of examples in Aborigine myth. A single example can suffice to give a general overview. In the Leagulamulmirree tribe, they sing of Wittee, the snake man. He got

1 Endicott, Kirk. *Batek Negrito Religion.* Clarendon Press, Oxford, 1979. p.185-189.

2 Berndt, Ronald M. and Catherine H. *The Speaking Land.* Inner Traditions International, Rochester, Vermont, 1994. p. 113.

3 Schmidt, Sigrid. *Tricksters, Monsters and Clever Girls.* 57. A Python Swallowed A Child. Rüdiger, Köppe, Verlag, Köln 2001. p.122-123.

4 Radcliffe-Brown, A.R. *The Andaman Islanders.* First Free Press, New York NY, (1922) 1964. p. 227.

5 Evans, Ivor H.N. *Studies in Religion, Folk-lore and Custom in British Borneo and the Malay Peninsula.* Cambridge University Press, United Kingdom, 1923. p. 155

6 Ibid. p. 188.

7 Roheim, Geza. *The Eternal Ones of the Dream.* International Universities Press, New York, 1945. p. 179.

a hankering for the two Waugeluk Sisters and followed them down the Roper River to the sea. While the rain poured down, Wittee changed into a giant snake, coiled around the camp of sleeping women and children and swallowed them. Shortly thereafter, Wittee began to worry that he might have swallowed his own sisters or daughters and he belched them out. Later, he swallowed them again and they became his Marraian, his sacred knowledge, and their spirits spoke to the people through Wittee.[1]

That we readily and regularly encounter snakes and swallowing of entire human beings among these widespread hunter-forager cultures suggests that these motifs are quite ancient, if not primordial among modern people. The most economical hypothesis would be that the motif accompanied the migration of the original population of modern people out of Africa[2] and experienced the individuation of localization in the Andaman Islands, the Malay Peninsula and Australia. Through language change, new generations of storytellers, changing environments and vast amounts of time, the motifs retained their basic shapes. This should not be surprising if we allow that the stories, in the fragmentary form of motifs, flowed along with the genes.

Throwing and Running

In *Guns, Germs and Steel*,[3] Jared Diamond imposes a grand and unavoidable perspective upon human history. His work came in response to a New Guinea highlander's simple question. Why was his village incapable of building things like airplanes? Many traditional historians dislike biological approaches to their specialty because it dwarfs human personality as a force in human events. Story gets lost in the sweep. Hitler purposefully killed six million Jews in twelve years. The Spanish Conquistadores inadvertently killed three million native Americans with smallpox, syphilis and flu in the first few years of the colonization of Hispañola and Cuba. The latter sobering facts come from Bartholomé de las Casas, who quoted church tallies of death lists maintained by each diocese. It would appear that the greatest danger that a European or black African slave posed to a Mesoamerican was not his bullet or his sword stroke but his handshake or his kiss. However, comparing the numbers of victims of various Eurasian genocides to that of the Mesoamerican one requires us to give full weight to biological perspectives.

1 Robinson, Roland. *Aboriginal Myths and Legends*. Sun Books, Sydney, Australia, 1966. p. 41.
2 Theodor Benfey was a German philologist who published the Panchtantra in 1859. It is a collection of Sanskrit animal fables. Benfey maintained that the stories found in the Panchtantra emanated from an original community of storytellers and represented the oldest stories known to literature. The Orion Complex is an original community theory concerning the myth of the hero pattern of Leavetaking-Adventure-Homecoming.
3 Diamond, Jared. *Guns, Germs and Steel*. W. W. Norton & Company; 1999.

Human culture, for all its grandeur and folly, operates as a relatively small part of life taken as a whole on planet Earth. Human culture needs the Earth. The Earth does not need human culture. It would recover its garden-like quality very quickly upon any hasty, self-induced, accidental disappearance on the part of people. The proper study of mankind continues to be man, but man as he fits into nature's guiding law.

Dr. Diamond's basic thesis rests upon a few simple facts. The widest stretch of land running east to west following the daily course of the sun is in the northern hemisphere extending from China to Europe. A huge population of people lived within this six-thousand-mile-wide band in many different environments. Plants can move east–west along a band of latitude much easier than north–south because the photo-period, or length of daylight, is the same east–west. This photo-period changes drastically the further north or south a traveler gets from the equator. It affects the success rates of seed germination and is why European wheat fares poorly in tropical regions. This wide landmass meant more people worked on the same problems going east to west than those going north to south. They shared and accumulated innovations on local variations of the same crops and barnyard animals on a landmass that stretched from the Pacific to the Atlantic. Simply stated, what made the Europeans able to colonize the world? They weaponized Chinese gunpowder which followed the course of the sun from Asia to Europe. Perfecting the gun was a six-thousand-miles-wide idea with sophisticated cultures on either extreme contributing and exchanging innovations over the course of centuries. However, germs always seem to kill more people than guns do.

Taking a page from *Guns, Germs and Steel*, we can modify Dr. Diamond's central question and ask, what was it that allowed hominids to become the dominant species in nature? Upright bipedalism which freed the hands to make tools? Fire use? Language? In mythology, man is often reckoned to be the weakest creature in nature. Man has not the claw of the lion, nor the speed of a horse. He has not the eye of the eagle nor the fang of a wolf. In what behavior do humans excel all other creatures? Is there any area of physical endeavor in which people are the superior athletes compared to animals? [1]In every regard, the least accomplished human throws with greater force and accuracy than the greatest chimpanzee hurler, our closest cross-species competitor. The best that the chimp can manage is an underhand sling. A chimp toss can be startling but not deadly.

---

1 In Chumash myth Coyote deals out traits to animals at creation. Size to bear, wings to hawk, etc. Man is last and there is nothing left to give. See Thomas Blackburn *December's Children*.

Throwing[1] imparts energy to a thrown object. It extends the kill zone and makes hunting safer. The simplest object thrown with speed and accuracy can do great damage. Israeli forces have had their share of casualties from rock throwing Palestinians. In the early 1990s, a Boy Scout troop killed a bear in Yosemite by stoning it after it wandered into their camp.[2] The U.S. Border Patrol regularly fire on people trying to cross the border illegally who have thrown rocks at agents. A thrown rock is considered to be a deadly weapon and a thrower can be charged with felony assault.[3] The baseball player Roy Chapman died when he ducked into a fast ball that struck his temple.[4]

The ability to throw with speed and accuracy provided a selective advantage for early hominids. Throwing is an activity that takes up a great deal of playtime among youths of all cultures. Throwing is a practiced art. Radcliffe-Brown mentioned how Andaman hunters will walk along a beach, aim at something up ahead and shoot an arrow or throw a spear at it. They go target to target as they walk along. Aborigine myth has hunters trailing boomerang tosses. Instinctively, ancient hunter-foragers knew that throwing made them the best hunters on the savannah. Throwing reveals a very high level of cognition. It requires a superior memory to be able to anticipate an animal's movements in response to being chased and attacked. A sense of the future is also required to store up experience. These traits are also revealed in tool making.

Another human physiological characteristic that led to early hominid top predator status was the ability to run long distances. There is no creature, however fast they can sprint short distances like the cheetah, that human hunters cannot chase down if they can get them up and running, track them and keep them running. Persistence hunting, or running game to exhaustion, was a highly efficient technique among the Bushmen.[5] ||kábbo, or Dream, the Bushman of whom the Bleeks recorded many tales, told of running a springbok down. "I chase it in the sun, that the sun, burning, may kill it for me, that I may eat it, dead from the sun. I was the one who chased it..."[6] The

1 Maki, Julia Marie. *The Biomechanics of Spear Throwing: An Analysis of the Effects of Anatomical Variation on Throwing Performance, with Implications for the Fossil Record.* Washington University in St. Louis. Thesis, 2103.
2 Filkins, Sexter. *"O.C. Boy Scouts Investigated in Bear's Killing."* Los Angeles Times, August 17, 1996.
3 Miller, Emily Russo. *"Suspected rock-throwers charged with felony assault."*. Juneau Empire, 9 November 2012.
4 Propert, Phyllis. *Carl Mays: My Pitch That Killed Chapman Was A Strike!* Baseball Digest, Vol. 16, No. 6, July 1957.
5 Liebenberg, Louis. *"Persistence Hunting by Modern Hunter-Gatherers,"* Current Anthropology 47, no. 6, Dec 2006. pp. 1017-1026. Also Attenborough, David. *The Life of Mammals* (program 10, "Food For Thought") BBC documentary, 2002. A bushman chased a kudu antelope to its exhaustion.
6 Scheub, Harold. *Story.* The University of Wisconsin Press, Madison WI 53718. p. 190.

Tarahumara of Mexico are famous for their ability to run one hundred miles at a stretch. Their manhood initiation rituals include running down a deer and strangling it once it has fallen in exhaustion and can go no further. Lumholtz, the famous Swiss explorer of the late 19th century, mentions an old Pagago hunter of the northern Sonoran desert who was famous for running down deer over a twenty-four hour period and shooting the exhausted beast with an arrow at the end of the chase.[1]

Persistence hunting would be impossible without the ability to follow footprints. People had millions of years of experience examining shapes and the conditions of those shapes before pictures were drawn on cave walls or letters written on paper. Cognitively speaking, the footprint led to the line drawing and the alphabet.

Hominids were hunter-foragers long before they evolved into modern people. The reason that humans became the top predator of the savannah was that they were the best throwers and the most enduring runners. But the ancestors of modern people were hunter-foragers long before they became throwers and runners. They brought hunting and foraging with them as they evolved out of animality. By this token, most primates could be considered hunter-foragers at one level or another. Chimps hunt colobus monkeys in packs.[2] Only man is the runner-thrower.

Running, as a motif, is ubiquitous in all mythologies. Monsters chase, heroes run away until it comes time to turn and make a stand. Heroes chase in order to exact retribution. Running is so apparent in myth that it is almost invisible. Twenty-six mile marathons are common all over the world in honor of Phidipides's run to warn the Athenians of the Persian army's advance. More noteworthy as a mythological motif is the ability to throw. Wilhelm Bleek noted that the origin of celestial bodies from Africa to Australia have humans throwing objects into the sky that become the sun, the moon and the stars.[3] In Bushmen folklore, baboons steal the son of Mantis's eye and play catch with it. Eventually it is thrown up into the sky where it becomes the moon. An angry young girl throws ash from the fire into the air and it becomes the Milky Way. Children steal a burning stone from the armpit of Old Man and when they throw it up into the sky, it becomes the sun. Among the Booroung of Southwest Australia, the Milky Way was created when wood-ashes were thrown into air by a girl of the ancient race. An *Aka-*

---

1 Lumholtz, Carl. *New Trails in Mexico*. University of Arizona Press, Tucson. (1912) 1999. p. 34.
2 Boesch, Christopher. *Hunting Strategies for Gombe and Taï Chimpanzees*. Chimpanzee Cultures, Harvard University Press, 1996. pp. 77-91. Also (Gilby)pp. 220-232.
3 Bleek, W.H.J. 'On resemblances in Bushmen and Australian Mythology', *Cape Monthly Magazine*, Cape Town, 1874, 8, pp.98-102.

Kede legend from the Andaman Islands claims that Bilika, the deity of the monsoon, made the sun by throwing a flaming brand into the sky.[1]

People threw spears long before they fired arrows. The Aborigines got to Australia before the invention of the bow. It was unknown to the entire continent at the time of contact. Throwing celestial objects into the sky is a very common motif in world mythology. On the coast of California, the hero twins of *Kumyaay* myth threw the moon up into the sky until it finally stayed up in the right place.[2] The motif of throwing objects up into the sky appears childlike to modern sensibilities. But like many aspects of mythology, what seems at first glance to be a childish trifle turns out to be of profound significance when placed within its cultural context. A good throw meant life or death for a hunter's family. It was the hunter's most crucial skill. Good throws brought honor and feasting. Bad throws brought hunger and shame. Ancient hunter-foragers knew that it was their mighty throwing arms that made them top predators. For them it was a creative act. Throwing created the uniquely human lifeway. It is a motif that shows up from Africa to Australia. The arc of a thrown spear or fired arrow mirrors the arc of the path that the sun follows east to west every day.

A further piece of evidence that confirms that the story telling technique traveled along with the flow of genes from Africa to Australia is how both Bushmen and Aborigine myths of the hero make similar use of images, patterns and parallels to propel a story linearly along to its conclusion. For Harold Scheub, the noted folklorist of African myth, image is the fundamental building block of storytelling. Image and motif are often used synonymously. They can be formed from fantasy or taken directly from reality and blended together. These images, coming one after another, create a line or a path to a conclusion. The images are patterned, not merely repeating the previous one. Each image, though similar to the one which preceded it, is slightly different, and with this difference, pushes the tale along.[3]

Here is an example of image patterning from !Han‡kasso, a Bushman prisoner who was under guardianship of the Bleeks in Cape Town.

!gaunnu-tsaxau went to get sticks for his father Mantis. These sticks were to be thrown at baboons. The boy wandered over to where a baboon troop was feeding. When questioned by an older baboon about his purpose, the boy innocently reveals his mission, to gather sticks that would be thrown at baboons. Outraged, the old baboon calls another one over to hear the child's admission. This old baboon comes over singing a song about "listening to

1 Radcliffe-Brown, A.R. The Andaman Islanders. p. 203.
2 DuBois, Constance Goddard. *The Story of the Chaup: A Myth of the Diegueños.* The Journal of American Folklore. Vol. XVII. October-December, 1904, No. LXVVII.
3 Scheub, Harold. Story. The University of Wisconsin Press, Madison WI 53718, 1998. p. 14-15.

the child yonder." He wants to know, "what does this child say?" The son of Mantis innocently repeats his admission, which in turn triggers a repetition of this scene, this image, five times in all. With each repetition, the knowledge grows among the baboons that the boy's efforts are directed against them. The last baboon to be called over is the eldest baboon. He confirms the boy is up to no good and exhorts his folk, "Ye shall strike the child with your fists." The poor boy is killed. His eye is knocked out of his head. It becomes a ball that the baboons all play with. Mantis comes looking for his child and finds the baboons playing his eye. He steals it back and hides it first in his quiver and then in water. The eye simultaneously rejuvenates the son of Mantis and becomes the sun when thrown into the sky.[1]

The next story with a pattern of images comes from Australia. It is a classic myth of the hero of ancestral beings told by Tonanga of the Aranda tribe, collected by Roland Robinson in 1954 on a myth-gathering expedition of Central Australian and Northern Territory tribes. It is called The Old Man.[2]

An old man came out of a cave. He had a tjurunga, a sacred inscribed stone, a spear, a womerah or spear thrower and a dilly bag which he carried around his neck. In this dilly bag, he kept six stones or namatoona. When he took them out and rubbed goanna fat on them, these namatoona grew into his sons. These boys the old man sent out hunting for him.

Once the old man came to a camp and made a big smoke. He took his sons out of the dilly bag and sent them off to hunt. When they returned laden with meat, the old man gave each of his sons to a woman in marriage. While the couples slept, the old man snuck up on them and pulled the namatoona out of his sons' hair and put them back into the dilly bag and fled in the night. When the women awoke, they found the old man and their husbands missing.

The old man goes to another camp. The image is repeated. Only this time, after he puts his sons back into his dilly bag, he does not flee, but hangs it up in a tree. When the women wake up and demand to know where his sons are, the old man open faced lies to them. The women wander the bush but come back home empty-handed and bewildered.

The old man moves on. He finds that a Mamu or devil dog is following him. Might be this is the evil spirit of a vengeful, abandoned woman left behind. The Old Man makes camp. As the Mamu sneaks up toward the fire light, one of the old man's sons spears it dead.

1 Bleek, W.H.I. and L.C. Lloyd. Specimens of Bushman Folklore. BiblioBazaar, London, (1911) 2007. pp. 43-52.
2 Robinson, Roland. Aboriginal Myths and Legends. Sun Books Pty Ltd. Melbourne, Victoria, Australia, 1966. pp. 5-8.

At the next camp, the image is repeated. The old man sends his sons out hunting and gives them in marriage to six women. But this time, as he was sneaking up and stealing the namatoona from his sleeping sons and returning them to his dilly bag, one of the women wakes up and sees what the old man is about. The old man immediately spears her dead.

The old man goes on and on like this until he dies and melts back into the earth. His six sons, trapped in the dilly bag roll around and around but cannot escape and become a big black stone. The old man is a classic ancestral being populating the Earth with people.

The pattern of images allows for an interesting analogy by comparing their differences. The wild Mamu is speared by one of the old man's sons. The woman who awoke at the wrong time and saw what she was not supposed to see was speared by the old man. Initiated men control life and death for both wild beasts and women, and this is emblemized in their spearing.

Both the Bushmen and Aborigine tales make use of repeated images, varied slightly with each retelling, to push the plot along linearly to the dénouement. There are two conclusions. Patterning images is a story telling technique as old in human myth as modern people's departure from Africa. It is a far flung technique that can be found in tales all over the world, for instance, in the Norwegian folk tale of the Pancake. [1]

There is a mythological continuum that originated in Africa and moved along the coast until people reached Australia. It is in these cultures that we will find the most ancient mythology that we can access and that it is a rich field to apply Lord Raglan's hero pattern in order to test its universality.

This next leg of our journey returns us to Africa and the Bushmen.

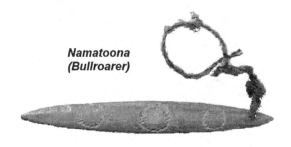

**Namatoona
(Bullroarer)**

1 Thompson, Stith. *One Hundred Favorite Folktales*. Indiana University Press, Bloomington IN, 1968. pp.430-433.

Hunter-Forager Myths of the Hero

It is assumed that the hunter-forager ancestors of modern people told myths of the hero. Therefore, in broadest outlines, the following catalogue of stories can be seen as variations on a theme originating from a location in Africa and of an antiquity of at least seventy thousand years and perhaps much, much older. The myth of the hero is recognizable in the myths and folktales of modern day hunter-foragers. Hundreds of examples could be assembled. However, for the purposes of brevity, only examples from certain hunting-foraging cultures will be selected.

Some hunter-foragers are refugees. The Mikea of Madagascar were farmers who fled war in the nineteenth century and sought refuge in the forest. Their agricultural past is still evident in their mythology. They have been dubbed re-specialized foragers in the technical literature.[1] The Pygmies were the original dwellers of the forests of central Africa. However, they all now speak languages related to their Bantu neighbors who have overwhelmed them. At the language level, their folklore is at one more remove from this hypothetical, original mythmaking population. The same can be said of the Negrito hunter-foragers of the Philippines. It is hard to cull their folklore from their Tagalog or Visayan neighbors. A recently published, weighty volume of Philippine folklore by one of the most widely respected scholars in the field contained only one myth that was directly attributable to a Negrito culture. And it is about the creation of the world thanks to the rage of Captan, a theme common also to non-negrito neighbors.[2]

1 Kelly, Robert L., Jean-Francois Rabemity and Lin Poyer. *Mikea.* I.IV.8. The Cambridge Encyclopedia of Hunters and Gatherers, ed. Lee, Richard B. and Richard Daly. Cambridge University Press, 1999. pp. 215-219.
2 Eugenio, Damiana L. ed. Philippine Folk Literature: An Anthology. The University of Philippines Press, 2007. *Legend about the Creation of the World as Told by the Mangians and the Negritos.* pp. 8-9.

Our filter will select only myths of the hero from those hunter-foraging cultures who live in territories demonstrated by archeology to have been continuously occupied by hunter-foragers from the Pleistocene period seventy thousand years ago up until recent times. These hunter-foragers exist as linguistic isolates from their neighbors. They are the clearest, most direct descendants of the hunter-foragers who left Africa. They are the direct inheritors of the hunter-forager lifeway and ethos if any can be said to survive. With an artifact as ephemeral as the myth of the hero, peering into their stories is as far back as we can reasonably expect to look in order to shape some idea what the original myth of the hero might have been like. We will start in Africa with the Bushmen and the Pygmies. The next stop will be the Semang of Malaysia, though they too have been linguistically overshadowed by newcomers like the negritos of the Philippines. Then the Andaman Islanders. Finally, the Aborigines of Australia. We will follow the coast Out of Africa across South Asia like the ancestors of modern people did, going myth to myth all the way to Australia. The superscripted numerals in brackets [1,2,3...] scattered throughout the text that follows correspond to those found in Raglan's hero pattern.[1]

The Bushmen

The Bushmen
of Southwest
Africa

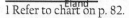
Eland

1 Refer to chart on p. 82.

Megan Biesele presents "oral forms from an evolutionary perspective"[1] in *Men and Women.* This champion myth of the hero is a captured live performance from the Bushmen. The audience is everyone within earshot around the campfire. The adults laugh. The children are open mouthed in shock at times.

It was told by *!Unn/obe N!a'an* in the village of Kauri Botswana in 1972. The storyteller was part of a population of Bushmen who were half-in and half-out of the traditional hunter-forager lifeway. The story was translated by an anthropologist who goes back to Africa almost every summer to visit and learn more from her friends. The hero of the myth is a desperate trickster. His lust has led him into a situation of having to bring home meat for not just one but for two wives and their children. There is a visceral realization of the radical oneness of the world in this farcical but deadly war between the sexes. It is a two-headed beast of burlesque and oedipal tragedy.

Any and all reference to circumstances of birth or parentage is omitted. The hero is the Creator, *Koaxa.* [1-8] There is an extended series of departures and returns over the course of a week. It is a downward spiral. The hero leaves camp to hunt. [9] He sees no animal and goes back to his wives empty-handed. He goes out the next day, but again sees no animal. He worries about what he can take back home to his wives. Remember how the Bushmen work Orion's and Leo's stars into a story about an unlucky hunter who shoots his last arrow at three zebras and is too afraid to go retrieve it because there is a lion waiting on the other side. So he sleeps outside the camp that night while his wives ridicule him in front of men dancing around the campfire.

Koaxa has a solution to his family's hunger. He climbs to the top of a tree and leaps out and when he hits the ground, his guts spill out of his anus. He butchers this meat, stuffs grass in his wounded rear end, and carries everything back to camp. As he enters, the little kids insult the meat and pester him about the grass sticking out of his backside. The women roast the meat and when the younger wife begins to pound a strip to tenderize it, it leaps out of her hand and bounces into *Koaxa's* lap. The flesh magically reincorporates itself back into the hero's body. The wives are astounded and determined to discover just what is going on. The episode repeats itself and this time the wives give up, hang the rest of the meat up in a tree and go to sleep. During the night, the rest of the meat reincorporates itself back into *Koaxa.* The wives wake the next day to the meat gone missing and know that they have been tricked. They want revenge. They gather melon seeds, cut strips off of their own vaginal labia, pound it all to paste and feed it to their husband. *Koaxa* wants to know where his wives came up with the strange meat. They lie and claim it is only rolled up rotten baby giraffe skin that

1 Biesele, Megan. *Women Like Meat. The folklore and foraging ideology of the Kalahari Ju/'hoan.* Indiana University Press, 1993. pp. 171-179.

they had just happened upon while they were out foraging. *Koaxa* thinks that it is good and falls asleep but has nightmares and wakes up with bad breath. He is angry and knows that he has been tricked. He sends his wives out to forage one way while he goes hunting another. He finds a gumball tree and hangs his testicles up on a branch and goes back and tells his wives that he has found good fruit. Incidentally, this is why gumballs are red. The next day the hero and his two wives go to the tree. The wives climb up and eat the dangling fruit. They are disgusted upon learning the truth and plot vengeance. They fashion a figure out of feces and tell *Koaxa* they have seen a baby giraffe. They advise him to tackle the beast rather than spear it because a man should be able to throttle such a small creature and then they will not lose the blood. *Koaxa* follows his wives' advice and comes up mired in filth. His anger is escalating. He ambushes his wives and beats them severely, thereby reestablishing the marriage bonds in a perverted way. [12-13] They all return home dejected. [10] Soon after, the youngest wife wants to visit her family but *Koaxa* refuses to allow her. [14-15] She runs off and a time of hunger follows with *Koaxa* rarely at home and the remaining wife wasting away. [16] The hero berates her over her fallen looks, takes his son and abandons her. [17] The son sneaks back and tells his mother to follow. They go to where *Koaxa* has killed an eland, and they butcher it and eat it. [11] The son sneaks meat to his mother who is revivified. There is a glimmer of a change of roles here. The mother reenters camp. *Koaxa* sees that her beauty has returned and begins to copulate with her right in front of his son. The boy kills his father with an ax [18] on flat ground [19] and claims the mother for his own wife. He allows insects to bite his penis which is supposed to make it grow large but the effect is overdone and the boy becomes too big for intercourse. In this respect, he does not quite succeed his father. [20] No burial, nor sepulcher. [21-22] Strictly speaking, *Men and Women* scores 10/22 but the myth of the hero pattern is deep in this story, even though Raglan's scheme might not be the best structural device by which to analyze it in order to reveal its unique details.[1]

The African Pygmies

The Birth of Bes was collected by Father Schebesta from the Pygmies of the Ituri Forest in northeastern Republic of Congo at the feet of perennially snowcapped Mount Ruwenzori. Wherever he did fieldwork, Father Schebesta sought out examples of monotheism. In Pygmy mythology, he

---

1 Scheub, Harold. *African Images. Patterns in Literary Art*. McGraw-Hill, 1972. Parallel image sets describe the sequence of episodes better here than Raglan's pattern does. Nevertheless, Leavetaking-Adventure-Homecoming is clear in the background.

certainly encountered the earliest known form of the widespread Garden of Eden motif. *The Birth of Bes* is a good fit in Raglan's myth of the hero pattern. There are extraordinary birth circumstances. The adventure ends with a twist and reveals yet another example of the swallowing motif. The hero marries and takes up the throne. Does *The Birth of Bes* reveal Bantu, even European, influences? This is well to keep in mind, especially since the Pygmies now speak the languages of their Bantu neighbors and serve them as hired hands for livestock and agriculture, and have done so for centuries. Pygmy culture might be more hybridized than Bushmen culture due to thousands of years of contact with outsiders. Pygmies were portrayed by the ancient Egyptians on the Metternich Stele dated at around 375 B.C., as the Dancers of God. Father Schebesta did not reveal by name the storyteller who told him *The Birth of Bes*.[1]

The Pygmies of the Ituri Forest

The *lulu* monster devoured all the people. [6] Only a pregnant woman escaped. [7] Her unborn child spoke to her from the womb. He announced that he would be born from a hole under the toe of her right foot. Upon birth, he suddenly grew up tall and war-like. [4] He wanted to know where everybody was. His mother informed him about the *lulu* monster and he sets out in search of vengeance. [9,10] He is led through the forest by his reluctant mother who believes he will be killed. With his father's spear, he kills the

1 Schebesta, Paul. *Les Pygmées du Congo Belge.* pp. 322-333. In Pygmy Kitabu. Jean-Pierre Hallet, Random House, New York NY, 1973. pp. 164-165.

lulu and frees all the people trapped inside. [11] The first one out was the hero's own father. [2] The freed victims are so grateful that they give Bes a beautiful young girl [12] for a wife and make him chief of the land. [13] Bes rates nine out of twenty-two in Lord Raglan's scheme of heroic attributes.

The hero is born in exile but is not exposed at birth. He is reared by his biological mother. The father is absent and only comes into the story at the end as the object of his son's heroic victory over the *lulu* monster. The son becomes a chief but was his father? Hunter-foragers living in small fission-fusion groups, have shamans and family heads, not hereditary chiefs. This detail smacks of Bantu influence, as they are agricultural, tribal and align themselves politically into chieftainships. The exact details of the conception are omitted but the birth itself is noteworthy. The hero comes out of his mother's right, big toe. This is bizarre to modern taste in fiction. As bizarre as the Bushmen Creator figure who had an eye on the bottom of his foot. But to hunter-foragers who had to be expert trackers, and readers of spoor, such imagination would perhaps seem less far-fetched. It might seem utterly practical. It gives new insight into the old notion of keeping a close eye on the ground.

The hero is born fully physically and cognitively mature. He has no childhood whatsoever. His departure upon his heroic quest begins with his first breath and is presented as a direct extension of his birth. He is literally born to adventure. He is devoted to a single purpose: vengeance. His own miracle-shocked mother is his helper and guide though she doubts his abilities. She passes on to the hero his father's spears with which he kills the *lulu* monster. All the victims that the *lulu* had swallowed are cut from the belly of the beast. First to emerge is the hero's own father. Most likely this alludes to the widespread swallowing motif and its ceremonial associations with rites of passages, transformations and metamorphoses. Those emerging are given a new birth of life. Grateful for their salvation, they bestow love and leadership upon the hero. Most conspicuously lacking in the pattern is the heredity leadership found in the first parts of Indo-European myths of the hero. There is no need for heroes who rise out of exile, divorced from their social advantages in life, in order to prove their natural superiority, in an egalitarian society where individual qualities are achieved individually rather than inherited familially.

The Semang of Malaysia

This myth of the hero was collected in 1918 by Ivor Hugh Norman Evans. He studied anthropology at Cambridge and became the curator of the Perak State Museum, the first of its kind in Malaysia. He held that position until his return to England in 1932. He recorded *Piagok* from Melpelam, the headman of Kintak Bong Negritos. Even in Evan's day, the population was tiny and shrinking. Their original language was long lost, having been submerged in the more populous tongue of the encroaching agriculturalists who were chopping back forests. The more common term in anthropological writings refers to these isolated hunter-foragers as Semang. This designation is of Malay origin. On the one hand, untangling the threads of hybridization of ancient Semang myth from the Malay overlay would end in a guessing game at best. There is only old myth, there is no pure myth. On the other hand, it is sad that there was no Bleek family for the Semang, to record their tales with linguistic sophistication and a commitment to long range study. The pertinent studies are frustratingly long on beliefs and practices but short on actual stories. The chance is lost to allow the body of Semang myth to speak for itself. Myths are the best artifacts or relics of a culture. Upon sensitive translation, myths allow you, an uninformed outsider, immediate access to people who do not look like you nor sound like you nor live, apparently, like you because at heart all human stories from the dawn of time spring from the same source. The main differences are local variations and details. The myth of the hero exemplifies the notion of the essential unity of humankind. It is a family story.

The Semang of Malaysia

A woman named Yak Kampeh dreamed that she was going to have a son. She went out the next morning to forage and sent her son Piagok up a tree to pick a particularly large fruit. Inside was a baby. Later Piagok had a dream of his own in which he met a beautiful woman. [1-8] When he went out hunting the next day, he actually met her. She wanted gifts of armlets of rattan, Jew's harps and combs. Piagok provided her with these wedding gifts and went with her to her village and made her his wife. One night, he had an unlucky dream. The next morning, he exchanged *Changlun* leaves with his wife and told her that if either one shriveled, it meant that the owner was dead. When he was long gone from home, he discovered to his great dismay that his *Changlun* leaf had shriveled. He hurried toward home. [9-10] In the meantime, his wife went to bathe with five other women. These women were false friends who wanted Piagok for themselves. In the bath, they drowned Piagok's wife. When the widowed hunter returned home and learned of his wife's fate, he summoned the five women and killed them with boiling water. Evil waters boiled up out of the ground and Piagok's hut turned to stone. He wrapped his dead wife in a rattan mat and carried her body up into the sky where they became stars. Whenever Semang shamans perform curing rites in a medicine hut, they call upon these two *Chinoi*, or star spirits, to return to earth and give them help and guidance.

All action is taken in response to dreams. There is a birth of unusual circumstances but it refers to the hero's little brother. The father is never mentioned. Dynastic struggle between despotic father and heroic son is replaced with sexual rivalry. It is a myth concerning the second big phase of life after surviving childhood, that is, getting a mate. Piagok is a myth of the hero shaped into a tragic love story. The hero himself is a grief-stricken Odysseus whose Penelope is dead upon his return. He slays no monsters out in the wild. His adversaries are his envious neighbors inside the sacred zone of home. Piagok exacts his revenge and departs the earth with his dead lover. They become healing saints to the Kintak Bong. Lord Raglan's motifs are fairly present but they are used in artful variations. However many missing details there are, the Leavetaking–Adventure–Homecoming is still strong in this myth of the hero.[1]

The Andaman Islanders

By contrast, the hero pattern must be applied synthetically to the Andaman Islander myth of *Perjido*, the Discoverer of Honey. British functional anthropologist A.R. Radcliffe-Brown was a collector of myth in the field. He

---

1 Evans, Ivor H.N. *Studies in Religion, Folk-lore and Custom in British Borneo and the Malay Peninsula.* Cambridge University Press, United Kingdom, 1923. p. 187-190.

was sensitive to local variations of a single myth, as well as to individual ways of telling tales. Like in our world, each performer "was eager to be original and so to enhance his own reputation... [and this is] a fertile source of variation in the legends."[1] He gives us a wonderful, living view of Andaman mythology but to fill in the hero pattern on *Perjido* takes extensive leafing through *The Andaman Islanders*. The information exists, but in many places, and not just in one tale. This cherry picking could be seen as forcing a synthesis upon the materials. Oral traditions maintain a large body of knowledge and folk beliefs that are brought to bear upon any story heard or told. What is known to be understood by the audience is left out of an oral recitation. We always enter Radcliffe-Brown's version *in media res*, jotted down in field notes from working men who were not well versed in storytelling.

The Andaman Islanders.

Dugong   Komodo Dragon

1 Radcliffe-Brown, A. R. *The Andaman Islanders*. p.141, p.187.

This is not a performance version of Perjido from an oko-jumu, an Andaman shaman and singer of tales, "the authorities of legendary lore."[1] The shaman tradition was already dying out in Radcliffe-Brown's day in 1906. There were no new initiates into the oko-jumu life and all of those who survived were old, old men who were not very open about sharing their sacred knowledge with uninitiated white foreigners.

The British anthropologist heard the tales in a piecemeal fashion. He criticized Mr. Man, an ethnologist who had preceded him to the Andaman Islands, for arranging the incidents of the stories that he collected into more coherent narratives than would normally be encountered in the field. This reflects Radcliffe-Brown's own experience as a collector of tales. Nevertheless, many of the missing incidents of Raglan's pattern can be fleshed out from the fragmentary, general body of Andaman mythology, available to the scholar, as well as to the storyteller and to his knowledgeable listeners. Lévi-Strauss would maintain that much implicit mythology from life in general supports any explicit, particular myth.

The mother of the hero *Perjido*, the Discoverer of Honey, is *Biliku*, the northeast monsoon wind. Not a princess but a natural force to be reckoned with. She is fecundity personified: powerful, not virginal. [1] His father is *Tarai* the southwest monsoon wind. This is a gross simplification. Depending upon which individual and which tribe is relating the story, *Biliku* and *Tarai* are male here, female there, married to each other or to others. About the only thing agreed upon is the directions that they represent. [2] Mother and father of the hero are the two fundamental directions of the prevailing winds and seasonal weather cycles but never specifically linked as siblings or cousins. [3] The circumstances of *Perjido*'s birth are not mentioned [4] but he is the son of gods or personified natural forces. [5] No attempt is made to kill him, nor is he spirited away, nor reared in fosterage far from home. [6,7,8] *Perjido* is a child playing at his mother's knee as he bumbles through the forest discovering honey in spite of himself. He has many adventures. Once he shot an eel and how it wiggled in pain across the countryside cut the creek beds into the terrain. His sisters are four birds. He invented the bow and arrow, fashioned the first pig by molding flesh with his playful fingers and transmogrified the dugong out of a pig by throwing a leaf at it. He is the culture hero of men's arts as his mother is the patroness of those feminine. [9] One day, *Perjido* goes out to shoot a fish. It disappears in a tangle of mangrove roots. On the water surface appears the reflection of a bee hive hanging from the branch of a tree. Stupidly, as only a classic Trickster can be, *Perjido* fetches fire to smoke the bees out of the reflection. The water keeps dousing his torch. He comes away disappointed. [10] He returns home to inform mother about his dilemma. She

1 Ibid. p. 187.

berates him as a fool and teaches him the error of his ways. He goes out the next day and gets the honey [11] but he does not share it with anyone. There is no marriage, no sustaining relationship established by his adventure. [12] Selfish *Perjido* relishes his honey all alone in secret. This is his kingdom and this is his reign. [13, 14] It was *Perjido* who discovered honey, [15] but he was not the one who presented it to humanity. Raglan's pattern is varied slightly but continues as a useful template to explore selfishness and the ultimate irony of the good that results unintentionally from an evil deed, the Trickster's grand province. *Perjido* loses exclusive rights to honey when Big Frog follows him into the forest and learns his secret by stealth. [16] Big Frog keeps the secret of honey to himself like *Perjido* did and does not share. Then Little Frog wheedles the secret out of his father, Big Frog. Home has not been lost, but exclusive rights and secret knowledge of honey have gotten away from the few, the select, the initiated. The generations of men are about to revolve and in the turmoil, a great gift to humanity becomes generally available. [17] *Perjido* survives but Big Frog is tricked into jumping from a tree and is impaled and killed by the stakes driven into the ground by his son Little Frog. A death by falling though not from a hill. Von Hahn's incident 15 deals directly with the hero's murder by a vengeful servant. [18, 19] Little Frog takes the honey and runs home with it. Implication: he assumes his father's place in all respects, now that the rival for his mother's affections is out of the way. Big Frog's son does succeed him. Among some Andamanese, *Perjido* is *Biliku's* husband and not her son. [20] There is no mention of burials or landscape associations or shrines with the heroes. [21, 22] but the Andamanese "personify the phenomena of nature," into landscape legends like the Selknam of Patagonia do.

This myth of the hero splintered and one character becomes two. The primary discoverer retires and his replacement is the culture hero that is tricked into giving honey to humanity by means of the machinations of his rival. The last phase of Raglan's pattern is played out in the career of Big Frog and his son Little Frog who comes into his own as a deadly rival to his father.

Synthesis manifests the pattern. This tale is pieced together out of snippets from the body of Andamanese mythology rather than being the transcript of a practiced performance of a single myth delivered complete at one setting to an appreciative audience by an accomplished performer. Perjido's discovery of honey is an example of oral literature. Storytellers in oral traditions suit their tales to their listeners. Shared understandings are omitted to get quickly to the liminal, where the story has the most scope for novel juxtaposing; the adventure. The missing incidents rest in the background of the listeners' minds as surely as the dark supports the stars. Competent storytellers leave the understood unsaid. This version of Perjido scores 10/22. It is admitted based upon the faith that there were fuller versions of this myth of the hero told by oko-jumus which sadly have been lost to time.

The Aborigines of Australia

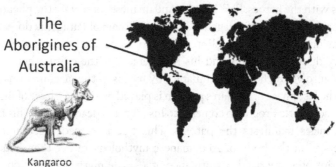

The Aborigines of Australia

Kangaroo

If the Bushmen are the genetic Parent People, then the Australian Aborigines could be said to be the cultural Parent People of humanity. They arrived in Australia before the invention of the bow and arrow, more than 70,000 years ago. Their hunter-forager lifeways could be reckoned as the most ancient on earth and the most faithful to our Pleistocene forebears who made the Grand Migration out of Africa. However, Aborigine culture is anything but uniform or crude, in spite of its relative technological simplicity. They lived by mythology, not machines. If sustainability is the measure, they are still far ahead of our super-civilization of science and technology. Many modern people cannot fathom how humans can continue living as they do in our day and age. The Aborigines came out of the Earth in the Dreamtime and have been here ever since. It is the white man who has wrecked their culture, not Mother Earth.

There is no body of myth more concerned with the land than that of the Australian Aborigines. Birth out of the earth itself is an example of ultimate land tenure. In a land of limited resources, it is important to know and respect your neighbor's territorial claims. It could mean your life. Stories support land tenure. A tally of landmarks mentioned in a given myth can map out a family unit's traditional hunting and foraging territory. In a very real sense, myth can serve as a deed and title to the land. It did for the ancient Greeks. Recall that the Athenian tyrant Peisistratus was accused of tampering with the first written version of the *Iliad* over the ownership of the isle of Aegina. The *Kumyaay* of San Diego, California, believe that their ancestors came out of the earth at the mountain Wikami in the eastern Mojave Desert lining the Colorado River.[1] Aborigine myth always solidly sets the story in a specific geographical location. The place is always real, but back in the Dreamtime, the ancestral era where everything happened for the first time.

Sometimes the entire myth of the hero is reduced to an incident within a larger myth like in *Erintja the Devil Dog*.[2] It was related to the Australian poet Roland Robinson by Albert Tonanga, a missionized member of the Aranda tribe, Flying Bat totem. Tonanga was an Aborigine artist renowned for his landscapes in the *plein-air* manner. This tale was published in 1966.

An old man lies down and is covered by sand. When he rises up, he is now a giant dog that pursues two women and swallows them whole. He hears the sound of a bull roarer and comes upon a mob of blackfellows having a *corroboree*. When the celebrants fall asleep, the devil dog quietly swallows them all whole. Now back when the old men were whirling the bullroarer, the string broke and the *namatoona*, the wooden weight, flew off and landed in the earth far away. From it, a young man rose up to greet the night. [1-8] He hears the sound of the *corroboree* (ceremony) and moves toward it feeling like something is wrong. [9] He draws out his *tjurunga*, a stone relic, and throws it at the devil dog. The monster is terribly wounded and it vomits all the people that it had swallowed. Once it has disgorged its load, it disappears into the Earth. The devil dog reappears out of the Earth where it had originally emerged and turns back into the old man.

Erintja scores 11/22. There is a slimmed down miraculous birth but not much post adventure. This is storytelling mostly concerned with the liminal

---

1 DuBois, Constance Goddard. *The Story of the Chaup: A Myth of the Diegueños*. The Journal of American Folklore. Vol. XVII. October-December, 1904, No. LXVVII.
2 Robinson, Roland. *Aboriginal Myths and Legends*. pp. 9-14.

region, the twilight zone, the out and away, the adventure, the chase, the danger, the betwixt and between, the place where you can lose sight of home. *Erintja* begins like it ends. Out of the Earth, back into the Earth, an almost vegetative resilience that defies death. The swallowed people, vomited by the wounded god, are reborn with new knowledge. They represent the initiates of the ritual linked to the myth, who, because of undergoing the ceremony, come away with deeper spiritual ties to everything and everyone around them.

The purpose of what went before was to establish a folkloric continuum of the myth of the hero that follows the Coastal Clan theory of the migration of modern humans out of Africa to Australia. The myth of the hero, in all its manifestations and permutations, followed the flow of genes. The proof of concept establishes the place of origin of the myth of the hero as Africa and that it was ancient in humanity long before people left the mother continent and struck out for new horizons across the globe.

Myths of the Hero in the Americas

To trace the myth of the hero pattern though northeastern Asia and Siberia would be to wander in an impassible thicket created by hybridization. The myth of the hero is everywhere and impossible to disentangle from neighboring versions. A check upon the process of hybridization occurred when modern human hunter-foragers reached the New World between twenty and thirty thousand years ago. Genetics seems to suggest that the New World was populated by a relatively small group of people. Their stories provide some deeper insight into the evolution of the myth of the hero pattern and a further piece of evidence pertaining to its universality. Hunter-foragers left the Old World for the New long enough ago that their myths of the hero reflect the ancient pattern clearly. Again, we are going for the taste of the droplet in acknowledgement of the vastness of the sea.

The Eskimo of Greenland

Henry Rink was a scientific explorer and Governor of Southern Danish Greenland. He studied the local varieties of the Inuit language on the shores of Davis Strait winter and summer for more than twenty years. He first published *Eskimo Tales*[1] in 1866. In *Kagsagsuk*, Rink presents us with a Cinderella story with an unforgiving twist. It is the compilation of nine different versions that he had jotted down in his notes over the years in Greenland and on Labrador Island. He was aware of possible Christian influence upon the old mythology and wrote with

---

1 Rink, Thomas. *Tales and Traditions of the Eskimos*. London 1875. Reduced to HTML by Christopher M. Weimer, Apr. 2003. 1. Kagsagsuk.

insight about the trials and tribulations of collecting folklore in the field and of witnessing public performance of stories with crowds gathered around.

The Eskimo of Greenland

Polar Bear

Tales are divided by the Inuit into two large categories. Ancient lore is the common property of all storytellers. Recent stories, like the 2001 movie version of the legend *Atanarjuat the Fast Runner*, belong to particular localities and are the private property of certain individuals and families. *Kagsagsuk* is an ancient figure, part Hercules, part Odysseus, known far and wide among the Inuit in the eastern Arctic.

The hero is an orphan. The parents are never mentioned and their death goes unexplained. [1-6] He does not live at home so the troubled circumstances of his birth are only implied. [7] His foster mother is a miserable old woman but the hero acknowledges her as his teacher. [8] We get a lot of childhood information, contrary to Raglan's pattern. He is poor, never allowed to eat in the living room with the family and has to sleep with the dogs. He is abused physically and emotionally. Ridiculously, all that grows on him is his nostrils. He is taught to pray by his foster mother. [9] He stands between two mountains and turns his face to heaven. An *Amarok*, a huge spirit wolf appears, chases the hero, and lassos him with its tail. A series of rituals begins that remove the witchcraft substance that has been enchanting the hero and holding him back in life. Invisible bones of animals and men have been clinging to him. This is an objectification of the pent up feelings caused by life as an abused orphan. Objectifying these natural resentments as bones associates them with death. *Kagsagsuk* agrees to return each day to the wolf and continue learning in order shake loose more of these bones and grow stronger. He takes the *Amarok's* counsel to delay vengeance and bides his time until winter when he will receive a portent. Three bears will appear out on the ice. In the meantime, he single-handedly drags a huge piece of driftwood out of the sea and secretly erects it behind his mother's igloo. The next morning, it is a mystery to one and all who gather around it. Liars claim credit for this fantastic feat of strength. Only when kayakers bring news of three bears out on the ice nearby does the hero allow his resentment to manifest itself. He rushes out and rips two of the beasts apart with his bare hands. The triumphant hero uses the third bear to beat those in the crowd who had treated him badly while he was growing up. He proudly presents the skins and meat to his foster mother and enters the living room to await his first properly-served meal in life. He has arrived home. [10] In spite of being accepted by his extended family, resentment over past treatment boils over and *Kagsagsuk* takes blood vengeance on all who have wronged him. [11] After victory, he does not marry, but he spares the people who were kind to him in his youth [12] and shares winter stores with them. By implication, he takes over as headman. [13-15] He does not lose favor with his people [16] but nevertheless departs from them in order to wander the world by kayak. He has countless adventures which establish customs and shape the land upon which the people live. [17] Nothing is mentioned of his death. [18-21] *Kagsagsuk* scores 11/22.

The character of the foster mother is noteworthy. She is portrayed as supportive, helpful, and knowledgeable; everything a real mother should be, in contrast to her often negative role in western myth and fairy tale. She is an Athena, with nothing of the wicked step-mother about her. The hero was lucky to have her.

The Chumash of the Central Coast of California

The American anthropologist John Harrington recorded Chumash myths and folk literature over a hundred and fifty years after this coastal, central California tribe had been forcibly converted to Christianity by the Spanish

Franciscans. He collected three versions of a myth of the hero about the twins Little Thunder and Little Fog from elderly informants in the 1920s.[1]

The genealogy of the characters in this myth goes back a couple of generations. The grandmother of the hero is a virgin who ignores her mother's caution not to spend too much time bathing in a pond. [1] The grandfather is a shape-shifter, a shaman who can take the form of a bear and appears while the girl is bathing. [2] The familial relationship is mentioned between the couple but glossed over by disguise. [3] She is killed by her bear husband grandfather. The girl's mother is *Momoy*, the personification of the powerful hallucinogenic *Datura meteloides*. She revivifies her daughter from a single drop of blood inside a magic bowl. Soon a baby girl appears. [4] Incidents 1-4 are repeated. When the revivified daughter/granddaughter reaches puberty, she is warned by *Momoy* not to spend too much time bathing in the river. [1] There, the girl is courted by a god, a personification of Thunder, and his brother Fog. [2] No family relation between the lovers is mentioned. [3] The girl becomes pregnant by both brothers and she gives birth to a son by each. [4] The fathers are natural forces, not chiefs or shamans. [5] No attempts are made on the boys' lives, they are not spirited away, nor are they raised by foster parents. [6,7,8] Nothing is mentioned concerning their childhood. [9] Because they want to follow in their absent fathers' footsteps, they go out hunting and traveling when they reach puberty. They meet their magical helper Coyote, an uncle of theirs. The boys visit distant relatives in a strange village in a huge cave where they humiliate Coyote, and they spend the night with a cannibal monster and his beautiful daughters. The monster *Hap* violently pursues the boys in the morning and creates prominent terrain features during the chase. On all of their adventures, the boys are guided by and playing tricks upon Coyote, who functions similarly to the foster parents of incident 3. Eventually they meet up with Turtle and run a race around the world. The boys win and Turtle forfeits his life in a bonfire. [10] There is nothing further so incidents 11-22 are missing though in other versions of the tale, Coyote leads them home. Turtle was thrown on the fire to cook so there is an implied return and a meal at the end of it. [11]

In another version, where the twins are merged into one character known as *Momoy's Grandson*, he is born under similar circumstances, hunts flies before he can speak and his first words are to demand a bow and arrow. He always pesters *Momoy* for bigger bows to go after bigger prey. Because she thinks that it is too dangerous, *Momoy* tries to stop the hero from descending into an arroyo to search out a Bear Shaman and kill him. But *Momoy's Grandson* flouts her fears, descends and wins the desperate fight. He drags the carcass home and frightens *Momoy* with it. Now that the Bear

1 Blackburn, Thomas. *December's Child*. 105-125.

Shaman is dead, she is delighted. She claims vengeance because this Bear Shaman had killed his wife, *Momoy*'s very daughter, the hero's own mother. *Momoy* tells the boy everything about the circumstances of his birth and who it was that he has killed. The hero proclaims that blood vengeance pardons even patricide.

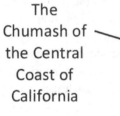

The Chumash of the Central Coast of California

Though much of the machinery of monarchy is missing, *Little Thunder and Little Fog* slips under the wire as a myth of the hero with a score of 7/22.

The Selknam of Patagonia

Father Matthias Guisande was a German Catholic priest who started studying the Selknam Indians of Patagonia at the tip of South America in 1918. He was of that generation of German anthropologists in search of monotheism in primitive culture. He collected *How* Šakanušóyin *Hunted Guanacos*[1] from his best informant, a shaman and headsman named *Tenenésk*.[2]

The hero's mother is a guanaco, a relative of the wool bearing llama. She is not a virgin [1] for she mates with the hero's father. The father is not mentioned as headman or shaman but he is an authority figure in the hero's life. [2] The father and the mother are not from the same family. But the animal marriage motif is the most unequivocal statement possible that all life forms one family. [3] Therefore, the hero's birth is highly unusual, [4] if not divine in the sense of being sanctioned by spiritual agencies of superhuman beings.[5] No attempt is made to kill the baby, [6] nor force it into exile. [7] The hero is raised at home by his father alone while his mother continues as a creature out in the wild. [8] No mention of his childhood is made except that he is such a fast runner that he can even run down guanacos. [9] Taking advantage of his skill, his people force him to hunt guanacos even though it makes the hero sad to kill his mother's kin. [10] He goes out often and brings meat back to his community and wins a race with his closest rival to confirm his status as the fastest. [11] He never marries. [12] Though he overtly prescribes no laws, [15] he introduced persistence hunting to the Selknam, that is, running prey to exhaustion. Persistence hunting is found worldwide. [13,14] The hero begins to lose favor as the guanaco herd dwindles and he becomes more and more reluctant to hunt. [16] His father drives him out of the house to run down the last guanaco, the hero's own mother. [17] He obeys his father and brings home the meat to the village but soon dies of a broken heart. [18] His death place is not mentioned. [19] The hero leaves no children behind to succeed him. [20] He is not buried and no resting place is mentioned, but in another myth, the dead Guanaco Man is buried head and shoulders above the bone white soil. [21] Mountains were commonly held to be transformed human ancestors from back when all the animals were people. Though not mentioned in the text, it is reasonable to ask if there is a prominent terrain feature named after Šakanušóyin [22] somewhere in Tierra del Fuego.

This myth of the hero scores 11/22. It could be argued that there existed fuller versions of this tale and that this is evident by the fact that the missing incidents are found in other tales and were therefore ready at hand for the storyteller to draw upon if needed. Joseph Campbell has been criticized for not applying his three part structure to a single myth *in toto*. This is less of a criticism when considering oral tradition and myth as an act of speech behavior. Did Father Guisande collect a performance version of this myth of the hero from *Tenenésk* or a mere summary? Good storytellers always fit the story to the situation in which the tale is told. The shaman would know the

---

1 Guisande, Martin. *Folk Literature of the Selknam Indians.* UCLA Latin American Studies Publication. Los Angeles, CA, 1975. p. 111.
2 Ibid. p. 13.

language abilities of the collector. Nevertheless, Šakanušóyin is at least half a hero myth by Raglan's tally and manifests the backbone.

The Selknam
of Tierra del Fuego

The Guanaco

The classic myth of the hero pattern, most detailed in Raglan, is a loose fit on stories from hunter-forager societies. The dynastic struggles of Indo-European style kingship and the need to propagandize the purported natural superiority of the rulers was absent in egalitarian, band level societies. The birth of the hero is not presented as a divinely sanctioned threat to the status quo. Stories of miraculous birth are to be found in the mythic traditions of all the societies mentioned above, but there was not the same social function attached to the hero's birth. In hunter-forager myth, heroes do what all common men do; they hunt for themselves. They do not try and get others to hunt for them. Status is earned, not inherited socially or purchased. There are no institutions of leadership to perpetuate father to son. It is the hero's adventures that set him apart, not his parentage. There is no need to breathe

the odor of sanctity upon his conception. Men and women can only increase status in hunter-forager societies by protecting, feeding, curing, teaching or entertaining people, never by merely inheriting it. Lastly, hunters marry their distant cousins from across the river or the next valley, not princesses from afar.

Just like much of the first part of Raglan's pattern is often left unsaid but understood in hunter-forager myth, so is much of the last part. The hero's life is not chronicled unto death and burial. Burial practices differed among hunter-foragers but they all tended toward the non-monumental, the temporary. There are at least two good reasons why hunter-forager bands do not maintain funerary shrines. Their nomadic lifeway does not permit it. But the Andaman Islanders' beliefs about the dead are insightful too. During the mourning period, the deceased's name is not to be uttered. The whole point of funerary ritual is to hasten the departed spirit on its way to the land of the dead and not encourage it to tarry among the living. The spirits of the deceased are considered to be malevolent, spiteful, terrifying and the cause of contagion and disease. They are best sent on their way to the land of the dead quickly. There was less incentive to remember outstanding individuals upon their death because the dead were regarded with superstitious dread. In lieu of graves or shrines, local heroes are often associated with prominent terrain features. Ancestor heroes became mountains for the Selknam back when all the animals were people.

Some of the selected tales are very folkloric, fairy tale like stories and seem almost childlike alongside mythology from grand literary traditions. Is a story a folktale or a myth? This is more a matter of character than plot structure. But to be fair, it is also one of the barriers preventing Raglan's pattern from fitting tightly to hunter-forager myths of the hero. For Raglan, myths are about divine characters who become kings on Earth, are founders of nations and require well rounded biographies. The adventures found in fairy tales are endured by common characters for humbler results. However, the underlying structure of the two kinds of story is similar enough for the purposes of this analysis.

Each myth of the hero is drawn from a corpus of traditional lore. The missing incidents of Raglan's pattern in any given tale can be filled in by the listeners and manipulated by the storytellers to suit the conditions of the performance. Absence of incidents does not automatically disqualify a myth from being heroic. What to leave in and what to take out depends on the individual storyteller. Though they may be absent in certain versions, the incidents of the first part, the birth, and those of the third part, the death, are always implied. Myths of the hero are always part of a corpus of traditional lore widely known and shared among the listeners. They are never invented out of the blue. The most originality that a performer can aspire to in oral tradition is to achieve a novel juxtaposition of well-known elements. There is small scope for the *avant-garde* in hunter-forager aesthetics, although the non-functional adornment of their tools might be called art for art's sake.

Raglan's pattern is a loose fit in particulars, but in general, under the divisions of incidents into three phases that he himself recognized and that parallel Van Gennep's divisions of ritual, the myth of the hero pattern holds up well. The natural phases hold a stronger claim to universality than do the individual incidents of the catalog. All hero myths start with a birth, elaborated upon or merely implied, an adventure where some fundamental aspect of the world is realized, and the return to his old home or the establishment of a new home in order to the share the benefit with and transform his society. Joseph Campbell will do much with a similarly reasoned three part approach to the myth of the hero.

Raglan makes small attempt to explain the origin of his pattern. He cites Krappe's outburst. "It is unthinkable that a tale with a plot as complicated... should have arisen independently."[1] However, he does not hold with any *similar-workings-of-the-mind* arguments either. If he were pressed to relate the myth of the hero to reality, he would maintain that myth is the verbal part of ritual, and no more. Perhaps he believed that no more could ever be determined upon this heading. He never defines ritual nor explores its origins. Raglan is strong on identifying form. For the origin, function and meaning of the myth of the hero, he is by turns silent or scornful, ever striving to remain a scientist whose discipline limits his observations only to those strictly demonstrable by empirical methods. He is not the writer to explore the implications of his observations because speculation is not science but metaphysics. Origin, function and meaning of the myth of the hero pattern were largely the purview of Otto Rank, of whom Raglan knew nothing and Joseph Campbell who was after his time.

---

1 Raglan, Lord. *The Hero: A Study in Tradition, Myth and Drama.* Dover, (1936) 2003. Part II: Myth, xii: The Folktale, p. 134.

THE HERO WITH A THOUSAND FACES

Joseph Campbell was an eclectic comparativist and popularizer who believed that the similarities between myths far outweighed their differences. His favorite tool for analysis was psychoanalysis, by turns calling upon both Freud and Jung, though leaning more toward Jungian concepts generally. He parallels dream and myth in that both phenomena employ archetypes, inheritable mental structures, in their creations and often for the same reasons. He follows a more Jungian approach in that dream is personalized myth and myth is archetypal dream. This was also Rank's approach to myth and dream. Because of the great similarities between them, Campbell believes that myths are not created spontaneously; rather, they are expressions of a "universal mythological formula."[1] His goal is to create a natural history of myth by compiling examples from all cultures, climes and times so that the "symbols speak for themselves."[2] Borrowing a word coined by James Joyce in *Finnegan's Wake*, Campbell calls his universal conception the Monomyth; the one, the shape shifting story of myth and dream of all human cultures. He believes that it is the goal of science to illuminate the laws that govern mutation and change and he compares his work to zoology and botany.

However, like Jung, Campbell is something of a mystic when he maintains that, "Myth is the secret opening through which the inexhaustible energies of the cosmos pour into the human cultural manifestation."[3] Fully actuated human beings cannot live in this world without myth. Myths do not stop at the hero

---

1 Campbell, Joseph. *The Hero With a Thousand Faces*. New World Library, Novato, California. 2008. p. xii.
2 Ibid. p. 1.
3 Campbell, Joseph. *The Hero With a Thousand Faces*, New World Library, Novato, California (1949) 2008. p.3.

achieving adulthood and marriage. They go on to integrate his consciousness into what it means to be a human being who must kill in order to live and will one day die him or herself and leave this beautiful world behind to grieving loved ones.

Like Raglan, Campbell cites Van Gennep as a source but he hardly mentions him in the text of his writing. However, Van Gennep's influence must have been profound upon Campbell. He adopts a three part structure to analyze myth that almost perfectly parallels Van Gennep's Separation–Initiation–Integration structure for ritual. The nuclear unit of the Monomyth is Departure–Initiation–Return. Robert A. Segal claims that "the universality of the pattern proves that the meaning of a myth must lie in it." [1] All heroes depart their original home, venture forth into the dangerous world upon adventures and return home or establish home, and share the benefits of their adventures with their people.

The work of Campbell represents a culmination of the traditional folkloric–ethnological–psychological branch of scholarship concerning myth. It provides a segue to another perspective that is just as vast and perhaps even more profound and certainly more startling. Campbell boils down the myth of the hero pattern to its essentials. It is hard to find a story in Indo-European or hunter-forager myth where his pattern is not applicable, or at least implied, in whole or in part.

It is not a crushing criticism that his pattern is never fully applied to a single myth taken *in toto*. Jesus is discussed under the separate chapters devoted to departure, initiation and return in *The Hero With A Thousand Faces*, if not all in a single passage. Campbell assumes that his readers will apply his pattern for themselves to the myths that they read or listen to. He was not the kind of teacher who would do that kind of leg work for his students. He empirically established the pattern for all to see. He also claimed that ultimately, the meaning of the pattern is self-realization. He even took a stab at how *the myth of the hero pattern originated in the human nervous system* and inspired the line of inquiry in the next section of the present work.

After his achievement of establishing the myth of the hero pattern plainly for all to see, his suggestion to locate this same pattern in the human nervous system is his second greatest contribution to the scientific study of the myth of the hero.

Campbell is a classic example of seeing further than the giants upon whose shoulders he has stood. Segal expressed surprise at how little scholarly writing is devoted to his work.[2] When you contemplate Campbell from a scholarly point of view, you contemplate his giants more than the

1 Segal, Robert A. *Joseph Campbell: An Introduction.* Penguin Books USA Inc. New York, 1987. p. 32.
2 Ibid. p. 10.

man himself. The reader is compelled to read Jung in order to judge how Campbell applies his ideas to myth. In attempting to suggest that the myth of the hero pattern is an artifact of the human nervous system, he turns to the pioneering German ethologists Konrad Lorentz and Niko Tinbergen to create his linkages. If anything, Campbell was a genius at throwing novel light upon his subject even if he were not the origin of that particular light. He was a widely read scholar in diverse disciplines, quick to establish parallels and adept at reasoning by analogy. He had an unshakeable belief in, and a talent for illuminating, the oneness of the cosmos.

The Singer of Tales

All of the above theories, apart from the ones which attribute faulty logic to myth making, are strong on identifying the form of the myth of the hero, and bold in assigning meaning to the pattern. On the other hand, they overlook its function as a speech act, a narrative associated with a performance, a visible, audible behavior that can be objectively observed. Only Rank and Frazier allowed that myths were the verbal remnant of a ritual and left it at that. Almost all of the theories utterly ignore the context in which the myth of the hero was composed.

If it is true that the myths were already ancient before they were ever written down, originally they must have been composed orally and are artifacts of language and speech. The scholar to whom we can gives thanks for enlarging upon this insight was Milman Parry, a Harvard classicist with an interest in the Homeric Question.[1] How were the epic *Iliad* and *Odyssey* composed and by whom? Voltaire had weighed in on this issue back in the 18th century when in *Candide*, he had Venetian senator Pococurante coolly lament that "Homer was no favorite of his... (due to) his endless repetitions..." Parry was convinced that most of what was strange and wonderful about the *Iliad* and the *Odyssey*, such as the errors and inconsistencies, the duplication of scenes and themes, and the repetitive heroic epithets, could be explained if they were viewed as *epic tales orally composed during live performances* line by line and deeply rooted in a social context of heroic values.

In 1933–35, Parry and his assistant A.B. Lord traveled around Yugoslavia recording Moslem and Christian oral epic traditions. Their goal was to make transcriptions of these performances and compare them with the works of Homer. The Milman Parry Collection of Oral Literature in the Widener Library

---

1 Lord, A.B. *The Singer of Tales*. Harvard University Press. (1960), 2003.

of Harvard University is the biggest collection of South Slavic heroic songs in the world. Béla Bartók, the world famous pianist, composer and ethnomusicologist, undertook some of the musical transcriptions. Parry and Lord were lucky enough to find Avdo Međedović, an illiterate farmer, a player of the one-string *gusle*, singer of tales, and for these two American scholars struggling to master the intricacies of sound recording equipment in the field, their Yugoslav Homer.

Avdo played at weddings, parties and in smoke-filled coffeehouses where women were forbidden. He sang night-long epic songs of up to 15,000 lines about the *Battle of Kosovo* and the *City of Bagdad*. The *guslar* had a repertoire large enough to sing a different tale for every night of Ramazan, the month long annual Moslem fast from dawn to dusk. Parry and Lord were interested to know how such feats of memory were possible without resorting to literacy. Avdo insisted that he sang his songs word for word and never made a mistake even though side by side comparisons of transcriptions of recorded performances demonstrated that this was not quite true. Parry and Lord set about understanding how *guslars* like Avdo learned his songs. He could hear a complete performance once and sing it himself the next night as well as, or even better than, his model.

The scholars were surprised by what they discovered. The path to become a master *guslar* typically began in the singer's mother's arms while she nursed him during performances at weddings and parties. As the boy grew, so did his interest in the music, singing and stories of any *guslar* passing through his village. Either by recognition of his talent or in fulfillment of a request, an older male relative, often a *guslar* himself, gives the apprentice his first instrument. Now he hangs around the fringes of every performance. Afterward, by trial and error, he imitates what he remembers until he finally gets it right.

For purposes of comparison, it is interesting to take note here of Tetsuro Matsuzawa, director of the Primate Research Institute at Kyoto University in Japan, and his observations of chimpanzee learning and teaching.[1] He calls it education by master-apprenticeship. Take as an example a young chimp learning from its mother how to crack nuts with a hammer stone. Education is based on the mother–child bond. There is no formal instruction, no positive or negative feedback by the mother as teacher. The young chimp has an intrinsic interest in learning because the immediate reward is tangible, food. The young learner watches his mother patiently crack nuts until the procedure clicks in his mind. Then it is lots of practice, lots of trial and error

---

1 Matsuazawa, Tetsuro. *The Chimpanzee Mind: Bridging Fieldwork and Laboratory Work, Education by Master-Apprenticeship.* pp. 12-13. The Mind of the Chimpanzee, Elizabeth V. Lonsdorf, et al. ed. University of Chicago Press, 2010.

until he gets it right. Matsuzawa claims that traditional Japanese arts are taught in such a manner. So is epic song in Yugoslavia.

At this point, there is no active teaching, no mentoring of the budding singer. Learning is all observation and experience, trial and error, and above all, persistence in devotion to a burning hunger in the heart and mind. It is during this lonely period that his honest resolve to become a singer of tales is revealed for all in his community to see, especially by the local masters who have taken notice of this youngster and will one day become his finishing teachers if his natural talent shows itself to be worthy of their attention.

The apprentice does not memorize entire songs note for note and word for word. What he works on for years is mastery of an ethno-poetic method of metrical line composition. This is a folk-linguistic mechanism by which to spontaneously generate poetic lines of a certain characteristic length, quality and theme *during* a live performance. Composition is a live, not a private act, for the *guslar*. We can only understand the work of the *guslar* by comparing it to how modern poets compose.

Metrics might well be the most underestimated word in modern, Western poetics. Historically, however, most of English poetry was composed in consciously metrical language. In other words, poetry traditionally has always been stringently rule governed above and beyond the call of grammar and syntax. It was Marlowe's Mighty Line that captured the universal themes of women, war and the ancient past in a single breath and provided a line for English poets to work with and to emulate. "Was this the face that launched a thousand ships?"[1] asks Faust upon seeing the conjured vision of Helen of Troy.

We can only know by comparison. English is an accented language. Some syllables are pronounced just slightly more loudly than their neighbors. This sets up a natural rising-falling pattern to spoken English, of which the poets of that language took advantage in order to express their thoughts rhythmically.

This is Shakespeare's guiding metric: an individual line ten syllables long, grouped into five units called feet, each foot comprised of an unaccented syllable paired with an accented one.

A perfect example is when Romeo first spied Juliet upon the balcony. "But soft, what light from yonder window breaks?"[2] Another from lamenting Macbeth. "It is a tale told by an idiot..." [3]Another from Calpurnia to

---

1 Marlowe, Christopher. *The Tragical History of Doctor Faustus.* V.i.110.
2 Shakespeare, William. Romeo and Juliet. II.ii.2
3 Shakespeare, William. Macbeth. V.v.27/28.

headstrong Caesar. "Your wisdom is consumed in confidence."[1] And lastly from Prospero. "Our little lives are rounded with a sleep."[2]

A slight variation of eleven syllables from pitiful Lear. "I am a man more sinned against than sinning."[3] Another from his bastard son Edmund. "Legitimate Edgar, I must have your land."[4]

In the mouths of competent actors, lines written under these constraints can project like the daily speech of man become a force of nature. This pattern of accents has also been parodied:

Te Dum Te Dum Te Dum Te Dum Te Dum.

Marlowe's Mighty Line has been likened to a blacksmith's set-tap hammer strike upon an anvil. It has been claimed that it was in response to the Victorian habit of stridently pattering out their iambic pentameter during deafening oral recitations in small parlors that incited the Modern movement in poetry. For modern poets, metrics is, at best, suspect. But the basic structure of Marlowe's Mighty Line allows for lots of variation in terms of number of syllables per line and pattern of accents. Iambic pentameter is one of the genius vehicles of human thinking and expression.

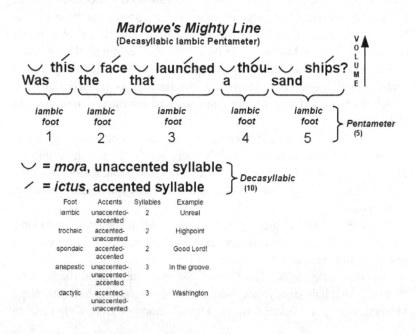

Marlowe's Mighty Line
(Decasyllabic Iambic Pentameter)

Foot	Accents	Syllables	Example
iambic	unaccented-accented	2	Unreal
trochaic	accented-unaccented	2	Highpoint
spondaic	accented-accented	2	Good Lord!
anapestic	unaccented-unaccented-accented	3	In the groove
dactylic	accented-unaccented-unaccented	3	Washington

1 Shakespeare, William. Julius Caesar. II.ii.51.
2 Shakespeare, William. The Tempest. IV.i.55-56.
3 Shakespeare, William. Lear. III.ii.59-60.
4 Ibid. I.ii.57.

Avdo's flexible line structure was also centered, though not strictly, on a ten syllable line, of various pauses and metrics. Comparing it to iambic pentameter in English poetics gives us a better appreciation of the restrictions that singers of tales were up against when composing aloud before audiences. Ten syllables is a good breath group both in English and in Slavic. In comparing iambic pentameter to Avdo's poetics, it is always good to keep in mind that poets compose in private on paper and *guslars* compose aloud publicly while playing a *gusle.*

Like in every *guslar* apprenticeship, Avdo listened and imitated and taught himself how to extemporize line by line, half-line by half-line, by means of metrical formulas organic to his native tongue. A formula is "a group of words which is regularly employed under the same metrical conditions to express a given essential idea."[1] These formulas are short phrases which are fitted into individual lines as needed to fill them out. In Homer, these are the renowned, oft repeated heroic epithets such as "wine-dark sea" and "rosy-fingered dawn," and "godlike Achilles." These epithets appear so often in the text that they lend credence to the suggestion that both epics were transcriptions of oral compositions. Incidents and themes appear in twos and threes. The on-the-spot assembly of metrical lines and half-lines by means of formulas and formulaic phrases is how the narrative is built up. The singer teaches himself to fit his thought within the metrical and rhythmic framework of the tradition. There is no fixed paragon to memorize and be transmitted word for word to the next generation. Instead, a mechanism of composition is mastered by which stories can be lengthened or shortened as appropriate to the spontaneous demands of the audience and the singer during any given unique performance.

Melodically, the songs of the *guslars* are monotonous, back and forth and sing-song. The *gusle* hums and growls under the bow. The rhythm is chopped out evenly, relentlessly, each syllable chanted heavily, inexorably. The melody is general, organic, full of slight variations to accommodate the flow of words, never fully resolving. It is trance inducing. Metrics and melody are devoted to story, never the other way around.

Once the young *guslar* has achieved a certain competence with his musical instrument, knows how to extemporize publically and has committed the plots to memory, he is ready to perform. If he is good enough to attract notice, only then will a master *guslar* step in and complete his education and instruct him on finer points and ornamentation.

Milman Parry passed away suddenly upon returning to America and his work was carried on by his assistant A.B. Lord. His book *The Singer of Tales* permanently changed the way folklorists looked at the myth of the hero,

---

1 Ibid. p. 30.

now as a public composition of oral tradition, as an artifact of language, as a speech act before an audience, "the presentation of tradition by the constant re-creation of it."[1] The myth of the hero as observable behavior.

Rap, in all its variety, is far more lyrical and personal in theme and less historical than Yugoslav epic. However Rap operates under a number of constraints and it is an ethno-poetic theory of public, spontaneously generated oral tradition. Heart-felt rhymes to a solid beat. A good rapper has to make it up on the spot, often in competition with other rappers for audience approval. Each rapper has developed his or her own techniques in order to do so, just like *guslars* each went through a long period of development before they could perform spontaneously. The *guslar* and the rapper both rely heavily upon oral traditions drawn from their climes and times.

The main purpose of this last section is to solidly root the composition of and performance of the myth of the hero in a behavioral context. Behavior is directly observable and permits linkages to the sources of story that are deep in each individual human being.

Last of the Bones

The myth of the hero has been identified in its essential form as a narrative, originally composed orally and preserved orally, with a basic three phase structure of Leavetaking–Adventure–Homecoming. Many of the finest minds of classical scholarship, psychology and anthropology have been fascinated with the form and attempted to interpret its meaning, historically, socially and psychologically. The myth of the hero is a universal feature of human mythology across time and terrain. As yet, no satisfactory explanation has surfaced to account for its ubiquity. Neither independent invention and diffusion nor the purported "psychic unity of man" fully account for all of the ramifications of the myth of the hero. The myth of the hero continues as a mystery that has remained popular in spite of its obscure origins. To continue our search, we must leave our folkloric roots and venture into other disciplines to trace the origins of the myth of the hero beyond our hunter-forager past, and into our evolution out of animality. The myth of the hero will be lifted from the pages of books and keyed into our essential humanity. We suggest that what the communicative cry is to a creature, the myth of the hero is to the human being. We bore the myth of the hero, our most spiritual story, with us as we evolved out of animality into the being that we are today.

Several of the writers above provide clues upon how to proceed. Great encouragement is gained by Segal's claim that "...the universality of the pattern proves that the meaning of a myth must lie in it." Franz Boas, the father of American ethnology, claimed that "Myth was everyday experience

---

1 Ibid. p. 29.

exaggerated, aggrandized in the play of imagination upon the stuff of reality." Otto Rank echoes this when he writes, "The mythologic evolution certainly begins on terrestrial soil, in so far as experiences must first be gathered in the immediate surroundings before they can be projected into the heavenly universe." Ultimately, the myth of the hero must be searched for in our daily lives and surroundings and it can be done so fruitfully.

Otto Rank once lamented that when all was said and done, "the origin of the first myth would still have to be explained,"[1] as if this were impossible or futile. We disagree, and believe, at least in concept, that the first myth of mankind can be clearly alluded to and that it is the myth of the hero. How can this claim be made?

It was the late Joseph Campbell who put the final polish on the pattern of the myth of the hero and achieved the most cogent expression of its form in *The Hero With A Thousand Faces*. It is again Joseph Campbell who points the way on the next leg of our journey. He wondered if the *myth of the hero pattern could have originated in the human nervous system*. Our journey now takes us out of the metaphysical realms and pushes us into those of the hard sciences.

1 Rank, Otto. The Myth of the Birth of the Hero. In Quest of the Hero, ed. Robert A. Segal, Princeton University Press, 1990. p. 5.

FLESH

Neurons and Narratives

If the mind is what the brain *does*,[1] then storytelling, and more particularly, the myth of the hero, is what human language *does*. The reason that humans excel in the world above their fellow creatures is that we have evolved the cumulative cognitive capacity to relate narratives and grasp narratives related by others. We guide our subsequent behavior, in work and in leisure, in response to them. Storytelling, as exemplified by the myth of the hero, has a natural history.

It is in story format that factual information is most readily passed and comprehended by the human mind. Narrative shaping politicians and ad-men know this all too well. Hollywood will make any distortion necessary in order to render history and biography into plots that better suit its audience's cinematic tastes and expectations. Quantum physicists have been known to lament this limitation of human cognition. The double slit light experiment has revealed the possibility of a single photon appearing simultaneously at points A and B. Unless the pilot-wave theory holds up, there is no discernible connection between them. This tears the net of the story filter of our minds and our common sense logic. This is why physicists claim that their discoveries are counter-intuitive and that they can be alluded to only by means of metaphor and analogy when they are rendered into everyday language.

Language and speech, the vehicles of story, all share the same evolutionary history. Story functions both in work and leisure behavior of humans. Language, speech, and narrative are skills deep within us. Even though it might be slightly less than precise to suggest that they are instinctual, it is a place to start our hunt

---

1 Pinker, Steven. *How the Mind Works*. W.W. Norton & Company, New York, NY 2009.

for where of the myth of the hero is located in our being beyond acquired, individual long term memory.

Chapter one of Joseph Campbell's *Primitive Mythology* is titled *The Enigma of the Inherited Image*.[1] In discussing the work of the pioneering ethologists Konrad Lorentz and Niko Tinbergen, he wonders how newly hatched turtles know that they must reach the sea and swim for their lives without ever being taught to do so. How do newly hatched chickens, with egg shell still stuck to their tails, already know the dangers of a hawk flying overhead only by the mere touch of its shadow? They react by running for cover, and can distinguish the hawk's shadow from those of other birds. Shadows of sparrows produce no run for cover. The chick is even able to distinguish a real danger from a contrived one. The image of the hawk shadow flown backwards over it provokes no key-tumbler response and the chick does not bother to hide. "The image of the inherited enemy is already sleeping in the nervous system and along with it, the well-proven reaction."[2] The key is the environment and the tumbler is the instinct. Experience of the environment accumulates at the deepest levels of our being as instincts. How these instincts were created and where they were located in the nervous system has remained an enduring mystery.

Campbell goes on to discuss innate releasing mechanisms in the nervous system that allow an animal to react to situations and circumstances without having been taught to do so. It is not the individual, but the member of the species that is reacting, and this reaction must be inherited for the animal has had no time in which to learn the reaction. These are isomorphs of the environment reflected in the central nervous system, imprints that have accumulated over generations of experience and are shared by all members of the species. Locke's notion of the mind as *tabula rasa*, or a blank slate, is largely incorrect. Archetypes, inheritable mental structures, are equated to innate releasing mechanisms, IRMs, or instincts. *"No one has yet been able to tell how it got there, but there it is!"*[3]

Campbell suggests, without being able to prove, that the myth of the hero pattern is somehow an artifact of the human nervous system, a complex of instincts. Much can be explained if something like it exists. Language is the key to tracing the linkages of the myth of the hero to our genes.

---

1 Campbell, Joseph. *Primitive Myth: Volume I The Masks of God.* The Viking Press, 625 Madison Avenue, New York, NY 10022. 1959.
2 Campbell, Joseph. *Primitive Myth: Volume I The Masks of God.* The Viking Press, 625 Madison Avenue, New York, NY 10022. 1959.
3 Campbell, Joseph, *Primitive Myth.* p. 31.

We Know Why the Wild Bird Sings

Each species of bird has its own repertoire of songs. Individual birds sing their species' songs individually like each human is the possessor of his or her own unique voice. The same bird songs can have local dialects within the geographic distribution of the species. This all depends upon environmental influences. It also depends upon genetics. Bird songs are reflections of learning as well as the operation of proteins and hormones in the brain. Some songs are innate and the bird sings almost from birth. Other songs are learned and the acquisition process follows predictable developmental stages much as human language acquisition does. The song control system of many birds has been mapped out with Magnetic Resonance Imaging (MRI). Activation patterns indicating neural responses have been plotted in their brains and associated with singing behavior.[1] Theoretically, the vervet monkey's communicative cry system that distinctly identifies the predator trio of eagle–cat–snake, could be subject to this kind of analysis. So could a chimpanzee's when it utters, "Hoo," upon examining a strange object.

Neuroscience has located language and speech in the human brain. They are identified as Broca and Wernicke's areas. They are on the left hemisphere, fore and aft of the ear and slightly above it in the temporal lobe. Developmental abnormalities in speech have been associated with lesions in Broca and Wernicke's areas. With Broca's aphasia, people can understand but not produce language. With Wernicke's aphasia, people can produce language but the words are incoherent. This demonstrates the specialization of function in language and speech of these two areas. Other parts of the brain play their roles in language and speech but as yet are not as well understood. MRI studies have mapped

1 Alcock, John. *Animal Behavior*. 9th Edition. Sinauer Associates, Inc. Sunderland, MA 01375. 2009. pp. 63-181.

activation patterns in Broca and Weirnike's areas associated with language and speech operations.

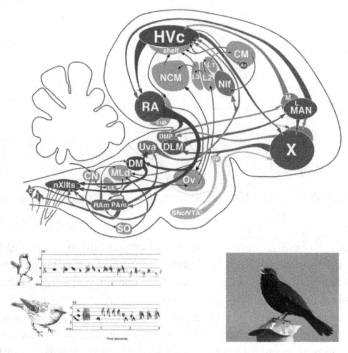

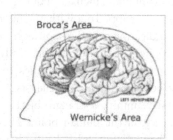

The Bird Song Control System

Endocranial casts of latex rubber have been made of many species. This process reveals the impression that the brain has made upon the inside of the skull. Many species, including chimpanzees, demonstrate development in Broca and Wernicke's areas. Some fossil hominid skulls also show similar development.

Paul Broca   Carl Wernicke

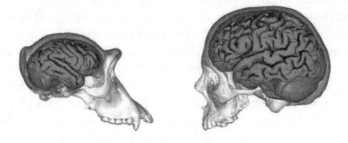

Endocranial casts of Chimpanzee and Human

Language and speech have been evolving for a long time. The story did not begin only with the rise of the hominids some 3.6 million years ago. Human language and speech have something of the waggle dance of the honey bee, which can reveal distance and direction of a nectar source to hive mates even hours after discovery. Speech is in us before we ever manifest it in words.

Neurons, nerve cells, pick up sensory input from the environment. They process all input and relay it to the brain. Neurons and complexes of neurons such as bird song control systems and Broca and Wernicke's areas, direct the appropriate motor responses in reaction to environmental input. We can no longer speak of nature without taking into account nurture, nor of nurture without taking in to account nature whenever we consider any behavior in isolation.

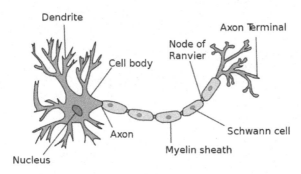

Neuron
(Nerve Cell/Brain Cell)

Feedback loops can be very complex structures to analyze. Nobody said it better than the German animal behaviorist Konrad Lorentz. "It is almost impossible to portray in words the functioning of a system in which every part is related to every other in such a way that each has a causal influence on the others."[1] When you are speaking of language, you are trying to speak about everything at once because you have to in order to try and describe what language does with the myth of the hero. However, researchers are now capable of looking at photos of MRI activation patterns in the brain and very accurately determine if the test subject had been looking at an igloo or at a hammer.[2] In fact, the complexity of the task of identifying the genes involved in language and relating narratives will most likely continue to baffle research for a good long while. The proof of concept, however difficult to achieve in fact, is scientifically plausible and points to the surest path of further discovery. The function of any neuron is an interaction of the feedback loop between the environmental input and DNA expression, and the DNA expression and the subsequent environmental change, and so on, and so on, and so on. We could never sing the myth of the hero were it not somehow coded in our DNA. The Earth made humans singers of tales and humans sing tales about their daily lives upon the Earth.

1 Lorentz, Konrad. *On Aggression.* Bantam Books, 1966. p. xi.
2 Shinkareva, Svetlana V. et al. *Using fMRI Brain Activation to Identify Cognitive States Associated with Perception of Tools and Dwellings.* Indiana University Press. 2008.

Put simply, genes are comprised of sections of DNA. They code for the production of proteins. The production of proteins is triggered by the environment. So which is the executive function, the environment or the genes? Nothing happens without input. The whole cell, most often in response to other cells, initiates the expression of a gene and the ensuing cascade of protein formation. The whole cell is considered to be the executive and the DNA is the anvil upon which the response is hammered out.

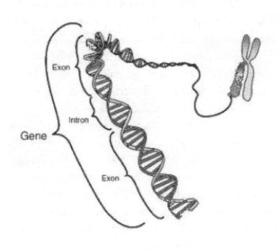

A Typical Gene

It was once thought that one gene-one protein was a rule. Research has shown that one gene can code for many different proteins or not function at all. It all depends upon environmental factors if a gene is expressed or repressed or mutated.

How does environmental

experience accumulate in the genes? DNA is not a static gift from mom and dad. It is a unique inheritance from both parents but it is not fixed at birth. DNA changes structure during the lifetime of the individual in response to the environment. This was discovered in identical twin studies. One twin gets cancer, the other does not. Why? One twin lives in an environment which triggers cancer. The other twin lives in an environment which represses it. Environment, most immediately to any given creature, means the air it breathes, the water it drinks and the food it eats.

Heredity plays its part. If you are missing a key sequence of genes on chromosome 15, whether you get Angleman's Syndrome or Pradovilli's Syndrome depends upon if you got the deletion from your mother or from your father. So how does a gene know where it came from?

DNA does not exist in the nucleus of cells as a naked molecule. When free floating in the nucleus, it is called chromatin. Chromatin winds around fist shaped protein molecules called histones. Tight coils repress expression of a gene. Loose coils enable expression of a gene. The histones function like a dial that opens or closes the coils. DNA is also "clothed" in chemically attached, organic molecules, the configuration of which is unique to each individual. Epigenetics is a new science that is concerned with how long lasting gene regulating attachments, often clusters of methyl (CH_3) molecules, are put in place or removed by the influence of environmental changes like food, famine, pollution, even social interactions and stress. Epigenetic processes take place where the environment meets the molecule. These same processes, considered as complexes, could be a contributing source of instincts. Instinct, to date has been a catch-all term to describe unlearned, universal behavior. Admittedly, this reasoning is provisional and is no doubt subject to further discovery and refinement upon future research.

Astounding claims are being made by the epigeneticists. The Swedish village of Overkaliks has maintained excellent genealogical records for hundreds of years. This made cross-generational statistical studies of the effects of famine possible. It has been established that the lives of parents, grandparents and great-grandparents can affect an individual despite that individual never having directly experienced what their ancestors experienced. In the case of this study, we are speaking about famine. When incidents of diabetes were checked against the history of grandparents, there was a strong correlation between the food supply of father's father and expression of the disease in the grandchildren. This appears to show that a transgenerational effect in response to famine is visited upon the descendants. There is a link between diet in one generation and life expectancy in another.

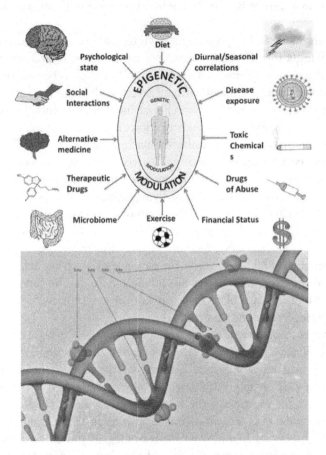

Methyl Molecules Influence Gene Expression

Similar studies with toxins and stress have produced similar results. Experience accumulates in the genes, by means of the addition of or the removal of the organic molecules that "clothe" them. A genetic memory of an event can travel through the generations. Environmental effects in one generation *can* be inherited by the offspring and *passed* in turn to the next generation.[1] Pavlovian conditioned response and other ecological systems theories of development come to mind. Lamarck's heresy is no longer so heretical. Part of the reason giraffes have long necks it that over the generations, the willful stretching of the neck to get at the top most leaves

1 Francis, Richard C. *Epigentics: The Ultimate Mystery of Inheritance.* W.W. Norton & Company. 500 Fifth Avenue, New York NY 10100, 2011.

of a tree does seem to have had a contributing effect to its lengthening over time.

About instincts, Joseph Campbell wrote, "No one has yet been able to tell how it got there, but there it is!" We are beginning to understand how the environment imprints itself upon our DNA, as well as how instincts are created. No behavior is possible without genetic underpinnings. This includes relating a myth of the hero around a hearth fire. The sheer complexity of the chemistry might forever confound our efforts to explain it step by step. The proof of concept has been plausibly established. The myth of the hero must ultimately be a feature of our natural history, of our genetics, of our DNA responding to the environment very similar to the vervet's instinctual cough- cough is a response to a martial eagle flying high in the sky above.

The individual expression of the genes of any individual of any species alive today is the result of an evolutionary history that goes back at least 4.5 billion years. The DNA in every human alive today goes back to the very beginning of life. The form of the molecule itself, changeable as it is, is immortal. It will continue and evolve as long as it can find an environment in which to replicate, just like a flame can burn as long as there are candles to keep lighting from it one after the other.

Experience of the individual accumulates in his or her DNA. Every creature alive today has an evolutionary history that goes back to the first cell, the primal ancestor of us all. Admittedly, the greatest confound to the theory of evolution and of the scientific origin of life itself is the mystery surrounding the creation of the first cellular membrane. The creation of the membrane stands today in the same position as did the eye in Darwin's day.[1] You either had an eye, went the reasoning, or you did not; and there were no intermediary stages that would constitute a favorable adaptation along the way. There is no instant complexity in evolution, it would seem. Such complexity as the membrane militates for instantaneous creation by a creator in some hearts and minds. The membrane is a complex, bi-layered structure with numerous protein receptors with binding sites to absorb larger materials from outside the cell. It is hard to imagine how evolution tinkered with existing structures available at the time and combined them in new ways to produce an entirely novel function. It is hard to imagine intermediary stages that would be favorable adaptations along the way. However, without the membrane, there is no inside and no outside. There is no regulation of the ebb and flow of materials in and out of the cell. Life happens inside membranes. The theory of evolution by means of natural selection cannot as yet account for the origin of the membrane and, therefore,

---

1 Bloom, M. and O.G. Mouritsen. *The Evolution of Membranes, Handbook of Biological Physics*, edited by R. Lipowsky and E. Sackmann, Vol. I, Chapter 2, 1995.

of the cell itself. Natural selection is only an explanation of the cell's function and mutability down the ages in nature.

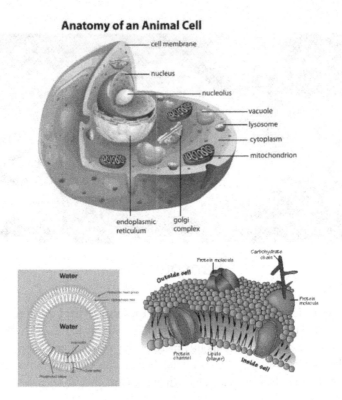

Anatomy of an Animal Cell

Cell and Membrane

Before Siddhartha became the Buddha, he sat under a Bodhi tree for seven years and meditated. At one point, he relived all the incarnations that he had lived as a human and as animals, from butterflies to elephants. It is mere speculation at this point, but it is intriguing to wonder how much of this kind of thinking is more than sheer imagination and metaphor. It makes us ponder Rumi's animal soul. If our DNA reflects our cumulative experience as a creature upon Earth, then how does this show up in our thinking?[1]

No one can say where the original strand of DNA came from. Is it the stuff of God? Did it generate spontaneously in the primal oceans out of non-organic substances? Was Earth seeded with life on a cosmic wind from outer space?[2] Perhaps we will never know. But as a flower sheds pollen to the

1 Shaw, Sarah. *The Jatakas: Birth Stories of the Bodhisatta.* Penguin Global, 2008.
2 Hoyle, B. and N.C. Wickramasinghe. *Astronomical Origins of Life- Steps Towards Panspermia.* Springer, 1999.

wind, Earth is now broadcasting genetic material out into space. Who knows where it will journey or upon what worlds it will land or what will happen when and if it does?

Panspermia

If the spirit is connected to the mind and the mind to the brain and the brain to the body and the body to the ancestry and the ancestry to the soil, water, wind and fire, then it no longer seems like mere poetry to wonder whether Earth is the mother of this creature called a human being, who seeks his or her spirit and sings of his or her adventures as the myth of the hero.

THE ORION COMPLEX AGAIN

In all the anthropological literature, there is no record of a purely foraging society of human beings. In all societies encountered under the diverse ecological conditions of Earth, if the women forage plant-based nutrition, the men hunt wild animals for meat. This is not to minimize the female contribution to the dinner table. It is now accepted that their efforts brought in the majority of the food for the family and accounted for the majority of small game as well. Men brought in big meat, the prestige food. What made humans hunters? *Women like meat!*

When Darwin wrote, "Origin of man now proved. Metaphysics must flourish. He who understands baboon would do more for metaphysics than Locke,"[1] he was anticipating someone like Jane Goodall. Young and untrained, she was nevertheless mentored by world-famous Kenyan paleontologist Louis Leaky who sent her out into the wild. The young Englishwoman had spent a long time observing chimpanzees at the Gombe preserve on the shores of Lake Tanganyika before she witnessed an older male dubbed David Greybeard eating meat from the carcass of a young bush pig.[2] She could not be sure whether the chimp had chased and killed his prey or merely scavenged the remains. Her husband Hugo soon after photographed a chimpanzee hunt of red colobus monkeys and their feast, where meat was shared among the hunters.

---

1 Darwin, Charles. *The Red Notebook of Charles Darwin.* 1 July, 1838.
2 Van Lawick-Goodall, Jane. *In the Shadow of Man.* Houghton Mifflin Company, Boston MA. 1971. p. 70.

Chimpanzees have been observed to use team tactics to hunt red colobus monkeys in the Taï Forest in Ivory Coast.[1] A group of five or six stalk silently along the trail until they spot their prey in the trees up ahead. The fastest chimpanzee takes off at a dead run down the trail. The others wait until they are sure that he has gotten out past the prey and has had time to climb a strategic tree in order to lie in wait. The youngest, most agile member is sent up into the trees in order to set the chase in motion. The others climb trees in order to funnel the prey toward the tree where the runner is lurking in ambush. A screaming red colobus is shepherded to his fate and once captured, the hunting party converges upon the kill to share in the feast up in the branches.

Humans hunt. Chimpanzees, with whom we share 98.3% similar DNA, hunt. Therefore, our most recent common ancestor also *probably* hunted. Some monkey species have been observed to hunt small rodents and smaller monkey species. Hominids hunted animals and ate meat long before they expressed language by means of anything that humans today would remotely recognize as speech. This should not be surprising in that our remote ancestors were insectivores. We did not become hunters as a transitional step toward evolving into *Homo sapiens*. Becoming hunters required no sudden light-bulb moment of inspiration. We brought our meat eating drive along with us step by step as we evolved into humans. What we selected for culturally was a human way of hunting. That means resorting to tools and tactics where once we only chased and grabbed.

Our first tool had to be the hammer stone. In Brazil, spider monkeys have been filmed using hammer stones to crack open nuts. Monkeys split off from apes about sixty million years ago. Chimps and orangutans have been taught to knap flints into sharp edges to cut things.[2] There is evidence of stone tools going back almost two million years. At some point, humans began to use one tool to make another tool. This was a crucial step in creating more complex and efficient tools.

It is reasonable to assume that the more highly developed the tools produced, the more accurate the throwing ability. The hand–eye coordination necessary to both skills probably evolved jointly, simultaneously. If all *Australopithecus afarensis* fossils of Hadar were puzzled together it would seem that Lucy of 1.8 million years ago had a hand that was capable of a three-fingered fastball grip. A rock in the right hand is a deadly weapon. Stoning as

1 Boesch, Christophe. "Hunting Strategies of Gombe and Taï Chimpanzees." *Chimpanzee Cultures*. Harvard University Press. 1994. pp. 77-94.
2 Matsuzawa, Tetsuro. "Field Experiments on Use of Stone Tools in the Wild." *Chimpanzee Cultures*, ed. Richard W. Wrangham et al, Harvard University Press, 1994. pp. 351-370.

capital punishment is as old as the Bible[1] and as contemporary as the newly created, constitutional nation state of Sudan, where in 2012 an unfortunate woman was convicted of adultery and sentenced to this punishment.[2]The deadly power of a group of coordinated rock throwers should not be underestimated.

Were the original rock-throwing hominids actual hunters or were they scavengers? Did they merely drive off big predators and appropriate the carcass? A hungry group of hunters with mouths to feed back home would take advantage of whatever came their way. Lion robbing is a hunting technique among the many African tribes. The hunters walk confidently up to a pride of lions devouring their kill. The lions are startled by the humans' nonchalant approach and scatter to the nearby grass to wait and see what this brazen act is all about. The hunters ignore the lions and quickly butcher a haunch and walk off with it before the lions have a chance to get angry. Once the human hunters walk away, the lions return to their meal. Rock throwing could kill in its own right or be used to drive off big predators from their kills.[3]

It goes against the facts to underestimate the power of our throwing arms in our evolution. When the course of natural selection led to a reduction of the snout and a shrinking of our teeth, then what would replace these features to ensure that we could defend ourselves in the arms race that is the working life out in the natural world? Rock throwing extends the kill zone. With thrown weapons, humans learned to kill from a safe distance. What we lost in the length and sharpness of our canine teeth we gained in the strength of our throwing arms and hands able to grip a rock with precision and throw it on target with power within a range of thirty meters.

Humans came out of animality with the digging stick in hand. Chimpanzees employ them. At what point did hominids haft a sharp stone onto a digging stick and make a spear? Humans became spear throwers. When the Israelites fought the Philistines at the Valley of Elah, we are told, David slew Goliath. The giant carried to his death a "spear [that] was like a weaver's beam; and his spear's head weighed six hundred shekels of iron."[4] The first hero chronicled in Western literature is Achilles.[5] He was

---

1 John 8:7. Let he who is without guilt cast the first stone.
2 Dziadosz, Alexander. *Young Woman Sentenced to Death by Stoning in Sudan.* Reuters. Thursday, May 31, 2012. http://news.yahoo.com/young-woman-sentenced-death-stoning-sudan-174901763.html.
3 Human Planet. Video: In southern Kenya, Dorobo hunters allow a pride of lions to kill a wildebeest, then steal their dinner from right under the predators' noses.
4 I Sam. 17:7.
5 Homer. *Iliad. Book 16: 140-145.* As Patroclus prepared to go out in Achilles' armor to drive the Trojans back from burning the Achaean's ships, "Only the spear of the incomparable son of Aeacus he took not, the spear heavy and huge and strong; this no other of the Achaeans could wield, but Achilles alone was skilled

renowned for throwing a mighty bronze tipped spear of Pelian ash and it was the emblem of his unstoppable war craft. Chimps throw sticks and hit with sticks. Jabbing is rarer but the spear may be very ancient indeed. The archaeology is hazy to date. Jane Goodall says that if chimpanzees had guns and knew their function, they would use them.[1]

It was not our throwing arms alone that made us top predator on earth. While we are by no means the fastest runner in the animal kingdom, there is no creature we cannot outdistance. Humans can run down any animal that they keep up and moving without allowing it a chance to rest. Persistence hunting,[2] the running of a beast of prey to exhaustion, is found among many hunter-foragers. The Selknam of Patagonia ran down guanacos. The Tarahumara of Mexico, famous for running distances of over one hundred miles at a single stretch, run down deer. The Bushmen run down eland and giraffe. It has been determined that statistically, persistence hunting is as successful as any other hunting strategy.

It was our throwing arms and running legs that made us the top predator of the Earth, all in service to the mother-child bond back in camp around the hearth fire. It was our family life, and the selection for social intelligence requisite for family life, that truly made us human.

The social intelligence, the bottom up empathy and the altruism that were selected for in the evolution of human families at some point in time transformed us into guilty hunters. We began to attribute the same grief to our prey that we knew that we would feel if we were in their place as quarry. Humans kill in order to live. We realized that it caused sorrow, not only to the victim, but also to the kin of the prey. We realized that hunting damaged our spirits. Our most basic need drove us to survive tragically. Our emerging consciousness evolved the vision to see both sides of the predator-prey issue.

Primates also know what it is like to be prey. It too is in their genes. In *My Friends the Baboons*, pioneering Afrikaner ethologist Eugène Marais described baboon life as one of almost unbearable anxiety. Studies have shown that an average baboon witnesses at least one troop member fall to predation per month. Compound this experience over millions of years, generation to generation and it becomes plausible to speculate upon how the image of and proper reaction to a hereditary enemy can come to sleep in the genes of a prey creature.

to wield it, the Pelian spear of ash, that Cheiron had given to his dear father from the peak of Pelion, to be for the slaying of warriors." Iliad, Books 13-24. The Loeb Classical Library, Harvard University Press. 1999.

1 Hess, Elizabeth. *Nim Chimpsky: The Chimp Who Would Be Human*. Bantam Books, 2008. p. 193.

2 Liebenberg, Louis. *"Persistence Hunting by Modern Hunter-Gatherers,"* Current Anthropology, 47:6, 2006.

In *An Instinct for Dragons*,[1] bio-anthropologist David E. Jones explores "the possible evolutionary or biological basis of universal cultural experience"[2] in the long relationship that primates have had with the fatal trio of big cat, snake and eagle and how the experience of these predators has imprinted itself into primate genes. The experience of predation by these three hunters has accumulated in the DNA of primates, including *Homo sapiens*. Jones' goal is to explore the biological and evolutionary foundations for the dragon in human folklore. He asserts that the cumulative experience of predation of primates over millions of years accumulates in the DNA, the genes of hunted species. The big cat, snake and eagle merge in a cognitive process known as "chunking" to become a mental construct, an instinct for the dragon. Taking a cue from the English philosopher John Locke's *Essay Concerning Human Understanding*, Jones begins his discussion of "chunking" with, "Wherein the mind does these three things: first, it chooses a certain number (of specific ideas): secondly, it gives them connection and makes them into one idea: thirdly, it ties them together by a name." [3]The dragon is more than a creation of the imagination of an individual artist imitated universally like a hit song. It is primate experience of the world as that experience pours out of human mouths in story because predation and language are riveted into our DNA. The vervet monkey's instinctual communicative cries for big cats, eagles and snakes demonstrates this. "Primate responses to predators and to dangerous situations can be argued to result from natural selection."[4] The cry for a big cat causes a leap for slender branches. The cry for a raptor causes a leap to the ground or a scurry for the bushes. The cry for a snake causes the vervets to stand up and mob the serpentine intruder. They do this from birth. There is no teaching. Natural selection etched this response into the DNA of the vervets and it is passed generation to generation hereditarily.

Jones is silent upon epigenetics, upon how the molecules clothing DNA encourage or retard the expression of genes in response to environmental influences and how the environmental experience of one generation can affect ascending generations even when the descendants do not directly experience what their forefathers did. Epigenetics bolsters Jones' notion of the dragon in folklore and provides it with a possible mechanism to account, perhaps only in part, for its existence and universality. Epigenetics lifts the folkloric motif of the dragon out of the ranks of previous amorphous mental constructs such as the id and the archetype because it indicates a plausible direction for the dragon to be chemically true in humans. The folklore motif

1 Jones, David E. *An Instinct for Dragons.* Routledge, 29 West 35th Street, New York, NY 10001. 2002.
2 Ibid., p.48.
3 Ibid., pp. 55-56.
4 Ibid., p. 53.

of the dragon exists as a biogram, a "bundle of adaptations, social relations and behaviors that are transmitted genetically..."[1]

The Deadly Trio

The dragon of folklore has also been reinforced by our day to day experience of bones and fossils. In *The First Fossil Hunters*,[2] Adrienne Mayor scoured ancient classical sources and discovered a wealth of references to "giant" bones that can be nothing other than dinosaur fossils. Greece stands at the crossroads of

1 Ibid. p. 59.
2 Mayor, Adrienne. *The First Fossil Hunters*. Princeton University Press. 41 William Street, Princeton, NJ 08540, 2000. p. 205.

dinosaur migration routes. The island of Samos is particularly rich in fossils that stick up out of the ground at the feet of the most casual observer. In the first century A.D., Pliny the Elder noted in his *Natural History* that after an earthquake on the island of Crete, a gigantic skeleton 22 meters long was uncovered. People wondered if it were not the bones of Orion, the Hunter who had been accidently killed by an arrow by Artemis, the Huntress, while swimming off shore .

The universal folklore motif of the dragon is an imaginative structure of the human mind that is also securely rooted in our DNA through language and our long experience of predation. It was reinforced in our daily lives by bearing witness to giant fossil bones left sticking out of embankments for our awe and wonder since our ancestors descended from the trees.

Marais goes on in *My Friends the Baboons* to describe a thrilling ambush of a marauding leopard that reads like the exploits of a pair of baboon hero twins. Two sexually mature but unmated young males lay in wait, hidden in some rocks. While one closed with the big cat fang to fang, his partner leapt upon his back. He snapped the leopard's neck with his long canines and killed it — but not before the dying leopard had gutted his brave companion throat to groin with its hind claws.[1]One baboon sacrificed himself for the other the way Castor took a spear for Pollux before Zeus set them in the stars as the constellation Gemini, forever chasing after Taurus the Bull and Orion, the Hunter.

1 Marais, Eugène N. *My Friends the Baboons*. Anthony Blond, Great Britain 1971. p. 44.

Primates know what it is like to be prey. The empathy and altruism selected for in camp also forced hunter-foragers to come to grips with what their prey felt out on the hunt. An acknowledgment of sorrow, reverence began to become part of hunting ritual. Hunter-foragers are well documented for feeling pity for their prey. Witness Black Elk of the Lakota nation who participated in the rubbing out of the 7th Cavalry under Colonel Custer, as he reminisces about his childhood:

> So I thought I would forget about it and shoot something. There was a bush and a little bird sitting in it; but just as I was going to shoot, I felt queer again, and remembered that I was to be like a relative with the birds. So I did not shoot. Then I went on down toward a creek, feeling foolish because I had let the little bird go, and when I saw a green frog sitting there, I just shot him right away. But when I picked him up by the legs, I thought: "Now I have killed him," and it made me want to cry.[1]

Hunter-foragers are also well known for the reverence that they show the kill. Again, witness Black Elk hunting with his father.

> While we were butchering and I was eating some liver, I felt sorry that we had killed these animals and thought that we ought to do something in return. So I said: "Father, should we not offer one of these to the wild things?" He looked hard at me again for a while. Then he placed one of the deer with its head to the east, and, facing the west, he raised his hand and cried, "Hey-hey" four times and prayed like this: "Grandfather, the Great Spirit, behold me! To all the wild things that eat flesh, this I have offered that my people may live and the children grow up with plenty."[2]

East is toward sunrise, the rebirth of day, the rebirth of life. Man only kills in order to live and prosper his family and regrets all pain caused by this awful necessity.

One of the most charming moments of Joseph Campbell's interviews with Bill Moyers in *The Power of Myth*[3] is when he relates *The Buffalo Maiden's Tale*. For the Blackfeet Indians, a mystic bond was created between man and beast. The food animal agrees to sacrifice itself to the reverent hunter if the hunter agrees to perform the proper revivifying rituals over the kill. This makes sacrifice out of slaughter. A proper kill is a prayer for reincarnation. It is a mythological motif found the world over in hunter-forager societies.

---

1 Neidhardt, John. *Black Elk Speaks*. University of Nebraska Press 1979. p. 51.
2 ibid. p. 65.
3 Campbell, Joseph and Bill Moyers. *The Power of Myth*. DVD. Mystic Fire Video, 2001.

Just as we gained insight into the myth of the hero by viewing it as a speech act, let us now take a look at the daily round of some hunter-foragers from that same perspective. Observers of animal behavior out in the field make every effort to link vocalizations with behavior. When we attempt this with some Bushmen still living in the traditional lifeway, what do we see and hear? John Marshall's poignant film *The Hunters*[1] a view of Bushman hunting techniques, provides modern witnesses the last best view possible of our ancestor's ancient lifeway.

We see nearly naked men rising from bed and taking leave of their camps, bearing weapons out into the dangerous world in order to hunt and bring back meat to expectant kin. After a period of wandering and following the tracks of elands or giraffes, and if they are lucky, the hunters make a kill and butcher it. Their dangerous work done, what they can shoulder, they take back home to their family. If the kill is grand, then the family might walk to the hunter instead.

The daily round of the typical hunter fits the pattern of the myth of the hero, Leavetaking–Adventure–Homecoming. Boys start hunting on their own at about the same age as heroes in myth go out on their adventures. Back in camp, we hear the hunters speaking about what they do and how they do what they do. Like people everywhere past and present, they largely talk about their work, which for them, mainly comprises stories about the

1 Marshall, John. The Hunters. Film, 1957. Directed by: Robert Gardner, Smithsonian-Harvard Peabody expedition1952-53.

hunt. "[M]en talk endlessly about hunting as they sit together repairing their equipment or poisoning their arrows. They recount over and over memorable episodes of past hunts, hear each other's news about recent hunts, and make plans...[The stories]...were told at night as people sat around their fires. The stories that were told were myth-like accounts of actual hunts, and these were told over and over."[1] In terms of natural selection, it is easy to see the adaptive value for creatures of being able to speak about their work, about how they fill their bellies and the bellies of their loved ones. Hunting techniques, tactics, prey behavior and past experiences can be shared and cultural wisdom accumulated. Being able to describe the location of prey and where a kill was left because it was too heavy to carry back to camp without help. How a beloved family member was killed or injured, or where one lies bleeding and who has to be rescued.

Seen from the perspective of evolution and natural history in search of emergent features, the myth of the hero almost becomes predictable leisure speech. The hearth fire is burning. The transformative power of fire is a constant before their eyes. The billowing smoke is a plaything of the imagination like clouds in the sky. Dreams get mixed with daily activities as people tell stories about the adventures of their ancestors, who were hunter-foragers just like they are. This is universal because not only is it in our genes but it is also reinforced on a daily basis. The only thing certain about life is that humans will wake up hungry and be forced to leave the safety of home in order to satisfy that inexorable drive by tragic means. People have forgotten that when they sing the myth of the hero, they are not venturing into the realms of fantasy. They are singing about themselves and reimagining their daily lives in grander terms. The parallel is exact, down to the violent encounter where the hero slays the monster just as the hunter kills his prey. The myth of the hero is nothing more than the daily round of the hunter-forager life rendered verbally, extravagantly. It became stereotypic though retelling.

The universality and continuing appeal of the myth of the hero is due to the fact that the individual life of humans on Earth has not fundamentally changed since our ancestors descended from the trees in spite of our science and civilization. In this respect, life never will change. Modern humans, like their hunter-forager ancestors, must leave the comfort of home, win the day at work and get back safely to share their gains with their family though where our ancestors threw spears, we twist wrenches and finger keyboards. The myth of the hero addresses the fundamental issue of life, day by day, birth to death, in words and imagination. Leavetaking-Adventure-

---

1 Thomas, Elizabeth Marshall. *The Old Way: A Story of the First People.* Sarah Crichton Press. 19 Union Square West, New York NY 10003. 2006. p. 95, 104.

Homecoming is the pattern for the daily round of many species. The myth of the hero was ancient in humanity long before we learned to sing it. As a species, we emerged from animality with the myth of the hero already in us, struggling for expression. For some people, such a conception of the myth of the hero debases the grand to the commonplace. For others, it elevates the profane to the sacred and pin points exactly where the animal soul ends and the true mystery of spirit begins.

People who just have adventures are not necessarily heroes. People who are merely brave and justify their violent means by appealing to so-called heroic values are not necessarily heroes. The tragedy of violent solutions applied to human problems was clearly summarized by the medieval Icelandic writer of *Njal's Saga*, the chronicle of the burning to death of an extended family in their home in order to satisfy honor and the thirst for vengeance by their aggrieved neighbors.[1] "The hand is soon sorry that it has struck." The Hatfields and McCoys perverted the heroic value of coming to the aid of a family member to the great profit of the local undertakers. Cool Hand Luke's repeated escapes from the chain gang were hollow endeavors because he had no home to get back to. The danger he braves is of no service to anyone, not even to himself. His truest prison is the isolation in which he imagines himself to exist. The contemporary anti-hero actually has very little to do with the myth of the hero. It is more a critique of the civilization in which the anti-hero finds him or herself lost and rejecting home, a civilization which makes it easier for the individual to be a sensual rather than a spiritual creature.

And if neuroscience can plot the song on the brain map of the songbird and if genetics can trace the influence exerted by the environment upon the expression of an individual's DNA, not only during his or her own lifetime, but also down into the lives of their grandchildren, it can be said, in theory, at the very least, that the myth of the hero, as a speech act, as revealed in its evolutionary history, is a reflection of the psychological imprint of the Earth upon the individual. It reveals the hunter-forager human kernel, the orientation of our being. It speaks to the species as much as to the individual. It is beyond gender. It speaks to the mother-child bond and the hunter's life in service to that bond. The myth of the hero is the overarching, guiding schema, the inescapable deep structure of the human mind. It is the compulsive force behind our personal thinking. It is what we do in life on a daily basis and what we speak about at leisure when we tell stories, the one and only story, everywhere the same no matter the terrain, the technology or the time. Fall or fly, the myth of the hero marks the threshold where the human animal leaves folklore behind and arrives at his or her own spirit.

---

1 Magnuson, Magnus and Hermann Paulson. *Njal's Saga*. Penguin Classics 1979.

SPIRIT

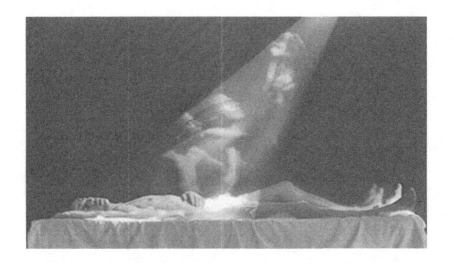

BRICOLAGE

Sometimes light must be shined from many angles to reveal the cogent details of a highly textured structure. The above words form an argument with support drawn from a diversity of disciplines and perspectives. It is a review of many commonly held assumptions in the manner that detectives do with cold case files. Some of it is a validation of common knowledge and common sense. Some of it is a valorization in the sense that Eliade meant the term; that is, a mythological insight that imposes meaning upon and gives encouragement to the daily struggle for existence. Some of it remains a Sassetti, a tantalizing but unprovable hunch. It is something of a jumbled assemblage, a patchwork of materials and sources, but none pushed too far outside of their original intention. Every effort has been made to curb enthusiasm for maverick reckoning. There is no reliance upon any extreme take from any subject from which material has been drawn. There is no appeal to esoterica or anonymous insider sources. It is a tinkering, in short, a bricolage (to borrow a term from Lévi-Strauss).

However, the Orion Complex is a more than a do-it-yourself construction from a diverse range of things that just happen to be available. The oppositions that it attempts to resolve by means of common sense logic are between academic disciplines rather than between lexical antonyms. It is more a proof of concept than a solid proof. It suggests a line of possible future research. It is a surrender of the old guard of poetry to the new guard of neuroscience regarding its most treasured feature, the myth of the hero. It is an attempt to outline that the myth of the hero is an "inheritable psychic structure," to echo Freud. I accept the criticism that it could be dubbed "armchair anthropology." It represents the tapestry that analogy has woven, analogies that are objective rather than subjective. This tapestry takes the structures of two universals, the daily round of hunter-foragers from work life and the myth of the hero from leisure life, and weaves them into a genuine homology which shares descent from a common ancestor and historical and genetic linkages down the ages. Human hunting and human storytelling evolved hand in hand out of animality and both endeavors share essential features with behaviors found in many species. It is a grand, unifying perspective with an insight from all vantage points. I also maintain that, although my evidence is largely gleaned from the research of others, my conclusions are original and can weather challenge. "We know the stories; we know their endings, the metaphors, the metonymies, all. It is the exhilaration of experiencing something new at the same time it is recognition or what we know already. What is inventive, what is singular is what the storyteller does with the familiar."[1] My only hope is that the thoughts and speculations presented here merit archiving in book form at the cost of even a single tree. The good of this work might be questionable. The good of a living tree is beyond question.

The hunt for the myth of the hero began in metaphysics. Mythology is generally seen as originating in the more spiritual realms of human thinking. However, a continuum of empirical perspectives has plausibly rooted the myth of the hero in every part of human life and history down to our DNA. The medieval churchmen Thomas Aquinas and Duns Scotus wondered if people were just matter capable of thought. For purposes of argument, something of this order has been attempted here.

The myth of the hero comes out of the pages of books as the imprint of the Earth upon the human hunter-forager's psyche. The Earth is the executive function of each individual creature. This mastery plays itself out in humans as the myth of the hero. Perhaps the complexity of the issue will forever remain too great to fully unravel chemically. Chuang Tzu claimed that the limited mind is incapable of apprehending the limitless universe. Even Harry Cliff, a particle physicist at the European Organization for Nuclear Research stated, "The next few years may tell us whether we'll be able to continue to increase our understanding of nature or whether maybe, for the first time in the history of science, we could be facing questions that we cannot answer."[2]

1 Scheub, Harold. *Story*. The University of Wisconsin Press, Madison WI 53718, 1998. p. 14.
2 Orwick, Jennifer. *The Two Most Dangerous Numbers in the Universe Are Threatening the End of Physics*. Business Insider. http://www.businessinsider.com/the-end-of-physics-as-we-know-it-2016-1. 01.14.16.

However, now that we have fully described our rigidly materialistic perspective, we find ourselves back in the metaphysical realm. Materialism appears to have turned back upon itself. Like the worm Ouroboros, it is a serpent that eateth its own tail.[1] The path to truth cannot begin with a false step. Wherever it leads must be accepted. What are the implications of the myth of the hero in the light of animal behavior and genetics? What does it say about science and spirit for the individual searcher in his or her life?

The words above constitute a reduction of sorts, but not one that purports to explain away the myth of the hero as merely the sum of its parts. This lands us right back on the note with which we started this complex melody. Paradoxically, the drive to root this artifact of human spirituality in the material world and in our physical being is in itself spiritually revealing.

How so?

1 Eddison, E.R. *The Worm Ouroboros*. Ballantine Books, (1926) 1967.

The Human Home

Science obtains knowledge by measuring perceptions. These are extended by means of engineered devices and the results are rendered to numbers. By flame, scalpel, scale, lens, battery and prism, revelations are interpreted by calculus. Rendered into everyday language, equations struggling to express change through time come out of the human mouth as myth minus spirits. Experiments and results are reproducible, if not in exact terms, then at least in statistically significant ones. Skepticism is the guiding light of science. Ideally, assumptions are always under review.

Spirituality, mythology, religion obtain knowledge and revelation by means of rich inner experiences of charismatic individuals. Jacob dreamed of the angel's ladder. Paul had a vision of Jesus on the road to Damascus. Black Elk fell ill and had what could only be described as a hallucination equal in grandeur to the biblical Book of Revelations. Moses was the only human acknowledged by the Judeo-Christian tradition of speaking directly with God after Adam and Eve. All of these rich inner experiences were transmitted to humanity by means of story. They are maintained by perpetuating story. If the stories stop being told, the knowledge will disappear from the cultural landscape. The stories cannot be corroborated based upon internal facts and procedures. They must be accepted on their own internal logic, on faith, if they are deemed to be true.

Jesus, as portrayed in the book of Matthew,[1] understood the use of story. In response to his disciples wondering why he told the gathering crowd so many parables, Jesus explained that the stories were for the illumination of less spiritually developed worshippers, not necessarily for those already "given to

---

1 Matt.13.10-11.

know." The logical implication is that the stories point toward a hidden truth rather than represent the historical, material and literal details of those stories as they form the truth itself apart from reality. How would Jesus respond to the notion that the map is not the territory? Would he sanction worship of the stories themselves, isolated from the unseen truths to which they allude?

But to return to our main argument: faith and skepticism, spirituality and science, meditation and experiment have uncovered startlingly similar insights in spite of their profoundly differing methods of inquiry. However, the vast distances between the extremes can only be bridged by analogy, that is, a carefully constructed string of analogies.

Many of the assumptions of hunter-foragers concerning human origins and relations with fellow creatures upon the Earth resonate harmoniously with the pre-Socratics and cutting edge science. Hunter-forager mythmakers rooted human origins, along with all other forms of life, in the material world, the earth, water, wind, and fire. Physics posits that the heavier elements that comprise the organic materials of our bodies were created by evolutionary processes of fusion in the center of collapsing-exploding suns. From here, it is a logical extrapolation to place humans into the family of animals and hunter-foragers did so. Is it mere coincidence that the ancient and modern perspectives align in this regard? Do the divergent methods by which myth and science confirm knowledge negate all serious considerations for analogy between the two perspectives? Or does empirical science here validate the intuition of myth and does phantasmagoric myth anticipate the rationality of science? In comparing their conclusions regarding human origins and our place in the cosmos, in what manner are science and spirituality not speaking about the same thing ultimately? Our hopes for the future are rooted in our trust of the past. Intuition and rationality clasp hands in the myth of the hero.

Humans are not strangers sojourning as spiritual exiles upon the Earth. To claim that humans are children of the Earth and relative to all other creatures with whom we share the Earth can no longer be viewed as a mere romanticism of priests and poets and primitives. Human unity with Earth and animal is demonstrable fact. *Homo sapiens* is an evolved animal species. What we do to the Earth and to our fellow creatures, we do to our home and to our family and to our very selves. Conservation is not mere jolly tree-hugging, nor is it the smug moral superiority of idle ingrates. It is an intelligent recognition that appreciates the long term effects of science and civilization upon the planet. It stands opposed to the heedless, short term conservatism under the aegis of fiduciary responsibility more expected of an accounting firm, where all that matters are figures that balance in the black during any given fiscal period, regardless of the long range conditions created out in the world. This ethos is incapable of creating a pragmatic government with a long range view. A geosophy, a love of Earth wisdom from the ground up, should come to dominate humanity through science and spirit. Will our consumer civilization align its course with that of the Earth or will the Earth itself have to discipline humanity back into its proper place in the family of life?

Humans can never live outside of nature, no matter how high up in the skyscrapers our apartments may one day reach. I hope and pray that these words that I have written will strike a green blow for the good of the Earth, for our children and for our sibling species. This is science and this is spirit. It results in sustainability. And until it becomes economics and politics too, human civilization will view the natural world as its battleground to plunder and misery will be the most predictable outcome of human activity. Human civilization has been an historical phenomenon. To sustain itself, it had better become an ecological one.

Or will we continue, even as our digital interconnectivity burgeons, to sow fear of one another? There is only profit in this fear for the few of us who make money the study of their lives. In our day through the internet, humans on all continents are aware of the material possibilities of the good life. The Declaration of Independence has been read in many languages. Each person who reads it cannot help but yearn for an opportunity at the "pursuit of happiness" too. The hunter-forager today might be a clerk and a clerk needs a job but he or she is still a hunter-forager at heart. E.O. Wilson says humans have Paleolithic emotions, medieval institutions and godlike technology.[1] Societies need governments in order to keep the roads open and free. Nothing happens without clear lines of transport and communication. That requires some compulsory collective effort. Individuals need freedom to dream and act upon their dreams. It is still the same old story for the individual. How to play your part on the team with no loss of self is part of the "discontent" of civilization. Is there a technological bill of rights? A material one? A nutritional one?

Is our fate as a global civilization one in which, as the population swells, we lurch quasi-democratically between oligarchy and socialism, a thieves' outing in the lifeboat? Or will humanity wolf and gulp until the resources are depleted? Will we all end up living in mazes of treeless slums with narrow corridors coast to coast? We can only submit our ways to the judgment of the Earth. If we are out of sync geosophically, we can only undermine the ground of our own being. Earth would be a garden without human beings.

---

1 Wilson, E.O. Harvard Magazine, Sep 09, 2009. Public discussion between Wilson and James Watson moderated by NPR correspondent Robert Krulwich.

What would we be without Earth? Is our civilization a facilitator of or a distraction from individual spiritual search?

There is a spectacular denizen of California tide pools that goes by the imposing name of *Hermissenda crassicornis*. It is an electric blue and orange sea slug with wavy appendages on its back called ceratae. At the white tips of these ceratae are cellular structures called cnidosacs. Housed in the cnidosacs are nematocysts, microscopic harpoons that hook and inject venom into the mouth of any creature that dares to try to make a meal of *Hermissenda*.

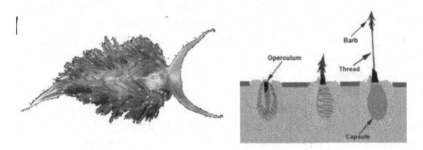

Hermissenda Crassicornis and Nematocyst

The truly amazing thing about the nematocysts of this Aeolid is their origin. *Hermissendas* do not grow their own nematocysts; they obtain them from their prey, in this case, the Proliferating Anemone. Instead of digesting the nematocysts along with their surrounding tissues, *Hermissendas* sequester them and transport them out to the tips of their ceratae via perpendicular tubes that line their guts called diverticulae. There they are incorporated into *Hermissenda's* metabolism whole and eventually function like they did back where they came from originally. It is a case of an intracellular symbiotic association called kleptoplasty. It would be like a human swallowing a baboon fang and metabolizing it as a sharp projection growing out of the fist for the purposes of attack and defense.[1]

Another example of the 'theft of body' of an intact organelle is the so-called "solar powered leaves that crawl." The marine sea slug, *Elysia chlorotica*, sequesters the chloroplasts of the algae *Vaucheria litorea*. These kleptoplasts reside within the cytoplasm of the digestive cells of Elysia and carry out photosynthesis. The sea slug provides carbon dioxide for the chloroplasts and the chloroplasts provide nutrients for the sea slug. Is there is a redirecting of animal nuclear encoded proteins to the chloroplasts as well as some lateral gene transfer from algae to sea slug? If so, this example of symbiosis represents a true mixing of separate genomes. Perhaps it is also a modern recapitulation of the ancient phagocytotic events theorized to have been the origin of the chloroplast in plant cells and the mitochondria in animal cells. It certainly speaks to the issue that the dividing line between species is more blurred than most of us are aware.

Symbiosis as a driving force in evolution is the theme of Frank Ryan's wonderful book, *Darwin's Blind Spot*.[2] It is a corollary mechanism to explain the staggering radiation of species descended from a common ancestor that Darwin's gradualism could not adequately account for. The discoveries of the pioneering role of bacteria and the influence of viruses upon the human genome could well signal that there is a paradigm shift in the offing about what it means to be a an individual human being on planet Earth.

Although it is completely unstated, there is almost a spiritual quality to *Darwin's Blind Spot*, perhaps more by content than by design. This spirituality is neither a violation of nor a negation of our senses. It resonates with a holistic view of life on this Earth. This oneness is expressed across such divergent times and venues as in the cutting edge physics of entangled subatomic particles whose forces are instantaneous across galaxies, as well as in the myth of the hero, whose manifestations are universal in human history.

Mary Shelley alluded to all of this back in 1819, albeit dimly, in her classic horror story. Doctor Frankenstein was likened to a modern Prometheus, the Greek Titan who stole fire for mankind. Like Prometheus, Shelley suffered for her audacity. Her life was nothing but tragic after she wrote *Frankenstein* at age nineteen. She created the central myth of the modern age though *Frankenstein* was meant to be taken as a crime against all tradition in general. Her work clearly stated the existential dilemma of modern man and the

---

1 Lindsey, Tabitha and Ángel Valdés. The Model Organsim Hermissenda crassicornis (Gastropoda: Heterobranchia) Is a Species Complex. April 22, 2016. Plos One. http://journals.plos.org/plosone/article?id=10.1371/journal.pone.0154265.

2 Ryan, Frank. *Darwin's Blind Spot*. Houghton Mifflin Company, 2002.

terrible inroads science was making into the notion of individuality. Inspired by Italian physician Luigi Galvani's work that demonstrated the electrical nature of muscular contraction in dead frog legs, Shelley imagined a human monster stitched together of parts harvested in graveyards and reanimated by the divine force of lightning. She was branded as the creator of an atheistic vision of the unsettling unity of the physical world. The individual spirit was ripped to shreds and loosed from its moorings in the cosmos she envisioned. It has not fully found its way back to safe anchorage since.

Art imitates life, and life imitates art. On March 14, 1970 at the Metro Health Medical Center of Cleveland Ohio, Doctor Robert White, Professor of Neurological Surgery at Case Western Reserve University, headed a team that successfully transplanted the head of one rhesus monkey onto the body of another. The patient awoke and promptly almost bit the finger off of one of Doctor White's assistants. The operation connected the blood vessels to the brain but did not connect the nerves to the spine. The monkey could not move its body but its face was animated for the eight days that it survived.

Doctor White believed that he had proved that the procedure was viable and that all that was lacking was further experience in order to perfect it. If the procedure could be made to work with rhesus monkeys, it would work with humans. In our day and age where human heart valves are replaced with ones harvested from pigs, the general public is still shocked by Doctor White's experiment. It rattles our notions of the individuality of our bodies and our souls. Is it ironic that this actual "Frankenstein" was a devote Catholic. Nothing much came from Doctor White's experiments in radical unity and their results are not well known. His research funding dried up and he went back to performing heart transplants until he retired.[1]

1   White, Robert Dr. http://userwww.sfsu.edu/art511_j/emerging.2001.f/kerrymaster/kerryartproposal2f/headtransplant.html.

ESEMPLASTIC

If a dilemma cannot be reduced to poetry, it is probably beyond universal understanding. We comprehend the world around us by means of story and manipulate ourselves, our fellows and our environment by our capacity to narrate sequences of events. As acts of speech, metaphor, narrative and story have always helped to get a lot of work done for humans while they were out on the hunt, down on the farm, up in the factory, and inside the office. Story has entertained us around the old campfire. And nowadays, in front of that technological evolution of fire, the television. Luckily, poetry can still help us cut through the knots that we cannot untie.

Humans are animals and constitute a single family of life. We are made of the same elements as earth and water and air and we are both driven by the same fire as the sun and the lightning. This knowledge is ancient myth and modern science. It is as fundamental as food. If clothes make the man, food becomes him, literally. Food comes from the Earth. We can make mere feces with it, or spirit. All this speaks to a cosmos that is radically one. Every "part" is somehow connected to every other "part" in time and space. There is only metamorphosis. Finality begins where imagination ends. The work of the poet is to reveal this fundamental, often unsettling truth, again and again, in infinite ways.

Wordsworth, his imagination bent on loss and sorrow, saw the crushing materiality and the empty oneness of the science of his day thus:

> The world is too much with us; late and soon,
> Getting and spending, we lay waste our powers
> Little we see in nature that is ours
> We have given our hearts away, a sordid boon!
> This sea that bares her bosom to the moon;

The winds that will be howling at all hours,
And are up gathered now like sleeping flowers;
For this, for everything, we are out of tune;
It moves us not.— Great God! I'd rather be
A Pagan suckled in a creed outworn;
So might I, standing on this pleasant lea,
Have glimpses that would make me less forlorn
Have sight of Proteus rising from the sea;
Or hear old Triton blow his wreathed horn.

Here science divorces humanity from its true nature. We no longer live our lives in a manner in which we are moved by our surroundings. The rectitude of empirical knowledge is not worth the loss of heartfelt connection to our world. Is the Earth no more than a ball-shaped stone circling around an even bigger one that is on fire, with everything floating on nothing? Even falling back upon old mythological, superstitious conventions beats living with the more unsettling implications which science was revealing to the senses. Spiritual beings were observed neither in the telescope out among the stars, nor under the microscope among the protozoa. Deprived of traditional founts of imagination, the world seemed so cold and lonely and dehumanized. Wordsworth was no futurist. He saw science as de-centering us from our imagined place in nature, as diminishing the human capacity for awe and wonder. Science provided a sordid, materialistic oneness with no possibility of angels.

Consider Jose Blanco White's sonnet *To Night*, which the Romantic poet Samuel Taylor Coleridge, who wrote *The Rime of the Ancient Mariner*, called the finest example of the form in the English language.

Mysterious Night! when our first parent knew
Thee from report divine, and heard thy name,
Did he not tremble for this lovely frame,
This glorious canopy of light and blue?
Yet 'neath a curtain of translucent dew,
Bathed in the rays of the great setting flame,
Hesperus with the host of heaven came,
And lo! Creation widened in man's view.
Who could have thought such darkness lay concealed
Within thy beams, O Sun! or who could find,
Whilst fly and leaf and insect stood revealed,
That to such countless orbs thou mad'st us blind!
Why do we then shun death with anxious strife?
If Light can thus deceive, wherefore not Life?

Out of the classical, Biblical tradition comes this intricate, ironic analogy that alludes to the oneness of the cosmos and the hope that lies at the heart of the mystery.

Sun:Light:Life:Blindness::Stars:Night:Death:Revelation

White was a futurist. He saw into the very heart of the problem of living life as an individual human being, even once the fundamental oneness of the cosmos is accepted.

Esemplastic is a word with a bit of a criminal record. Coleridge stands accused of lifting a term from the German philosopher Schelling, *ineinsbildung,* a compound of in+one+cultural tradition or education. He then translated it back into Greek, and anglicized it as es+em+plastic. "Plastic" in Greek has the meaning of to form, to shape, to mold. Etymologically, denotatively, esemplastic means "into one shape." Connotatively, *ineinsbildung* means an interweaving of opposites. Esemplastic is an adjective most often associated with poetic imagination and connotatively means an object being molded into a unity, simplifying the difficult, the mysterious power to shape all into one, to extract hidden details and meanings from this fundamental oneness. Esemplastic is an unlovely sound with a wonderful meaning. It all relates to the grand oneness of the cosmos. It is one of the major tasks of the poet to explore this hidden reality and make it common knowledge among men.[1]

No one expressed the esemplasticity of the cosmos with greater audacity, clarity or humor than Chuang Tzu, one of the great sages of Taoism. The Tao, the oneness, is referred to as the Way.

Master Tung-kuo asked Chuang Tzu, "This thing called the Way — where does it exist?"

Chuang Tzu said, "There's no place it doesn't exist."

"Come," said Master Tung-kuo, "you must be more specific!"

"It is in the ant."

"As low a thing as that?"

"It is in the panic grass."

"But that's lower still!"

"It is in the tiles and shards."

"How can it be so low?"

"It is in the piss and shit.[2]

---

1 Coleridge, Samuel Taylor. *Biographia Literaria.* Princeton University Press; First Paperback Edition (February 1, 1985).
2 Watson, Burton. *Basic Writings of Chuang Tzu.* Columbia University Press, April 15, 1996.

All humans are siblings. All humans are related to the animals from the bacteria on up to chimpanzees. All creatures are made of the same stuff as trees, rocks, oceans, stars and hurricanes. Doubting Thomas put it like this. "The kingdom of the Father is spread out upon the earth, and men do not see it."[1] Are we finally at the threshold of the spirit? A thought experiment puts this radical materialism into a day to day perspective.

Imagine a person sitting in a café enjoying a cup of coffee. Looking out the window, this person suddenly witnesses a small child get run down by a car and killed instantly. How might this person react? This would depend upon his or her own personal spiritual theory of the cosmos.

A theist might ask how could God allow such a thing to happen to an innocent child. A theist must surrender to the mystery and contradictions of any answer that is based upon superhuman beings functioning as powerful arbiters of his or her personal fate.

An atheist might ask how anyone could believe in a God who permits such things to happen. To create by miracle and then watch your creations suffer and die by whimsy? In light of manifold contradictions, an atheist must reject the muddled mystery in order to stay true to his or her rational mind.

An agnostic might ask, if there is a God somewhere, how could things like this happen? An agnostic teeters between his or her perceptions and his or her hopes and dreams. It was Darwin's bulldog, Thomas Huxley, who coined the term in 1869. From Greek he took *a*, "without," and *gnosis*, "knowledge," and formed agnostic. "Agnosticism is of the essence of science, whether ancient or modern. It simply means that a man shall not say he knows or believes that which he has no scientific grounds for professing to know or believe."[2]

Blind faith is impossible and even out of sorts with human evolutionary design. So is abandoning all spiritual search. How so?

Both theists and atheists have made up their minds upon a fundamental question that cannot be answered fully by the human heart and mind. Both positions require leaps of faith. They are opposite sides of the same coin. They represent a certain weariness in the face of enduring mystery. The extremes of both are shrill and close minded. They both reason as if faith and rationality are by nature at odds. What makes these points of view antagonistic is their insistence that they represent mutually exclusive truths. Both vested interests, pulpit and laboratory, find their supremacy over their believers threatened by one another's point of view. The difference is more politics than logic.

---

1 Patterson, Steven J. and James M. Robinson. *The Gospel of Thomas.* Fragment 113. http://gnosis.org/naghamm/nhl_thomas.htm.
2 Dixon, Thomas. Science and Religion: A Very Short Introduction. Oxford University Press, 2008. p. 63.

Do agnostics do nothing more than dither in the ground left between theism and atheism? Or is it the default spiritual perspective of a hunting, foraging creature formed by evolutionary forces? For the purposes of argument, humans, both physically and behaviorally, can be largely accounted for by means of material perspectives. What about spiritually? If humans evolved out of the materials of Earth, what did the Earth produce in us? Science and experience reveal that humans are hunters and seekers subject to recurring hunger. Curiosity and the drive to search our surroundings are in us from birth. The structure of the human mind also has an evolutionary history and development. It is linked to our physical evolution. Curiosity can be likened to mental hunger. The hunger of the belly can never be fully satisfied nor satisfied once and for all. Curiosity can never be fully satisfied nor satisfied once and for all. Curiosity is an assumption that requires constant reviewing as living augments experience. The search for spiritual connection is a journey with more rest stops than final destinations. Evolution and life as a hunter-forager upon Earth have taught humans that questions, like hunger, always recur. True questions remain questions. Spiritual hunger is a consequence, intended or unintended, of human evolutionary design. It evolved in response to Earth's requirement of courage in each life lived. Agnosticism is the true, heartbreaking, uplifting spirit of a hunter-forager. It might be called an exploratory spirituality that enthusiastically questions its own beliefs until the mystery itself teaches you how and where and when to bend a knee. It is too busy seeking to rest in much argument along the paths of discovery.

THE END AND THE BEGINNING

Ashes to ashes and dust to dust. Even after laying out all the evidence side by side, there are those who still reject the unified, symbiotic view of life and humans' place in this world that science and ancient spirituality proclaim. For many disbelievers, it is an intolerable violation of sacred scripture. For many it is not even very important information because the unified, symbiotic, pantheistic view of life does not address the major concern of their existence; that is, their personal mortality and their personal fate upon dying. Most people care more about what will happen to them than where they came from. Ashes to ashes and dust to dust is no truth upon which to build a spirituality capable of succoring a person in the hour of deepest need.

In the harshest glare of science, a human being seems to be not much more than a "pig's head on a stick,"[1] an acquisitive intelligence cut off from its foundations by the flimsiest of constructions, subject, like any other creature, to the "conqueror worm"[2] once his underpinnings fail him. Just another entity among entities all hunting each other, making body or feces with their food, nothing beyond that can be demonstrated empirically. Freud saw religion as a corral for the instincts, a wish fulfilling illusion that soothes our fears of death but which will soon vanish as scientific reason becomes more widespread.[3] Humans may lack the immortality of Tolkien's elves,[4] but for science, human fate, like the fate of the elves, is tied to the fate of the Earth. And that is the rub. Most individual humans

---

1 Golding, William. *Lord of the Flies*. Perigee Trade, 2011.
2 Poe, Edgar Allen. *Complete Works. The Conqueror Worm*. Create Space, 2011.
3 Freud, Sigmund. *The Future of an Illusion*. Create Space, 2011.
4 Tolkien, J.R.R. *The Silmarillion*. Houghton, Mifflin Harcourt, 2004.

will never be satisfied with tying their personal fate to the fate of the Earth. Why is that?

Death breaks our hearts, yet we reject its finality. There is a stubborn hope of continuance beyond mortality in the heart of humans that cannot be extinguished no matter the impressive list of facts that seem to militate against it. To many people it would seem like a violation to even try. Others claim that this rejection is only childish wish fulfillment in denial of death. But if this were all there were to it, how could we, once we mature, forget for a single instant that we are born to die and that those whom we love are born to die as well? In light of the tragic finality of it all, what is the point of subjecting ourselves to the arduous business of living? It requires great endurance and effort to continue on, day by day, caring for loved ones, but we are also capable of setting aside our cares and celebrating this life in our leisure and of doing things unselfishly for others. How can the pain of dying and the horrors of decomposition ever leave our minds if that is the only end to life? Is our pleasure-seeking consciousness that distractible, moment to moment? Nietzsche hated hope, for he claimed that it only prolonged the individual's suffering.

Or does this hope that "springs eternal in the human heart" reflect our dim understanding of a vast, inchoate, steadying truth which resides at the core of our thinking; that however much things seem to change, nothing is ever lost, somehow, some way? Our teeth will be the last part of our body to decompose in the soil, but they too will ultimately rejoin the flow of material cycles. So what happens to our thoughts upon dying? Is our visionary thinking, for all its scope and reach, ultimately trapped inside the bones of our skulls and subject to decomposition as well? Or is there something happening in our being that lies underneath our thinking and functions like the soil supports the roots of a tree? Can this hope which resonates so harmoniously with our best yearnings and earnest hungers ever be dismissed by mere logic? Or must we stay forever hunter-foragers in order to pursue happiness?

Humans are creatures of animal origins, each in search of his or her own spirit. An article posted on the internet asked, "Will Science Someday Rule Out the Possibility of God?"[1]Science and rationality cannot extinguish the human intuition for spirit. Theological disputes and atheism can all ultimately be reduced to a sad haggling over folklore and parliamentary procedure. These sidetracks and extremes ignore the essential need of a sentient being.

---

1 Wolchover, Natalie. *Will Science Someday Rule Out the Possibility of God?* Sep 17, 2013. http://www.livescience.com/23251-science-religion-god-physics.html.

As life is lived, humans will always watch loved ones die. The final word will be uttered and then there will just be no more and no matter how natural or welcome the relief at the cessation of suffering, it will still be strange to watch the light go out of a dear one's eyes. Something that was there is no longer there. We will always wonder where the spark, the animating presence went, and if the person is close to our hearts, we will always hope to see him or her on the other side when our own time comes. Humans will always have near death experiences bathed in white light and beckoning arms. Humans will have out-of-body experiences and call the essential being that stands revealed to them apart from their corporeal bodies, their soul, their spirit. Humans will spontaneously pray in times of danger and some of their prayers will appear to be answered, to their unshakable personal satisfaction. Finally, humans will never stop dreaming, and some of those dreams will mysteriously reveal the future. And those who have these experiences will share them with friends and loved ones in the form of stories. It creates cognitive and emotional dissonance for an individual to go against his or her own best hopes, even if he or she will never understand the existential basis for those hopes. A central element of faith in a ground up, science accepting spirituality might start with a thought from Walt Whitman. "Has anyone supposed it lucky to be born? I hasten to inform him or her that it is just as lucky to die, and I know it."[1] Freud liked to remind us that each life lived owes Nature a death. So no matter if you have sailed the ocean blue, or slain a dragon or two, your greatest adventure is always dead ahead. People die sleeping, crying, screaming. People die smiling and laughing. Is it memory of the past that provokes these responses? Or is it the path unfolding ahead as their bodies become pure mind and anticipated spirit?

Unavoidably, heroes kill and heroes die. The myth of the hero, as a complex of instincts, is a vast cascade of protein synthesis in response to environmental pressure to get out into the world and hunt. It resides at the core of our being. It is our sum total. It compels our behavior. The myth of the hero as a story teaches us to transform hunger into spirit. Our fundamental hunting nature reveals that our deepest happiness is in the search. Our crowning cognitive achievement is the awestruck question, never the final answer. If the human mind is incapable of certainty, then the highest wisdom is hope and hope rendered verbally is prayer. The myth of the hero, the primal pattern of all stories, teaches us that Earthly existence will inexorably lead each individual to bend his or her knee in prayer. The only hope is to love the mystery that unfolds. Paradoxically, is this not the reward of life and the good of living for the alpha hunter-forager on this lovely planet Earth?

---

1 Whitman, Walt. *Leaves of Grass*. "Song of Myself," 1859. 7.123-12.

A New Birth of Mystery

Open your heart and mind and sing that the myth of the hero is made of Earth. Sing it now that you know the story, from the morning, through the noon and deep into the night. It was not the gods who gave humans the myth of the hero. Like their bodies and their food, the Earth cultivated it in her grandest children to help each individual discover his or her own soul, if it exists, and to prepare him or her to meet the gods, if they exist. It is the cry of the hunter staring into flames beneath the stars rolling overhead while the family huddles close and sings along. The myth of the hero was ancient in humans long before they found the right voice to share it with their fellows. What the song is to the songbird, the myth of the hero is to humans. In Earth it began and to Earth it will return. Where the myth of the hero ends, all true search begins. What else could these words create but a journey towards the mystery that is the discovery of self?

BIBLIOGRAPHY

A.R., Radcliffe-Brown. *The Andaman Islanders*. New York, NY: The Free Press, 1922.

Aczel, Amir D. *Entanglement*. New York, NY: Wiley, 2002.

Alberts B, Johnson A, Lewis J, Raff M, Roberts K, Walter P. *Molecular Biology of the Cell. (6th ed.Chapter 4: DNA, Chromosomes and Genomes.* Garland, 2014.

Alcock, John. *Animal Behavior. 9th Edition*. Sunderland, MA 01375: Sinauer Associates, Inc., 2009.

Anonymous. *The brains of Neanderthals and modern humans developed differently*. Max Plank Gessellschaft, Nov 08, 2010.

—. *The Epic of Gilgamesh*. Assyrian International News Agency Books Online www. aina.org. Tablet I., n.d.

—. *The Holy Bible*. King James Version, n.d.

Anonymous. *The Aryan Expulsion-and-Return Formula in The Folk and Hero Tales of the Celts*. UK: Lightning Source UK Ltd. Milton Keynes , 1881.

Ardrey, Robert. *African Genesis: A Personal Investigation into the Animal Origins and Nature of Man*. New York NY: Atheneum, 1961.

—. *The Territorial Imperative*. New York NY: Dell Publishing Co., 1966.

Bartlett, F.C. *Remembering*. NewYork, NY 10011: University of Cambridge, 1995.

Bellows, Henry Adams. *The Poetic Edda.*. www.sacred-texts.com., 1936.

Berlin, Brent and Paul Kay. *Basic Color Terms: Their Universality and Evolution*. Center for the Study of Language, 1999.

Berndt, Ronald M. and Catherine H. *The Speaking Land.* . Rochester, Vermont: Inner Traditions International, 1994.

Bierhorst, John, editor. *The Red Swan: The Myths and Tales of the American Indians.* New York, NY: Farrar, Straus and Giroux, 1976.

Bierhorst, John. *The Mythology of North America.* New York, NY 10016: William Morris and Company Inc., 1985.

Biesele, Megan. *Women Like Meat.* Bloomington, Indiana 47404: Indiana University Press, 1993.

Blackburn, Thomas C. *December's Child-A Book of Chumash Oral Narratives.* Berkeley, California: University of California Press, 1975.

Bleek, W.H.I. and L.C. Lloyd. *Specimens of Bushman Folklore.* London: BiblioBazaar, (1911) 2007.

Bleek, W.H.J. *'On resemblances in Bushmen and Australian Mythology'.* Cape Town South Africa: Cape Monthly Magazine, 1874.

Bloom, M. and O.G. Mouritsen. *The Evolution of Membranes.* Handbook of Biological Physics, edited by R. Lipowsky and E. Sackmann, Vol. I, Chapter 2, 1995.

Blust, Robert. *Terror from the Sky: Unconventional Linguistic Clues from the Negrito Past.* Digital Commons @ Wayne State. Human Biology, Volume 85, Issue 1, Special Issue on Revisiting the "Negrito" Hypothesis, Article 18, 2013.

Boas, Franz. *The Mind of Primitive Man.* Washington D.C.: Heath & Co., 1938.

Boeree, C. George. *Carl Jung.* Http//www.ship.edu/edu-cgboeree/jung.html., n.d.

Boesch, Christopher. *Hunting Strategies for Gombe and Taï Chimpanzees, in Chimpanzee Cultures.* Harvard University Press, 1996.

Bordes, Francoise. *The Old Stone Age* . New York NY: McGraw-Hill Book Company, 1968.

Bowler, Peter J. *Evolution: The History of an Idea.* . Berkeley CA: University of California Press., 2003.

Bullfinch, Thomas. *Bulfinch's Mythology. Author's preface.* The Project Gutenberg EBook, n.d.

Burnett, John. *Early Greek Philosophy.* New York NY: Meridian Books , 1960.

Campbell, Joseph and Bill Moyers. *The Power of Myth. DVD.* Mystic Fire Video, 2001.

Campbell, Joseph. *Primitive Myth: Volume I The Masks of God.* New York : The Viking Press, 1959.

—. *The Hero With A Thousand Faces.* Novato, CA 94949: New World Library, 2008.

Capelloti, P.J. *The Theory of the Archaeological Raft: Motivation, Method and Madness in Experimental Archaeology.*. EXARC. http://exarc.net/issue-2012-1/ea/theory-archaeological-raft-motivation-method-and-madness-experimental-archaeology, 2006.

Cassier, Ernst. *The Myth of the State.* 1946.

Cassirer, Ernst. *Essay on Man.* 1944.

Chomsky, Noam. *Syntactic Structure.* London, New York: Mouton de Gruyter, (1957) 2002.

Cipriani, Lidio. *The Andaman Islanders.* London: Weidenfeld, 1966.

Coleridge, Samuel Taylor. *Biographia Literaria.* Princeton NJ: Princeton University Press; 1985.

Cook, Arthur. *Zeus.* 1914.

Cornford, Francis. *From Religion to Philosophy.* 1913.

Danielsson, Bengt. *From Raft To Raft: The Account of a Fantastic Raft Voyage from Tahiti to Chile and back to Polynesia.* London: George Allen & Unwin, 1960 .

Dart, R.A. "The Predatory Transition from Ape to Man." . International Anthropological and Linguistic Review, 1, 1953.

Dart, R.A. *Australopithecus africanus: The Man-Ape of South Africa.* Nature, Vol.115, No.2884, 1925.

Darwin, Charles. *Transmutation of Species, Notebook B.* 1837.

Darwin, Charles. *The Descent of Man. Chapter 6. On the Affinities and Geneology of Man.* New York NY : D. Appleton & Co., 1871.

Darwin, Charles. *The Origin of Species by Means of Natural Selection.* John Murray, London, England., 1859.

—. *The Red Notebook of Charles Darwin.* 1 Jul, 1838.

De Angelis, Franco & Benjamin Garstad. *Euhemerus in Context.* Classical Antiquity, Vol. 25, No. 2, 2006.

De las Casas, Bishop don Fray Bartolomé. *A Short Account of the Destruction of the Indies.* 1542.

Diamond, Jared. *Guns, Germs and Steel.* W. W. Norton & Company, 1999.

Diodorus. *v.41.4–46, vi.1.* n.d.

Dixon, R. M. W. *The Languages of Australia.* 1980.

Dixon, Thomas. *Science and Religion: A Very Short Introduction.* Oxford England: Oxford University Press, 2008.

DuBois, Constance Goddard. "The Story of the Chaup: A Myth of the Diegueños." *The Journal of American Folklore.* Vol. XVII. , No. LXVVII, October-December, 1904.

Dumézil, Georges. *Mitra Varuna: An Essay on Two Indo-European Representatives of Sovereignty*. Zone Press, 1990.

Dundes, Alan. *The Hero Pattern and the Life of Jesus*. Protocol of the Twentyfifth Colloquy, 1976.

Durkheim, Emile. *The Elementary Forms of the Religious Life*. Oxford, England: Oxford University Press, 2008.

Dziadosz, Alexander. *Young Woman Sentenced to Death by Stoning in Sudan*. Reuters, Thursday, May 31, 2012.

Eddison, E.R. *The Worm Ouroboros*. Ballantine Books, (1926) 1967.

Endicott, Kirk. *Batek Negrito Religion*. Oxford England: Claredon Press, 1979.

Eugenio, Damiana L. ed. *Philippine Folk Literature: An Anthology*. Manila: The University of Philippines Press, 2007.

Evans, Ivor H.N. *Studies in Religion, Folk-lore, & Custom in British Borneo and the Malay Peninsula*. Charleston, SC 29413: Cambridge University Press, 1923.

Filkins, Sexter. "*O.C. Boy Scouts Investigated in Bear's Killing.*" Los Angeles CA: Los Angeles Times, August 17, 1996.

Finley, M.I. *The World of Odysseus*. London, England: Penguin Books Ltd. , 1954.

Francis, Richard C. Epigentics: The Ultimate Mystery of Inheritance. *Epigentics: The Ultimate Mystery of Inheritance*. New York NY 10100: W.W. Norton & Company, 2011.

Frazer, James George. *The Golden Bough. A Study in Magic and Religion. 3rd ed.* New York, NY: Macmillan Press, 1926.

Freidel, David and Linda Schele and Joy Parker. *Maya Cosmos: Three Thousand Years on the Shaman's Path*. New York NY 10022: HarperCollins Publishers, Inc., 1993.

Freud, Sigmund. *New Introductory Lectures*. New York, NY 10110 : W. W. Norton & Company, 1990.

—. *The Future of an Illusion*. New York, NY: W.W. Norton & Co. , (1927) 1989.

—. *Totem and Taboo*. New York NY: Norton and Co., 1950.

Garlake, Peter. *The Hunter's Vision: The Prehistoric Art of Zimbabwe*. London: British Museum Publications, 1996.

Gennep, Arnold. *The Rites of Passage*. Chicago IL 60637: The University of Chicago Press, (1909) 1960.

Gilby, Ian C. and Richard C. Connor. *The Role of Intelligence in Group Hunting: Are Chimpanzees Different from Other Social Predators*. 2010.

Goldberg, Christine. *The Historic-Geographic Method: Past and Future*. Journal of Folklore Research. University of Indiana Press, Vol. 21, No. 1, Apr 1984.

Golding, William. *Lord of the Flies*. New York, NY: Penguin Publishing Group, 1999.

Graves, Robert. *The Greek Myths. Volumes I & II*. Great Britain: Penguin Books Ltd., 1953.

—. *The White Goddess*. London: Faber & Faber, 1948.

Gray, Richard. "Archicebus Achilles could be humanity's earliest primate cousin." *The Telegraph*, 05 Jun 2013.

Gribbin, John and Jeremy Cherlas. *The First Chimpanzee*. Barnes and Noble Books, 2001.

Guisande, Martin. *Folk Literature of the Selknam Indians*. Los Angeles CA : UCLA Latin American Studies Publication, 1975.

Hallet, Jean-Pierre. *Pygmy Kitabu*. New York NY: Random House, 1973.

Harrison, Jane. *Prolegomena to the Study of Greek Religion*. 1903.

Harrison, Jane. *Themis*. 1912.

Hawkings, Steven. *A Brief History of Time*. New York: Bantam Dell Books, 1995.

Herodotus. *The Histories. Book II, chapters 121–124*. n.d.

Hesiod. *Works and Days*. Leob Classical Library, Harvard University Press, n.d.

Hess, Elizabeth. *Nim Chimpsky: The Chimp Who Would Be Human*. New York NY: Bantam Books, 2008.

Heyerdahl, Thor. *Kon-Tiki: Across the Pacific by Raft*. Chicago: Rand McNally & Company, 1950.

—. *American Indians in the Pacific: The Theory behind the Kon-Tiki Expedition*. London: George Allen and Unwin, 1952.

Homer. *The Iliad*. Leob Classical Library, Harvard University Press, n.d.

—. *The Odyssey*. Leob Classical Library, Harvard University Press, n.d.

Hoyle, B. and N.C. Wickramasinghe. *Astronomical Origins of Life- Steps Towards Panspermia*. Springer, 1999.

Jones, David E. *An Instinct for Dragons*. New York: Routledge, 2002.

Jones, Sir William. *Discourses delivered before the Asiatic Society*. 1824.

Jung, Carl. *Man and His Symbols*. Dell, 1968.

Kelly, Robert L., Jean-Francois Rabemity and Lin Poyer. *Mikea. I.IV.8*. The Cambridge Encyclopedia of Hunters and Gatherers, 1999.

Kinsella, Thomas. *Tain Bo Coulaigh*. Oxford, England: Oxford University Press, 1969.

Krohn, Julius, (Welsch, Roger L., translator). *Folklore Methodology: Formulated by Julius Krohn and Expanded by Nordic Researchers*. Austin, TX: University of Texas Press , 1981.

Labov, William. *Principles of Linguistic Change*. Blackwell Publishing, 1994.

Lanman, Charles R. ,. *The Sacred Books and Early Literature of the East. Vol. IX: India and Brahmanism, Rig Veda*. Parke, Austinand Liscomb, Inc. , 1917.

Lee, Richard B. and Richard Daly ed. *The Cambridge Encyclopedia of Hunters and Gatherers*. Cambridge University Press, 1999.

Lévi-Strauss, Claude. *The Raw and the Cooked*. Chicago, IL: University of Chicago Press, 1983.

Lévy-Bruhl, Lucian. *Primitive Mentality*. London: George Allen & Unwin , 1923.

Liebenberg, Louis. *"Persistence Hunting by Modern Hunter-Gatherers"* . Current Anthropology 47, no. 6, Dec 2006.

Lindsey, Tabitha and Ángel Valdés. *The Model Organsim Hermissenda crassicornis (Gastropoda: Heterobranchia) Is a Species Complex*. Plos One, April 22, 2016.

Long, M., et al. *The Origin of New Genes: Glimpses From the Young and Old.* . Nat. Rev. Genet. November , 2003.

Lonsdorf, Elizabeth V, et al. ed. *The Mind of the Chimpanzee*. Chicago IL: University of Chicago Press, 2010.

Lord, A.B. The Singer of Tales. *The Singer of Tales*. Boston MS: Harvard University Press, (1960), 2003.

Lorentz, Konrad. *On Aggression* . New York: Bantam Books, 1966.

Lumholtz, Carl. *New Trails in Mexico*. Tucson AZ: University of Arizona Press, (1912) 1999.

Magnuson, Magnus and Hermann Paulson. *Njal's Saga* . Penguin Classics, 1979.

Maki, Julia Marie. *The Biomechanics of Spear Throwing: An Analysis of the Effects of Anatomical Variation on Throwing Performance, with Implications for the Fossil Record*. Washington University in St. Louis, Thesis, 2013.

Malinowski, Bronislaw. *Myth in Primitive Psychology*. 1926.

Mann, Thomas. *Freud and the Future*. Daedalus Vol. 88, No. 2, Myth and Mythmaking, Spring, 1959.

Marais, Eugène N. *My Friends the Baboons*. Great Britain : Anthony Blond, 1971.

Marlowe, Christopher. *The Tragical History of Doctor Faustus, Christopher Marlowe: Five Plays*. New York NY: Hill & Wang Inc., 1956.

Marshall, John, Directed by: Robert Gardner. *The Hunters*, Film. Smithsonian-Harvard Peabody expedition1952-53, 1957.

Matsuazawa, Tetsuro. *The Chimpanzee Mind:Bridging Fieldwork and Laboratory Work, Education by Master-Apprenticeship* . The Mind of the Chimpanzee, 2010.

Matsuzawa, Tetsuro. *Field Experiments on Use of Stone Tools in the Wild*. Boston MA: Chimpanzee Cultures, ed. Richard W. Wrangham et al, Harvard University Press, 1994.

Mayor, Adrienne. *The First Fossil Hunters* . Princeton, NJ 08540: Princeton University Press, 2000.

Meletinsky, Eleazar. *The Poetics of Myth* . New York, NY, 10001: Routlege, 1998.

Milbrath, Susan. *Star Gods of the Maya: Astronomy in Art, Folklore, and Calenders.* Austin TX 78713-78: University of Texas Press, 1999.

Miller, Dean A. *The Epic Hero*. JHU Press, 2000.

Miller, Emily Russo. "*Suspected rock-throwers charged with felony assault.*" Juneau AK: Juneau Empire, 9 November 2012.

Müller, Max. *The Sacred Books of the East*. New York, NY : Parke, Austin, and Lipscomb, Inc. , 1917.

Neidhardt, John. *Black Elk Speaks*. University of Nebraska Press , 1979.

Neurendorf, Kimberly A. *The Content Analysis Guidebook Online*. http://academic.csuohio.edu.kneundorf/content/., 2002.

Nietzsche, Friedrich. *The Birth of Tragedy Out of the Spirit of Music. The Portable Nietzsche, translated by Walter Kaufman*. London, England: Penguin Books, 1977.

Orpen, Joseph. *Mythology of the Maluti Bushmen*. Capetown, South Africa: The Capetown Gazette, May, 1874.

Orwick, Jennifer. *The Two Most Dangerous Numbers in the Universe Are Threatening the End of Physics* . Business Insider. http://www.businessinsider.com/the-end-of-physics-as-we-know-it-2016-1., Jan 14. 2016.

Pane, Ramón. *La relación of Fray Ramón Pane*. . http://faculty.smu.edu/bakewell/bakewell/texts/panerelacion.html, n.d.

Patterson, Steven J. and James M. Robinson. *The Gospel of Thomas. Fragment 113*. http://gnosis.org/naghamm/nhl_thomas.htm, n.d.

Paul, Marla. *Your Memory is like the Telephone Game: Each time you recall an event, your brain distorts it*. Northwestern Now, Sep. 9, 2012.

Pausanias. *Description of Greece with an English Translation by W.H.S. Jones, Litt.D., and H.A. Ormerod, M.A*. Harvard University Press; London, William Heinemann Ltd. 1918., n.d.

Petrich, Perla, editor. *Literatura Oral de los Pueblos del Lago Atitlán. Casa de Estudios de los Pueblos de Lago Atitlán*. Guatemala, C.A: CAEL, 1996.

Pinker, Steven. *How the Mind Works*. 2009: W.W. Norton & Company, New York, NY.

Plato. *Meno*. n.d.

—. *Phaedo.* n.d.

—. *The Republic.* n.d.

—. *Theatetus.* n.d.

Poe, Edgar Allen. *Complete Works, The Conqueror Worm.*. Create Space, 2011.

Premack, David and Guy Woodruff. *Does the chimpanzee have a theory of mind?* England: Behavioral and Brain Sciences, Volume 1, Issue 4, Dec . Cambridge University Press, 1978.

Pritchard, James B., ed. *The Ancient Near East, Volume I: An Analogy of Texts and Pictures.* Princeton University Press, 1958, n.d.

Propert, Phyllis. *Carl Mays: My Pitch That Killed Chapman Was A Strike!* Baseball Digest, Vol. 16, No. 6, July 1957.

Propp, Vladimir. *The Morphology of the Folktale.* Austin TX: University of Texas, 1968.

Pseudo-Apollodorus. *The Library, with an English Translation by Sir James George Frazer.* Harvard University Press; London, William Heinemann Ltd. 1921., n.d.

Pulford, Mary, H. *Peoples of the Ituri.* Orlando, Florida 32887: Harcourt Brace Custom Publishers, 1993.

Radcliffe-Brown., A. R. *On Social Structure.* Journal of the Royal Anthropological Institute of Great Britain and Ireland, 1940.

Raglan, Lord. *The Hero.* Mineola, NY 11501: Dover Publications, Inc., (1956) 2003.

Rank, Otto. *The Myth of the Birth of the Hero. In Quest of the Hero ed. by Robert A. Segal.* Princeton NJ: Princeton University Press, 1990.

Rink, Thomas. *Tales and Traditions of the Eskimos.* London, 1875.

Robertson Smith, William. *Lectures on the Religion of the Semites. Fundamental Institutions. First Series.* London, England: Adam & Charles Black , 1889.

Robinson, Roland. *Aboriginal Myths and Legends.* Melbourne, Victoria, Australia: Sun Books Pty Ltd , 1966.

Roheim, Geza. *The Eternal Ones of the Dream.* New York NY: International Universities Press, 1945.

Ryan, Frank. *Darwin's Blind Spot* . New York, NY: Houghton Mifflin Company, 2002.

Sagan, Carl. *Cosmos.* New York, NY 10019: Ballantine Books, 1980.

Sagan, Carl. Foreward to Story, Ronald. *The Space-gods revealed. A close look at the theories of Erich von Däniken (2 ed.).* Barnes & Nobles, 1980.

Sarbin, Theodore R. *The Storied Nature of Human Conduct*. Praeger, Wesport, Connecticut, 1986, n.d.

Sassetti, Filippo. *Lettere di Filippo Sassetti*. Reggio, Dalla Stampería Torregiani E.C., 1844.

Scheub, Harold. *African Images: Patterns in Literary Art*. McGraw-Hill, 1972.

Scheub, Harold. Story. *Story*. Madison WI 53718: The University of Wisconsin Press, 1998.

Schilling, von, F.W. *Historical-Critical Introduction to the Philosophy of Mythology*. State University of New York Press, 2008.

Schmidt, Sigrid. *South African |Xam Bushman Traditions and Their Relations to Further Khoisan Folklore*. Rüdiger Köppe Verlag, Köln , 2013.

—. *Tricksters, Monsters and Clever Girls*. Rüdiger, Köppe, Verlag, Köln, 2001.

Seattle, Chief. *Chief Seattle's Thoughts*. http://www.kyphilom.com/www/seattle.html, n.d.

Segal, Robert A. *Joseph Campbell: An Introduction*. New York, NY. 10014: Penguin Books USA Inc., 1987.

—. *Joseph Campbell: An Introduction.* . Penguin Books USA Inc., 375 Hudson Street, New York, NY, 10014, USA, 1990.

Segal, Robert A.ed. *In Quest of the Hero*. Princeton, NJ 08540: Princeton University Press, 1990.

Shakespeare, William. *Complete Works*. New York NY: Doubleday & Company, 1936.

Shaw, Sarah. *The Jatakas: Birth Stories of the Bodhisatta*. Penguin Global, 2008.

Shinkareva, Svetlana V. et al. *Using fMRI Brain Activation to Identify Cognitive States Associated with Perception of Tools and Dwellings*. Bloomington IN: Indiana University Press, 2008.

Sophocles. *Oedipus Tyrannis. Edited and translated by Hugh Lloyd Jones*. Cambridge, MA: The Loeb Classical Library, Harvard University Press , 1994.

Spence, Lewis. *An Introduction to Mythology*. Moffat Yard & Company, 1926.

Spyridakis, S. "Zeus Is Dead: Euhemerus and Crete." *The Classical Journal*, Vol. 63, No. 8, May, 1968.

Sturlusson, Snorri. *The Prose Edda*. www.sacred-texts.com, n.d.

Tedlock, Dennis. *Popol Vuh: The Definitive Edition of the Mayan Book of Life and Glories of Gods and Kings* . Touchstone Rockefeller Center, 1230 Avenue of the Americas, New York, NY 10023, 1996.

Thomas, Elizabeth Marshall. *The Old Way: A Story of the First People*. New York: Sarah Crichton Press, 2006.

Thompson, Stith. *One Hundred Favorite Folktales*. Bloomington IN: Indiana University Press, 1968.

Tolkein, J.R.R. *The Silmarillion*. Houghton, Mifflin Harcourt, 2004.

Tylor, Edward B. *"Professor Adolf Bastian."* London: Man 5., 1905.

—. *Primitive Culture*. New York NY: Harper & Row, (1871)1958 .

Utley, Francis. *Lincoln Wasn't There or Lord Raglan's Hero*. Washington, D.C. : CEA Chapbook. Supplement to CEA Critic 22, no. 9., 1965.

Van Lawick-Goodall, Jane. *In the Shadow of Man*. Boston MA : Houghton Mifflin Company, 1971.

Van Over, Raymond. *Sun Stories: Creation Myths from around the World*. . New American Library, Inc.,1633 Broadway, New York, 1980.

Von Daankan, Erich. *Chariots of the Gods*. Berkley Books, 1999.

Von Hahn, Johan Georg. *Sagawissenschaftliche Studien*. Jena: Mauke, 1876.

Walls, Jan and Yvonne Walls. *Classical Chinese Myths*. Hong Kong : Joint Publishing Company, 1984.

Watson, Burton. *Basic Writings of Chuang Tzu*. New York NY: Columbia University Press, April 15, 1996.

Wells, Spencer. *The Journey of Man: A Genetic Odyssey*. Princeton NJ: Princeton University Press, 2002.

White, Robert Dr. *Dr. White Webpage*. http://userwww.sfsu.edu/art511_j/emerging.f/kerrymaster/kerryartproposal2f/headtransplant.html., 2001.

Whitman, Walt. "Song of Myself." *Leaves of Grass*, 1859.

Whorf, Benjamin Lee. *Language, Thought and Reality*. M.I.T. Press, 1964.

Wilbert, Johnannes. *Folk Literature of the Selknam Indians*. Los Angeles, California: University of California , 1975.

Wilkinson, Richard H. *The Complete Gods and Goddesses of Ancient Egypt*. . Thames & Hudson. (2003), n.d.

Wilson, E.O. "Interview with Robert Krulwich." *Harvard Magazine*, Sep 09, 2009.

Wolchover, Natalie. *Will Science Someday Rule Out the Possibility of God?* http://www.livescience.com/23251-science-religion-god-physics.html., Sep 17, 2013.

Wolf-Knuts, Ulrika. *On the history of comparion in folklore studies* . Thick Corpus, Kalevala Institute, 1999.

Wrangham, Richard W. ed. et al. *Chimpanzee Cultures*. Boston MS: Harvard University Press, 1996.

INDEX

A

Aborigine, 73, 74, 86, 93, 134, 137, 139, 141, 154, 155
accented language, 173
accumulation of environmental experience in genes, 187, 197
Achilles, 16, 23, 41, 107, 175, 195, 235
activation patterns, 183, 184, 186
adaptive value of speech, 202
adventure, 6, 11, 16, 18, 81, 84, 89, 96, 147, 148, 150, 153, 155, 156, 165, 176, 201, 227
Agamemnon, 67
analogy, 5, 19, 28, 29, 38, 64, 65, 78, 84, 94, 112, 141, 169, 181, 207, 212, 221, 238
Andaman Islanders, The, 31, 104, 126, 133-135, 137, 139, 144, 150-152, 164, 231, 233
Anima/Animus, 69
animal behavior, 10, 37, 94, 183, 201, 209, 231
animism, 63
anthropology, 7, 44, 58, 61, 63-65, 91, 92, 101, 103, 105, 127, 137, 148, 176, 196, 207, 236
anthropomorphism, 67, 73
anti-hero, 203
Apollo, 53
apprenticeship, 175
archetype, 69, 129, 197
Arctic, 32, 158
art for art's sake, 165
Artemis, the Huntress, 53, 199
audience, 17, 145, 151, 153, 175, 176, 181
Australia, 31, 74, 122, 124, 125, 127, 133-135, 138-141, 144, 154, 156, 233, 238

B

Back when all the animals were people, 27, 28, 30, 33, 37, 162, 164
Bastian, Adolphe, 36, 63, 68, 240
Bible, 2, 19, 20, 39-41, 116, 195, 231
Bierhorst, John, 32, 77, 232
Biesele, Megan, 30, 104, 126, 145, 232
Big Dipper, 51
biogram, 198
biography of Everyman, 18
bird song control systems, 185
Black Elk, 200, 211, 237
Bleek, Wilhelm, 27, 105, 138, 140, 149, 232
Boas, Franz, 8, 64, 85, 105, 176, 232
brain, 36, 37, 47, 69, 71, 86, 89, 101, 122, 181, 183-186, 192, 203, 217, 237-239
Broca and Weirnike's areas, 122, 183-185
Bushman, 54, 92, 103, 104, 137, 139, 140, 201, 232, 239

C

Campbell, Joseph, 8, 9, 162, 165, 167-169, 177, 182, 190, 200, 232, 239
carpenter's square, 56, 57
Cassirer, Ernst, 62, 67, 73, 233
cave paintings, 29
celestial equator, 55
central myth of the modern age, 216
characotel, 67
charioteer, 69, 70
chimpanzees hunting, 138, 193, 194, 232,

Printed in the United States
By Bookmasters